THIS MODERN WORLD

DEREK E. WOOD

Second Edition

HEINEMANN EDUCATIONAL BOOKS
LONDON

Heinemann Educational Books Ltd
LONDON EDINBURGH MELBOURNE AUCKLAND TORONTO
HONG KONG SINGAPORE KUALA LUMPUR NEW DELHI
NAIROBI JOHANNESBURG LUSAKA IBADAN
KINGSTON

ISBN 0 435 31951 5

© Derek E. Wood 1966, 1976

FIRST PUBLISHED IN THIS EDITION 1967
REPRINTED 1969, 1970
REPRINTED WITH ADDITIONS 1972
REPRINTED 1973
SECOND EDITION 1976

Published by
Heinemann Educational Books Ltd
48 Charles Street, London W1X 8AH
Printed Offset Litho and bound in Great Britain by
Cox & Wyman Ltd, London, Fakenham and Reading

CONTENTS

LIST OF ILLUSTRATIONS

PREFACE

In common with many other history teachers the author has long felt the need for a textbook for a course on contemporary world history. It is hoped that this book will provide an introduction to the methods and skills necessary for a more advanced study of history and that it will also help pupils to understand contemporary problems in relation to their historical background. Such understanding should help them to form more balanced judgments and so develop attitudes of tolerance and fair mindedness that will equip them to take their places as responsible citizens in this modern world.

I have tried to make each study self-contained, while at the same time maintaining the essential continuity of development and interplay of events that are typical of the period. Comparisons and cross-references have been liberally used to achieve this but careful teacher guidance will be necessary for full understanding by pupils. As they are unlikely to read all chapters, a selected study of related topics will help them to realise the inter-relationships and appreciate the significance of different movements, people and events.

Because this book is to be read and studied by pupils with little experience of historical method, the notebook summaries at the end of each chapter are an important feature. They may be used in a variety of ways. Early in the year they should provide a framework on which pupils will be able to build their own notes. As pupils gain maturity and experience in note-making, the summaries could become references against which pupils could check the coverage of essential features in their own notes. Finally, for revision purposes, the summaries offer skeleton outlines that do not provide a lot of factual information but rather test ability to remember and recall — vital skills which the successful student of history must develop. The vocabulary list at the end of each chapter is also intended to help to develop historical skills by emphasising words and terms commonly used in historical writing.

Related reading varies considerably from topic to topic. In listing the books at the end of each chapter the aim has been to concentrate on recent publications and, where possible, to provide a range in depth of treatment. Individual teachers will be able to recommend titles according to the ability and maturity of their pupils. A number of other general works related to the period would make useful additions to any school history library, and these are included as a separate list on page 298.

The satisfaction derived from writing this book has been heightened by the willing co-operation of both pupils and colleagues. History students of Form 5P1 at Burnside High School in 1965 gave valuable assistance through their pertinent comments and questions as they worked from many of the chapters during the year. I am also grateful to Mr E. J. Brewster, whose assistance in the early stages was most helpful, and to colleagues in other schools who used sample chapters with their classes. Most especially, I am indebted to Mrs N. S. Mitchell, lately of the Secondary Inspectorate, for her sustained interest and encouragement and for her scholarly guidance. Criticisms and suggestions that have come from her reading of the manuscript have been responsible for many improvements. Finally, the assistance I have received from my wife has been incalculable. In particular, her unflagging enthusiasm and support have created the atmosphere and environment essential for undertaking work of this nature. To all who have materially assisted me in so many ways, I offer my sincere thanks.

D. E. WOOD

November 1966

Preface to the Second Edition

A number of small up-datings have been made in the various reprintings of this book. However after the passage of nearly ten years since it first appeared, it has been necessary to recast the sections dealing with the most modern period. At the same time the opportunity has been taken to include more photographs and to revise the reading lists.

June 1976   D. E. W.

ACKNOWLEDGEMENTS

The author and the publishers wish to thank the following for permission to reproduce the photographs in this book:

Associated Press Ltd: Figure 35
Camera Press Ltd: Figures 28, 29, 30, 38, 39, 41
Keystone Press Agency Ltd: Figure 13
Library of Congress: Figure 22
The Mansell Collection: Figure 40
Novosti Press Agency Ltd: Figures 14, 15, 16
Radio Times Hulton Picture Library: Figures 1, 2, 5, 7, 8, 11, 12, 17, 20, 23, 24, 27

FIG. 1 — Kaiser Wilhelm II (1859–1941) with the King of Greece at German Army manoeuvres. The Kaiser has his arm outstretched and the King of Greece is on his left and wears a German uniform as a compliment.

FIG. 2 — The Great Review at Vincennes in 1903. King Edward VII, salutes the French parade.

1

THE CAUSES OF
WORLD WAR I

The Allied and Associated Governments affirm and Germany accepts the responsibility of Germany and her Allies for causing all the loss and damage to which the Allied and Associated Governments and their nationals have been subjected as a consequence of the war imposed upon them by the aggression of Germany and her Allies.

Article 231, Treaty of Versailles

It is quite obvious that, in the eyes of the victorious nations in 1919, there was no doubt as to the cause of World War I — the 'Great War'. It had been caused, they declared, by the aggression of Germany and her allies. However, this war-guilt clause rankled with the German people and was later to provide an important rallying cry for Hitler when he began his attack on the unfairness of the peace settlement of 1919. Although the motives of Hitler were open to question, there is no doubt that history will at least support his claim that the verdict of Versailles was unfair.

If we wish to find the real causes of the Great War of 1914-18 we must examine not only the incidents of the immediately preceding years but also the pattern of events at the close of the nineteenth century. While these in themselves would probably not have caused an international war, it is equally true that without them war would have been most unlikely.

NATIONALISM

Nationalism is not just the wish of people with common traditions to be united but it also implies their desire, even their determination, to exist as independent units among other nations. Just as in the present century Africa and Southern Asia are witnessing the growth of new independent nations, so in the last century did Europe see the rise of great new nations on that continent. In the years since World War II we have seen the emergence of nations such as India, Pakistan, Malaysia and Indonesia and the revival of the ancient land of China. Although we are separated from them by many thousands of miles we regard them, in this shrinking world, as our neighbours and become concerned, and sometimes even involved, when they have disputes.

We realise also that, in some cases at least, these nations have been formed at the expense of the empires of older established countries, notably France, the Netherlands and Great Britain. In the same way the latter half of the nineteenth century saw the emergence of new States on the map of Europe and the decline in size and strength of older nations. Thus Italy became a nation in 1860 and Germany followed ten years later, while the empires of Austria and Turkey, which included many minority racial groups, were gradually weakened and disappeared completely in 1918. Russia too was beginning to take a more active part in European affairs and, rather like China in the present century, was somewhat of an unknown force but obviously one which had to be respected. Finally, in the remote southeastern corner of the continent, the Balkan peoples were struggling to win their national independence from Turkey. These small nations hardly merited a place in the main stream of European history but later events were to prove that their problems and aspirations could alter the course of history.

Common problems. Whether large or small, these new nations all had the same problems and hopes. They were anxious to bring all people of the same race under their national flags and they were also anxious to establish themselves in the world, perhaps by extending their trade, perhaps by establishing an overseas empire, or perhaps by building up a strong army to let other nations see that they were not to be trifled with. Whatever their desires and whatever the actions they took, it was soon apparent that the path to nationhood would not be a smooth one.

Nations can be compared with people in this respect. Just as a teenager, struggling to become established as a person in his own right in a highly competitive and difficult world, may sometimes fly in the face of authority and demand greater privileges and rights from reluctant adults, so may a young nation consider it is underprivileged and is being unfairly treated by those whose national unity has been longer established. Thus the problems of nations are simply the problems of people. In civilised societies people usually settle their differences by peaceful means and nations, too, can often settle their disputes by diplomacy (simply international good manners). But when diplomacy fails war often results. The hopes and fears and the national pride, patriotism and jealousies that were typical of the fifty years preceding 1914 did not make war inevitable but certainly helped to make it extremely likely.

Rise of Serbia. Some nations were anxious to extend their rule over people of the same nationality. For instance, Serbia had emerged as the most powerful of the new Slav States in the Balkans. During the nineteenth century she had gradually freed many of her fellow countrymen from the rule of Turkey and, by the end of the century, she was anxious to complete this task and to wrest from Austria territory on the Adriatic coast which was also inhabited by Slavic peoples. Italy had similar hopes in Trentino and Trieste.

France and Germany. Some nations wanted revenge for former defeats and to recover lost territory. France, in 1871, after the Franco-Prussian War, had been forced to cede the rich industrial provinces of Alsace and Lorraine to the newly-created German Empire and to submit to the bitter humiliation of allowing a victorious German army to march through the streets of Paris. In many nations there was a spirit of blustering patriotism which showed little regard for the concerns and rights of others. This was probably most marked in Germany, where the Prussian Junkers (a semi-feudal class of military landowners) believed that war was the noblest of all occupations and that the Germans were the greatest race on the continent of Europe. As the Junkers provided most of the officers in the German army, their ideas were even more dangerous and they infected many ordinary Germans with their beliefs in German greatness and German destiny.

And so the growing pains of the new nations were felt throughout Europe. There became an increasing number of pressure points where national differences and frictions remained unsettled. These were most serious on the Franco-German border and in southeastern Europe. In some cases, especially where territory was involved, there did not appear to be any immediate or peaceful solution, while in others the attitudes of those involved did not make such a solution seem likely. The problem was not confined to the continent of Europe but spread to the rest of the world as European nations continued to extend their influence overseas.

IMPERIALISM

The Industrial Revolution, which had its beginnings in England in the late eighteenth century, had spread across most of Europe by 1900. This had greatly increased the demand for raw materials for the factories of Europe and cheap food for the factory workers. It also meant that, as production increased, new markets were needed for the factory products. Thus, as the nineteenth century progressed, the European countries became more and more interested and active in overseas expansion.

Great Britain. The first country to develop a large trading empire was Britain. With the early development of industrialisation in that country there was a need for foreign raw materials, markets and foodstuffs. However, in the first part of the century British overseas expansion was economic rather than political. By this we mean that she was more concerned with the establishment of trading posts and the investment of surplus capital (mainly the profits from industry) than with the acquisition of colonies. Her experience with the rebellious American colonies was still sufficiently recent for many British statesmen to consider that colonies were more trouble than they were worth. It was commonly believed that, when their colonies reached a certain stage of development, settlers in such lands as Canada and New Zealand would demand their independence in the same way as the Americans had done. Thus, as the free trade movement grew in strength in nineteenth century Britain, less importance was attached to the actual ownership of overseas markets and sources of raw materials. Similarly missionaries such as David Livingstone in Africa and Samuel Marsden in New Zealand were more interested in the conversion of native peoples to Christianity than in the extension of the British Empire.

Growing competition. But from about 1880 onwards, a marked and quite sudden change took place. British manufactured goods which, until this time, had found a ready market in Europe were now shut out by high protective tariffs as France, Belgium, Germany and others sought to develop their own industries. Britain was forced to seek additional markets beyond Europe. As European industrial production continued to grow, Britain found that her former European customers were now trade competitors, who were also seeking overseas markets for their growing industrial surplus and underdeveloped areas in which to invest their surplus capital. The attention of the countries of Europe thus became focused on the only large undeveloped areas remaining in the world — Africa, Asia and the Pacific. Competition became so keen that there was a growing danger of being excluded from areas where trade was already established. Powers therefore became convinced of the necessity to own such areas to protect their interests. Within less than thirty years much of these areas had been acquired in fact, if not in name, by one or other of the European Powers as colonies, protectorates or 'spheres of influence'. A study of the map opposite shows how this transformation took place.

However, the growth of empires and even the rivalry between colonising nations is not in itself necessarily a cause of war. To

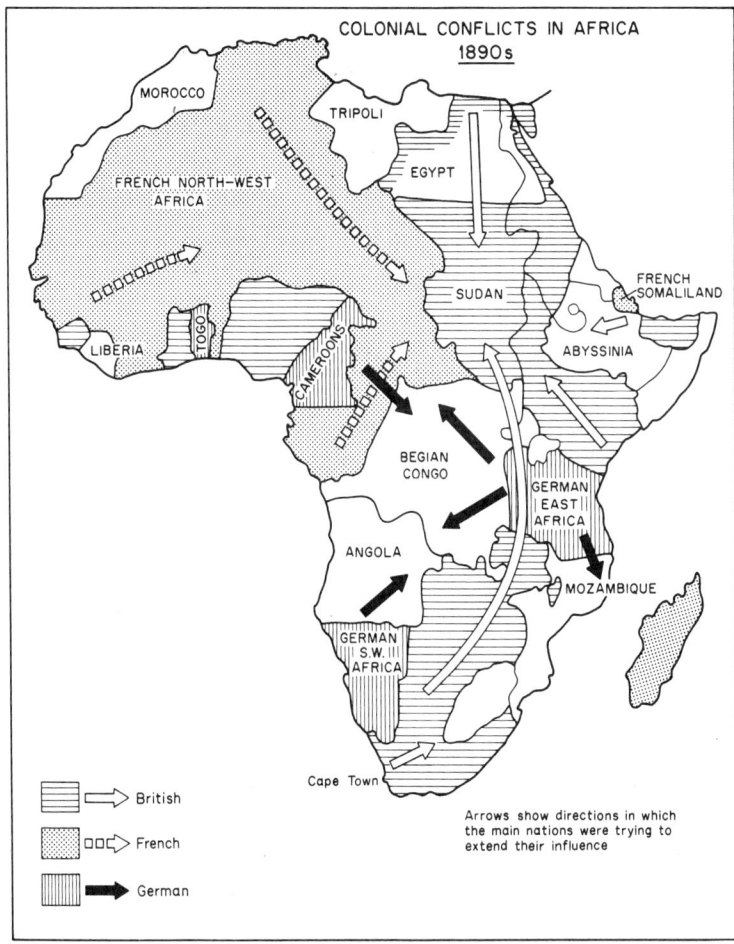

FIG. 3

understand why imperialism in this period can be regarded as a cause of World War I we must remember what we have already read about the growth of nationalism in this same period. We have seen that the nations of Europe were very much concerned with their own ambitions and their own interests. It is easy, therefore, to understand that the rivalries and jealousies that were to be found on the continent of Europe would quite naturally be transferred to the overseas activities of the European nations. There was no League of Nations or United Nations to oversee the scramble for colonies and no world court to which disputes could be referred. It was largely a question of 'every man for himself and the devil take the hindmost'. Britain sought to protect her trading rights by bringing them under the flag; Germany, late in the race, sought 'a place in the sun' worthy of her growing strength; France began a rapid inland penetration from her north African colonies; and Spain and Portugal hastily revived claims to trading posts they had established on the West Coast of Africa in the Age of Discovery. In the climate of national rivalry that prevailed differences were bound to be magnified and disputes and armed clashes were almost inevitable.

Clashes in Africa. In Africa the two dominant colonial Powers were France and Great Britain, the one in the north and the other in the south. Although a large section of central Africa was under Belgian control (in the Congo), the only real threat to the influence of these two Powers came from the German territories ranged on either side of the continent. As the map on page 17 shows, each of these three nations was anxious to link its territories. Cecil Rhodes dreamed of a Cape to Cairo railway which would be an 'all red route' linking British South Africa with Egypt (at the time under British control). This dream helped to lead, in 1899, to the Boer War and to real hostility between Britain and Germany which hoped to link its possessions in east and southwest Africa.

Further north, British interests had clashed with those of France at Fashoda, in 1898. An Anglo-Egyptian army under the command of Lord Kitchener was reconquering the Sudan when it met a French force intent on linking France's west African territories with French Somaliland on the east coast. Only the dignity and diplomacy of the British and French commanders prevented war between the two countries. Although most of the African colonial disputes had been provisionally settled by 1904, German jealousy of French aims in Morocco remained to cause a series of international crises in the years immediately preceding 1914. Also Italy, which had been least successful in the race for colonies, was anxious to demonstrate its nationhood and, following its failure in Abyssinia, cast covetous eyes on Tripoli, the only remnant of the former Turkish Empire in North Africa.

Emergence of Japan. The situation in Africa was repeated in Asia and the Pacific islands where, however, the position was complicated by the emergence of a new imperial Power — Japan. Britain and France were securely established in trade with China by 1880 but their position was soon threatened by the ambitions of Russia, Germany and Japan. As we will examine the consequences of this more closely in Chapter 8, it is sufficient to say here that further international tensions resulted. Meanwhile, in southeast Asia, French acquisition of Indo-China prompted Britain to annex Burma in 1886 and, at the same time, she began to extend her control in Malaya and Borneo. With the development of steamships the Pacific islands became valuable as coaling stations as well as sources of tropical products and native labour and areas of missionary activity. Increasing activity in the Pacific produced tensions in the New Hebrides, New Guinea, and Samoa, which involved France, Britain, Germany and the United States. Finally, on the continent of Asia, Russia's expansion east of the Caspian Sea brought her into contact with Persia and Afghanistan which were regarded by Britain as buffer States protecting her interests in India. Although Anglo-Russian differences were apparently settled at Pendjeh in 1885, they were further complicated by the development of Persian oil resources and suspicion remained between the two Powers.

German-Russian conflict. The final area of colonial conflict was in the Balkans and the Near East where the ambitions of Germany and Russia clashed. A great Pan-Slav movement ('unite the Slav peoples') developed in Russia which, if successful, would have brought much of the Balkans and central Europe and large areas of Turkey under Russian control. Russian designs on the Balkans and Turkey and her hopes for access to the Mediterranean from the Black Sea had helped to cause a number of wars in Europe in the nineteenth century. These aims had been thwarted largely by the actions of Britain and France. But now a new and much closer threat had arisen. In 1891 a Pan-German League was formed which had as its ultimate goal German world conquest. In keeping with this ideal was the German plan for a railway from Berlin to Baghdad which would carry German trade and influence right through the Balkans to the Persian Gulf and would bring Turkey into the German sphere of influence. Although the railway was barely begun by 1914, the clash of German and Russian interests in this area was an important cause of increasing world tension.

We have seen that, for one reason or another, the remainder of the undeveloped world came largely under the control of the European nations in the thirty years preceding World War I. Whether the colonies gained were to provide new markets or raw materials, whether they were to increase manpower for national armies or to allow missionaries to preach the gospel, whether they were to be used as coaling depots or naval bases, the result was the same. In the eyes of the people of the time a nation's prestige could, at least in part, be measured by the size and wealth of its empire. How that empire had been acquired seemed, in comparison, a much less important matter.

MILITARY RIVALRY

But power and prestige cannot be measured by the size of an empire unless a country is strong enough to defend its possessions. And nations cannot be united and defended from attack unless they have strong armies. Thus a natural accompaniment of the growth of nationalism and imperialism was the growth of large armies and navies. Germany emerged from its wars of unification in 1870 with the largest and strongest army in Europe, and this army was retained not only to defend the new nation from possible attack, especially from defeated France, but also as a symbol of German greatness. Other countries followed this lead and, by the start of the present century, the European nations possessed larger peacetime armies than at any other stage in their history. Compulsory military training was typical of all countries and vast sums of money were being spent annually on armaments. German, Russian and Italian defence expenditure trebled in the twenty-five years before the war broke out, while that of Austria and Britain more than doubled. France, which was spending in 1890 more per head of population on defence than any other country, also increased its expenditure. By 1914 there were over three-and-a-half million regular soldiers in Europe and millions more who were trained reserves. As each country tried to secure its own safety by increasing the size of its army, the nervous tension grew and the danger of war increased.

The naval race. The only country that was not involved in this race to build armies was Great Britain. The British have always relied on their navy to defend their islands from foreign attack, and ever since Drake had defeated the Spanish Armada some three-and-a-half centuries earlier, the British navy had been the almost unquestioned 'mistress of the seven seas'. But German colonial ambitions required the development of a strong navy to support them and the growth of the German navy after 1897 was regarded by Great Britain as a direct threat to her seapower. Believing that, for safety, her navy needed to be as large as the combined fleets of any two European Powers, Britain embarked on a vast shipbuilding programme. She developed a new type of battleship, the 'Dreadnought', with such strength and firepower that no other ship could hope to come within range of it without being blown out of the water.

When the Germans began to build a similar type of ship the naval race developed in earnest. The British believed that the only reason for the greatest military nation in the world to build a great navy was because it intended to use that army outside of Europe, and this belief was intensified when the Germans rejected the British offer of a 'naval holiday'. In 1912, to offset the growing German naval threat, Britain agreed to defend the North Sea while France was to safeguard the interests of both countries in the Mediterranean.

It was not likely that international competition in the building of armies and navies would, in itself, cause a war, but as the nations of Europe devoted increasing sums to military expenditure and were obviously becoming steadily more prepared for war the actual danger of war also increased. The danger was made even more acute by the formation of the alliances which finally split Europe into two opposing camps, each armed to the teeth.

THE ALLIANCES

In the concluding years of the nineteenth century a great Triple Alliance had been formed uniting the major Powers of central Europe — Germany, Austria and Italy. This was matched, in the early years of the twentieth century, by a similar, if less formal, agreement which included Britain, France and Russia. By 1914 these two opposing groups, each with its supporting allies, faced each other on the European stage. While a dispute between them need not necessarily have caused a war, it is apparent, from all that we have so far discovered about their attitudes and ambitions, that the chances of this were considerable (see map, next page).

Following the defeat of France by Germany in 1870 the German Chancellor, Bismarck, was determined to prevent any attempts by the French to regain the valuable industrial lands of Alsace-Lorraine or to find allies in Europe who would be prepared to assist them in a war of revenge. One of the methods he adopted to secure these ends was to build up a series of alliances with the other European Powers. By clever diplomacy he managed to secure the friendship of both Austria and Russia in the *Dreikaiserbund*, or League of Three Emperors, in spite of the conflicting ambitions of these two countries that we have already noted. But the secretly signed Dual Alliance with Austria in 1879 showed where Germany's real sympathies lay.

The Triple Alliance. In 1882 Austria and Germany were joined by Italy who resented French expansion in North Africa. This Triple Alliance was a defensive agreement designed to protect Austria against attack by Russia, and Germany and Italy from attack by France. At the insistence of Italy it was agreed

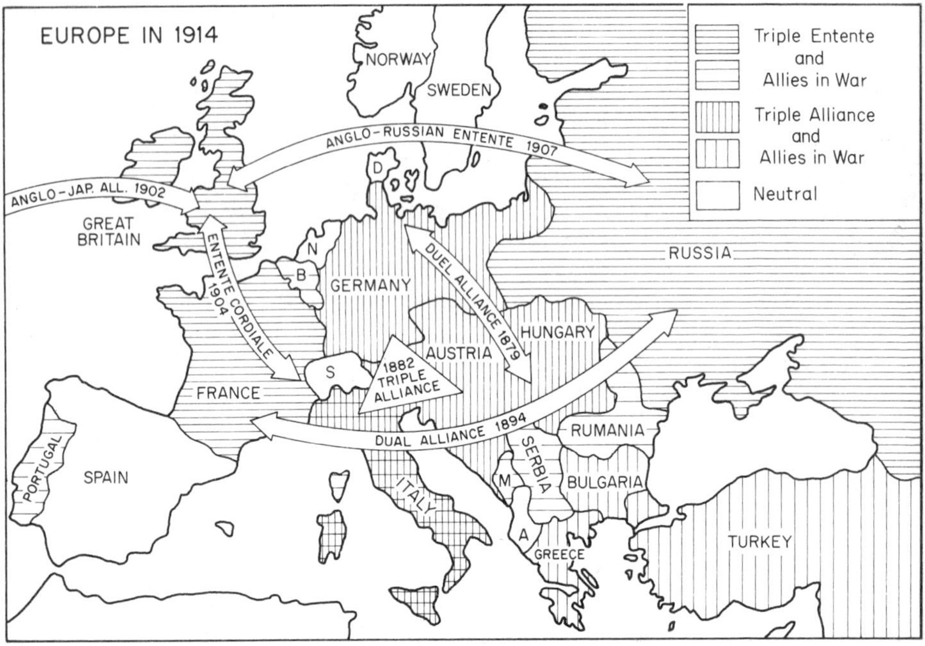

EUROPE IN 1914

NORWAY
SWEDEN

Triple Entente and Allies in War

Triple Alliance and Allies in War

Neutral

ANGLO-RUSSIAN ENTENTE 1907

ANGLO-JAP. ALL. 1902

GREAT BRITAIN

D

N

B

GERMANY

ENTENTE CORDIALE 1904

DUEL ALLIANCE 1879

RUSSIA

HUNGARY

S

AUSTRIA

1882 TRIPLE ALLIANCE

FRANCE

DUAL ALLIANCE 1894

SERBIA

RUMANIA

PORTUGAL

SPAIN

ITALY

M

BULGARIA

A

GREECE

TURKEY

FIG. 4

FIG. 5 — A German munitions factory in 1914.

that, under no circumstances, would it operate against Great Britain to whom the Italians still felt gratitude for assistance in the movement for the unification of their country. The alliance was joined in the next year by Rumania and later, although rather unwillingly, by Turkey. Although the existence of the Triple Alliance was known throughout Europe its terms were kept a closely guarded secret until the end of the war. This secrecy helped to increase the fears of other nations, especially France, who therefore began a frantic search for allies to counter the Triple Alliance.

Dual Alliance. As German friendship with Austria became more obvious after the Kaiser's dismissal of Bismarck in 1890, Russia's need for an ally became more apparent. With France similarly placed, it is hardly surprising that the two nations drew steadily closer together, in spite of the great political differences between democratic republican France and autocratic Tsarist Russia. French loans began to pour into Russia to help with industrial development and, in 1894, the two nations signed the Dual Alliance to protect Russia from attack by Germany or Austria, and France from her fear of Germany and Italy. Thus, within the space of fifteen years, the major nations of Europe, through fear and suspicion of each other, had divided into two opposing groups.

Britain stays aloof. Britain alone remained aloof. Separated from continental Europe by the English Channel, she remained, apparently safe, in her island kingdom which had not suffered a European invasion since William the Conqueror's landing almost nine hundred years earlier. Meanwhile her colonisers were steadily painting increasing areas of the map of the world with 'British red' and the sealanes were crowded with British merchantmen distributing her industrial produce and creating additional wealth for the 'workshop of the world'. But the days of unquestioned British naval, commercial and industrial supremacy were almost over. The events we have described in the preceding pages indicated to alert statesmen in Britain that the indefinite continuation of this policy of 'Splendid Isolation' would be extremely foolish. Thus the turn of the century saw Britain becoming anxious for her position as a European and a world Power. Britain, too, had to seek allies.

Triple Entente. But what would Britain do? Would she join France, her traditional opponent for centuries, with whom she had so recently clashed in Africa and Asia, or would she join Germany and her allies in spite of their naval and colonial differences? She chose neither of these courses and, in

1902, signed an alliance with Japan directed against their common enemy, Russia.

Britain, embittered by the German encouragement of the Boers and suspicious of increased naval competition, next began to settle her differences with France. This had been accomplished by 1904 and, although the formal agreement was limited to colonial matters, it marked the beginning of a new era in Anglo-French relations. The *Entente Cordiale* (friendly understanding) of 1904 recognised French interests in Morocco and British interests in Egypt. It made no provision for a military alliance, but the settlement of their colonial differences made it easy for the two countries to draw closer together and we have already seen evidence of this in the naval agreement of 1912.

The defeat of Russia by Japan in 1904-5 largely removed British fears there and, prompted by the French who were anxious to draw their two allies closer together, Britain and Russia settled their differences in Persia and Afghanistan in 1907, thus completing the Triple Entente. Once again no promises were made of assistance in the event of war but the direction in which Britain was moving was becoming fairly apparent and the events of the following years were to confirm it.

TOWARDS 'INEVITABLE' CONFLICT

Modern historians are in general agreement that no one wanted war in 1914 but they also agree that many accepted war as inevitable. The fear and insecurity that had been aroused by blustering nationalism, greedy imperialism, the armament race, secret treaties and hostile alliances, newspaper sensationalism and the tactless public statements of the Kaiser, made many believe that it was only a matter of time before a serious war would break out. In order to appreciate the significance of the events in Morocco and the Balkans in the decade preceding the war, it is necessary to set them against this background of fear and insecurity and increasing acceptance of the inevitability of a major conflict.

Testing ground. Morocco became the testing ground for the new friendship between Britain and France. The Kaiser had already declared that Germany was being 'encircled' by the alliance between France and Russia and he realised the possible serious consequences for Germany of the Anglo-French entente of 1904. In the following year he challenged French influence in Morocco when he landed at Tangier and declared that Germany would support Moroccan independence. However, when the conference he demanded met at Algeciras the next year his only support came from Austria and, although the independence of Morocco was recognised by the Powers, France was given special responsibilities there. The arrest of German deserters from the Foreign Legion almost sparked off another international incident at Casablanca in 1908 but the dispute was settled peacefully. Things came to a head in 1911 when the French occupied the capital, Fez, and appeared to be preparing to establish a protectorate over the country. Germany immediately demanded a piece of the French Congo as compensation and sent a gunboat, the *Panther,* to the Moroccan port of Agadir to back its claims. Europe was on the brink of war but, when Britain openly declared her support of France, Germany reduced its demands and the matter was settled peaceably. Europe breathed again. All that German intervention in Morocco had achieved was a strengthening of the bonds between Britain and France.

Balkan crises. Meanwhile, in the Balkans, events were taking a more serious turn. In 1908 Austria openly annexed (or took possession of) the Slav province of Bosnia (see map, page 27) which she had occupied since 1878. This infuriated Serbia which, as we saw at the start of the chapter, was anxious to unite all the Balkan Slavs under its rule. War was probably only averted because Russia, weakened by its recent defeat by the Japanese, was not prepared to come to Serbian assistance against Austria. Another chance soon presented itself. In 1912 the Balkan States of Serbia, Greece, Montenegro and Bulgaria combined to defeat Turkey and to drive it almost completely out of Europe. As a result of their victory each acquired additional territory and Serbia, in particular, became stronger and more confident than before. Although the victors quarrelled over the division of the spoils, the Second Balkan War of 1913 made little difference except that Bulgaria lost some of its gains.

And so, by 1913, a proud and angry Serbia stood as a challenge to Austrian hopes for expansion in south-eastern Europe. Serbia now blocked any chance of Austria reaching the valuable port of Salonika on the Aegean Sea, while Austria's refusal to allow Serbian annexation of Albania prevented Serbia from gaining a coastline on the Adriatic. Neither was prepared to accept the situation as permanent and each was ready to seize the first opportunity to humiliate and overcome the other. (Study the map on page 27.)

THE COMING OF WAR

Immediate cause. The chance came at Sarajevo, capital of Bosnia, on June 28, 1914, when the Archduke Francis Ferdinand, the heir to the Austrian throne, was assassinated. The spark had now been lit which was shortly to turn the whole of Europe into a furnace and engulf the world in the most extensive and frightening war to that time. The events and attitudes and alliances of the preceding years now combined to make a European war inevitable although there were few in 1914 who could have foreseen the carnage and destruction that was to take place.

Austria hoped for a local war with Serbia which would effectively solve its problems before Serbia's Russian ally could be mobilised. With this in mind, Austria handed Serbia an almost impossible ultimatum (or list of demands) which had to be accepted within forty-eight hours. War could still have been avoided because Serbia accepted all but two of Austria's demands and asked that these be decided by arbitration. But Austria rejected Serbia's reply and declared war on July 28.

To the climax. From this date events moved quickly to a climax. In response to a request for help from Serbia, Russia prepared for war. Germany demanded that the preparations be stopped and, when Russia refused, declared war. Two days later this was followed by a German declaration of war on Russia's ally France, and the invasion of Belgium began. The violation of Belgian neutrality, which had a European guarantee, gave the British Government reason to enter the conflict and, by August 4, Europe was at war. Of the great Powers, Italy alone remained a spectator until May, 1915, when, anticipating the greatest gains from joining the Allies, she declared war on Austria-Hungary.

For four years the war raged in the trenches of northern France and on other battlegrounds. The opposing sides seemed to be so evenly matched that although fortunes seesawed with attack and counter-attack no ultimate victory seemed possible. Meanwhile men died in their thousands on the fields of Flanders, on the beaches of Gallipoli and in the freezing cold on the Russian front. In 1917 revolution overthrew the Tsar and Russia withdrew from the war but within a month the Allies were joined by the Americans and the tide of battle began to turn slowly but surely against Germany and her allies. Finally, at 11 a.m. on November 11, 1918, the guns ceased firing and the war was over. More than twenty million men had been either killed or permanently disabled, while the losses in money, buildings, stock and industrial production were impossible to calculate.

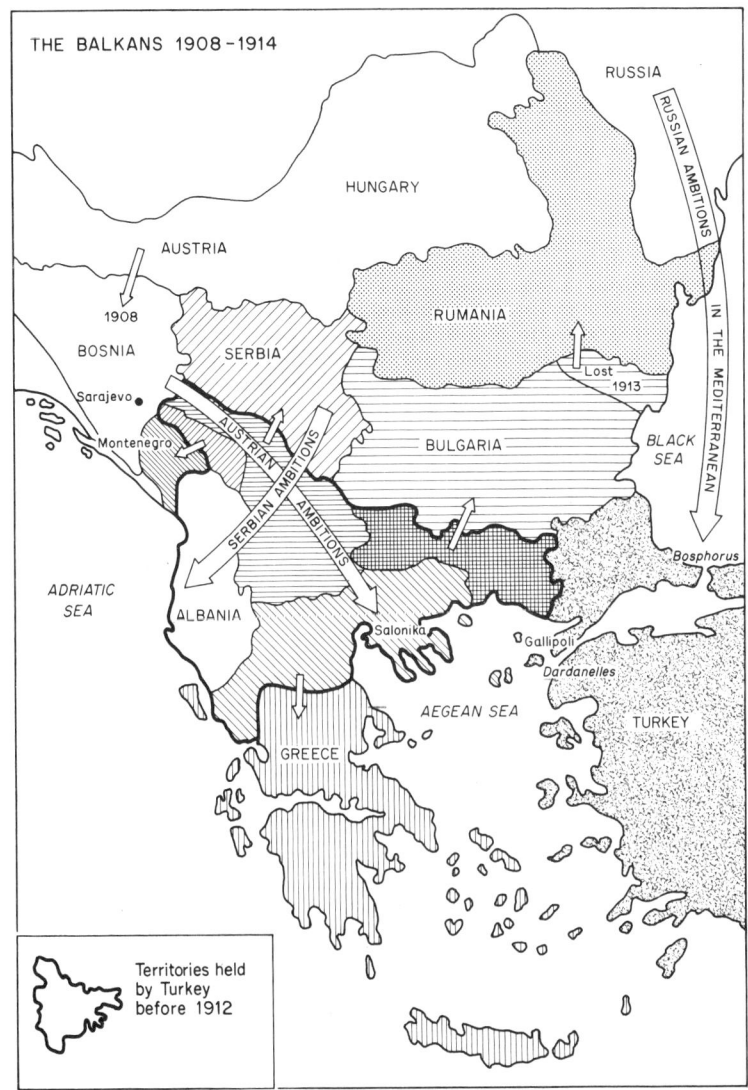

THE BALKANS 1908–1914

RUSSIA

RUSSIAN AMBITIONS

IN THE MEDITERRANEAN

HUNGARY

AUSTRIA

1908

BOSNIA   SERBIA

Sarajevo ●

Montenegro

AUSTRIAN AMBITIONS

SERBIAN AMBITIONS

RUMANIA

Lost 1913

BULGARIA

BLACK SEA

Bosphorus

ADRIATIC SEA

ALBANIA

Salonika

Gallipoli

Dardanelles

AEGEAN SEA

TURKEY

GREECE

Territories held by Turkey before 1912

FIG. 6

RESPONSIBILITY FOR THE WAR

In the fifty years since World War I historians have argued about who was really responsible for the war. Immediately after it public opinion in the various countries was strongly biased in favour of national interests but historians now make it clear that all nations must bear some of the responsibility. This is amply illustrated by Professor Fay, whose *Origins of the World War,* published in 1930, is still regarded as one of the authoritative accounts of the causes of the war.

Austria and Serbia. The original combatants were Austria-Hungary and Serbia. Austria believed that it was acting in self-defence because of Serbia's obvious territorial designs. However, Austria was still prepared to 'rattle the German sword' and to drag the whole of Europe into the war if necessary. Serbia, too, was not guiltless. Later historians have shown that the Serbian Government was fully aware of the assassination plot and took no steps to stop it or to warn Austria. This was not known in Austria at the time and cannot excuse Austria's actions but it is clear proof that Serbia must bear its share of the blame for the events that followed.

Germany. What of the other great Powers? Were they also implicated or were they simply victims of circumstances? Germany neither plotted nor wanted a general European war, though she certainly had ambitions to dominate continental Europe and was quite ready to fight to achieve this. In any case she felt compelled to support Austria which was her only dependable ally. The alternative was to be left isolated between France and Russia, neither of which was friendly. Germany certainly wanted to avoid fighting Britain as well as Russia and France at the same time and here German leaders miscalculated the British reaction to the crisis.

Russia and France. The Entente Powers must also take a share of the blame. Russia had frequently encouraged the Serbian idea of a national Slav State and Serbia expected its support. Although Russia had not fully recovered from the war with Japan, it was prepared to act in 1914 provided it received support from its allies in western Europe. It was Russia's secret military preparations and general mobilisation of its army while still discussing the problem with Austria that prompted Germany to call up its reserves and declare war. France had promised Russia its support if it came to the assistance of Serbia and made no real attempt to stop the Russian preparations for war. The French President appeared to have accepted that the war was inevitable and was more concerned in ensuring that Britain would give her support.

Britain. The British Government was anxious to preserve peace but could not decide whether to support France and Russia until the German invasion of Belgium made sure that public opinion would support a war against Germany. If Britain had openly declared her intentions soon enough, other countries, notably

Fig. 7 — Off to war: Conscripts arrive in Paris 1914.

Austria and Germany, might have been forced to think carefully before they acted. But Britain's move came too late.

'In the forty years following the Franco-Prussian War, there developed a system of alliances which divided Europe into two hostile groups. This hostility was accentuated by the increase of armaments, economic rivalry, nationalist ambitions and antagonisms, and newspaper incitement. But it is very doubtful whether all these dangerous tendencies would have actually led to war, had it not been for the assassination of Francis Ferdinand. That was the factor which consolidated the elements of hostility and started the rapid and complicated succession of events which culminated in a World War, and for that factor Serbian nationalism was primarily responsible.' [1]

[1] Fay, Professor S. B., *Origins of the World War*, New York, 1930 Vol. 2, Macmillan Co.

NOTEBOOK SUMMARY
The Causes of World War I

NATIONALISM
1. Definition
   Aims
   Examples of nationalism in 19th century Europe
   Common problems
2. Nationalism at work (Use these examples to show different features of nationalism)
   In Serbia and Italy
   In France
   In Germany
3. The importance of nationalism

IMPERIALISM
1. Definition
   Reasons for European overseas expansion
   Britain overseas before 1880
   Reasons for colonial competition after 1880
   Results (in general terms)
2. Imperialism at work (In each case note the Powers involved, the reasons for their clashes, and the areas where these occurred)
   In Africa
   In Asia and the Pacific
   In the Balkans and the Near East
3. The importance of imperialism

MILITARY RIVALRY
1. The reason for it
2. The arms race in Europe
3. The Anglo-German naval race (Note causes and results)
4. The effect of military rivalry

THE ALLIANCES
In each case note the date, reasons, members and terms
1. The Triple Alliance
   Three Emperors League (Note its weakness)
   Dual Alliance
   Triple Alliance
2. Anglo-Japanese Alliance
3. The Triple Entente
   Dual Alliance
   Entente Cordiale
   Triple Entente
4. The importance of the alliances

THE CRISES
1. The background
2. Morocco (Note each event and its significance)
   Tangier and Algeciras

Casablanca
Agadir
3. The Balkans (Note each event and its significance)
   Annexation of Bosnia, 1908
   Balkan Wars, 1912 and 1913
   Sarajevo incident, 1914

THE WAR
List the main stages by which the European nations became involved
in the war

RESPONSIBILITY FOR THE WAR
Note the attitude and actions of each of the nations involved: Serbia,
Austria, Russia, Germany, France, Britain

WORDS TO KNOW

The following words used in this chapter need to be understood. Most
of them have been explained in the text but all of them should form
part of a history student's vocabulary. Make a list in the back of your
notebook, with meanings, of those words that are new to you. Learn
these and use them in your essays:
   Alliance, arbitration, autocratic, capital (referring to money),
democratic, diplomacy, enter.te, Junkers, Kaiser, nationalism, Pan-
Slav, protective tariffs, republican, Tsar, ultimatum.

BOOKS TO READ OR CONSULT

Alington, A. F. *The Lamps Go Out*, London, Faber, 1964.
Koch, H. W. *The Origins of the First World War*, London, Macmillan,
   1972.
Schmitt, B. E. *The Origins of the First World War*, London, Historical
   Association (Pamphlet G 39), 1958.
Trainor, L. *The Origins of the First World War*, London, Heinemann
   Educational Books, 1973.

QUESTIONS FOR ESSAYS OR DISCUSSION

1. Why did France, Russia and Britain sink their differences between
   1900 and 1914? Discuss the agreements that were entered into.
2. (a) Discuss the causes of World War I, 1914-18.
   (b) Indicate briefly the reasons for Britain's entry into the war
       against Germany in 1914.
3. (a) Show how and why Europe came to be divided into two
       armed camps in the years 1871-1914.
   (b) To what extent was this division of Europe into two camps
       responsible for general war in 1914?
4. Write an account of the causes of World War I, stressing the TWO
   which you consider to be most important.
5. 'The murder at Sarajevo made European war inevitable'. Discuss.

2

THE GROWTH OF NAZI POWER IN GERMANY TO 1934

By November of 1918, after a year of changing fortunes, the 'war to end all wars' was finally over. In June the Germans were threatening the safety of Paris but by September they had been driven almost completely out of France. In October Germany's allies, Bulgaria, Turkey and Austria-Hungary, withdrew from the war and the German navy mutinied. In November the Kaiser abdicated and the armistice was signed. It only remained to draw up the peace treaties, to 'make the world safe for democracy' and to forget as quickly as possible the horrors of the preceding four years.

And yet, a short twenty years after the Treaty of Versailles was signed, the world was again at war. Within Germany a new and extremely powerful political party, the Nazis, emerged during that period and, led by Adolf Hitler, set out to regain for Germany the position that had been lost in 1918. To understand the reasons for its growth and its success we must turn first to the peace settlement that ended World War I.

THE TREATY OF VERSAILLES

Considering the tremendous losses suffered by the allies during the war and the emotional propaganda directed against the Germans by allied newspapers and politicians, it is not surprising that the demands of the victorious nations were harsh. Also France, the greatest sufferer from the war, had been invaded by German armies twice within fifty years.

The conference was dominated by the French Prime Minister Clemenceau, 'the tiger', whose sole aim was to ensure security for France and prevention of any further German aggression. British public opinion, spurred on by such newspaper headlines as 'Hang the Kaiser' and 'Make Germany Pay', made it difficult for her representative, Prime Minister Lloyd George, to be moderate in his attitude to the defeated enemy. From across the Atlantic and unembroiled in the national interests of the European Powers came President Woodrow Wilson, the champion of international idealism which was to have a partial although far from satisfactory recognition in the formation of the League of Nations.

The 'Big Four' at Versailles were completed by Prime Minister Orlando from Italy who, because of the ineffective part played by his country in the war, had only a minor voice at the conference table.

Germany not invited. Although the other victorious nations were also represented they took little part in the framing of the settlement and simply endorsed the decisions of the 'Big Four'. It is significant to note that neither Germany nor any of the other defeated nations were invited to attend. In later years, the Germans could with some justification claim that they had been forced to sign a *diktat* (a dictated settlement). When the German representatives were finally presented with the treaty to sign they were dumbfounded. Instead of a settlement based on the Fourteen Points as proposed by President Wilson when the armistice was signed they found a set of demands based largely on the selfish interests of the European victors. When they objected they were told that their choice lay between signing in Paris or in Berlin. They signed.

German losses. The map on the next page shows Germany's principal territorial losses in Europe. The valuable industrial lands of Alsace-Lorraine (1 on the map) seized in 1870 had, once more, to be returned to France, while the important coal field of the Saar (2) was to be administered by the League of Nations for fifteen years. Its future would then be decided by a plebiscite (popular vote). Meanwhile the coal was to be used by France. In the northeast further losses of territory resulted from the re-establishment of Poland (3), which had been under Russian control for a hundred years, and the creation of the new nation of Czechoslovakia (4). The important German Baltic port of Danzig (5) was declared a 'free city' to be administered by the League of Nations and Memel (6), another main port, was given to Lithuania. By the reappearance of Poland, Germany lost over three million citizens of whom about one-third were Germans while the 'Polish Corridor' (3a) which gave Poland access to the sea severed East Prussia (7) from the rest of Germany. Smaller areas were ceded to Belgium (8) and Denmark (9). All told Germany lost, in Europe, over six million inhabitants (10 per cent of her population) and a large and strategically important land area. As well as this all German colonies were ceded to the Allies to be distributed as mandates of the League of Nations (see Chapter 4) and all German trading rights were cancelled.

To prevent future German aggression, strict controls were placed on her military strength. Her air force was abolished and her army and navy were greatly reduced in size and strength. For

FIG. 8 — 'The Big Four' 1918 — Orlando, Lloyd George, Clemenceau, Wilson.

FIG. 9

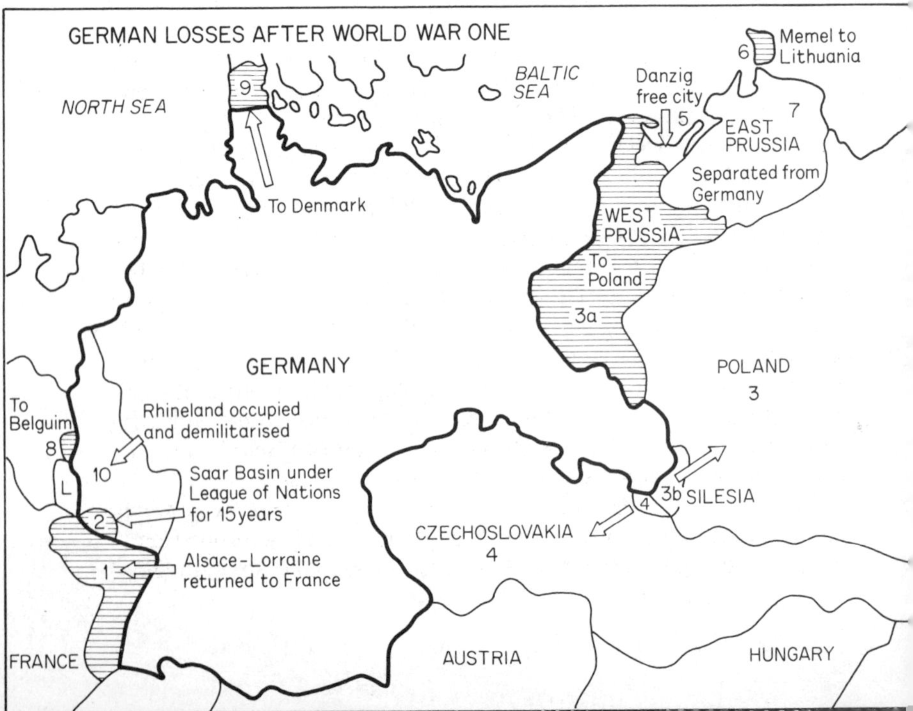

GERMAN LOSSES AFTER WORLD WAR ONE

NORTH SEA

BALTIC SEA

9

To Denmark

Danzig free city

5

Memel to Lithuania

6

EAST PRUSSIA

7

Separated from Germany

WEST PRUSSIA

To Poland

3a

GERMANY

POLAND

3

To Belguim

8

L

10

2

1

Rhineland occupied and demilitarised

Saar Basin under League of Nations for 15 years

Alsace-Lorraine returned to France

4

3b SILESIA

CZECHOSLOVAKIA

4

FRANCE

AUSTRIA

HUNGARY

instance, tanks and submarines were banned. She was never again to build fortifications on the banks of the Rhine and, as an immediate guarantee of this, the Rhineland (10) was to be occupied by the Allies for the next fifteen years. And so Germany, which in 1914 had possessed the greatest army in the world and an immense navy, was reduced to the position of a second-rate nation with no apparent hope of ever reviving its military traditions.

Enormous reparations. But this was not all. Germany was also to pay compensation for damages caused by the war. The actual amount of these reparations (or payments for damages) was never fixed, although something in excess of £6,000,000,000 was envisaged. As well as making this cash settlement it was forced to surrender almost its entire merchant navy to Britain, and large quantities of cattle to Belgium and coal to France. Germany's ability to pay and the effect that an impoverished Germany would have on world trade were scarcely considered. France for one was pledged to make Germany pay even if it was ruined in the process. With this object in mind the French occupied the Ruhr industrial district in 1923 to collect by force the amounts that were owing when Germany fell behind with its payments. France failed in this and created further opposition in Germany. However, as a result, the Dawes Plan of 1924 and later the Young Plan of 1929 modified the reparation payments. But in spite of occupations, modifications and American loans it became increasingly apparent that Germany could not and would not pay anywhere near the amount demanded. When payments finally ceased in 1932 the Germans had paid little more than they had borrowed and the Allied demands had only served to create serious antagonism in Germany and unfortunate economic problems for the world.

'War-guilt clause'. Finally, as we saw in Chapter 1, Germany was forced to admit the complete responsibility for the war in the now famous 'War Guilt Clause' (see page 13). Within Germany the reaction was immediate. The representatives of the new German Government who had been forced to sign the treaty were denounced as traitors. Many cried that Germany had been 'stabbed in the back' and that she was 'beaten but not defeated'. Germans considered that they had been cheated by the Allies who had ignored the high ideals expressed in Wilson's Fourteen Points in preference for a harsh and vindictive peace settlement. If people of the same nationality were to be grouped together in nation States then, the Germans argued, this rule should apply to the German people as well as to the Czechs, Poles and Slavs.

Yet, as a result of the treaty, over two million Germans were now living under foreign flags. Furthermore, Germany was excluded from the League of Nations which therefore tended to appear, in German eyes, as a body concerned with maintaining and enforcing the provisions of the Treaty of Versailles rather than as a truly international organisation seeking peace and justice for all. It is scarcely surprising that those who sought to destroy the Treaty of Versailles found a large amount of support in Germany.

POSTWAR GERMANY

Germany also had problems at home. Soldiers, coming back from the war in their thousands, found there were no jobs for them. Farmers and farm workers were able to return to the land but many city workers found offices shut and factories closed down. The situation was worsened by a serious shortage of food during the winter following the war as it was not until January 1919 that the German Government agreed to use its own ships and pay in gold (of which it had considerable reserves) for the food that the Allies were willing to supply. Soldiers who had been trained to live off the land during the war carried their violent methods over into the postwar period and resorted to robbing and killing to find food for themselves and their families. For the ordinary German, hunger and unemployment were added to the bitterness he already suffered from military defeat.

Economic chaos. Under the strain of the postwar economic problems the German money system, based on the *mark,* collapsed. The following table shows how the *mark* rapidly lost its value in the early 1920s:

DATE	MARKS	£ STERLING
1914	1	1/-
1921	1	½d
January 1923	100	½d
September 1923	1,000,000	½d

The German housewife who, before the war, had taken her money to town in her purse and her purchases home in her basket now found that she needed her basket to carry her money but that she could put her purchases in her purse! In other words, before the end of 1923, German money was not worth the paper it was printed on. German shopkeepers soon refused to accept money in exchange for goods and people were forced to resort to the ancient system of barter to get the goods they required. This created difficulties for those with goods to sell but for those who were paid in money wages the position rapidly became impossible. Although it is easy to see the effects of the fall in the value of money the reasons for it are less obvious.

Gold and paper. Before 1914 most countries used coins made of gold, but during the war governments needed their gold to buy war materials from other countries because gold was the money generally accepted for international dealings. They replaced their gold coins with paper notes and promised to give anyone with a note a gold coin in exchange if he asked for it. As long as the amount of paper money was carefully controlled and the Government was able to pay its debts people were happy to accept this arrangement.

In states such as Britain today, although it is no longer possible to exchange paper notes for gold, this does not cause anyone concern. However, because of the great shortage of money in Germany after the war, the Government began to print more and more paper money. The value of money, like the value of building sections, bananas and boots and shoes, varies largely according to the supply. When there is an oversupply the value falls. By 1923 over two thousand printers were working nonstop to provide Germany with paper money which, when it came into circulation, was so plentiful that it was worthless. The great landowners (the Junkers) were not affected because their land still kept its value, while those with large debts were able to pay them easily with the new cheap money. But those who depended for their incomes on wages or salaries paid in cash were ruined. These included most of the professional classes, the small businessmen, the white-collar workers, old-age pensioners and the bulk of the working class. As their life savings and hopes disappeared before their eyes they became ready to listen to anyone who would promise them a better future.

THE WEIMAR REPUBLIC

The defeat of Germany in 1918 introduced a new age in German politics. The abdication of the Kaiser and the establishment of the new Weimar Republic produced, on paper at any rate, the first truly democratic government in the history of the German people. As in our own Parliament the real power of government was in the hands of the Chancellor (Prime Minister) and his Cabinet. But instead of being responsible to the Emperor as previously, they were now responsible to the House which represented the people and which was elected, by secret vote, by all adult Germans — the Reichstag (pronounced Rīshstāg). The second House, or Reichsrat (pronounced Rīshrāt), like the British House of Lords, had limited powers, while the President, elected by popular vote every seven years, had a position similar to the British monarch. However, there was one important difference. If the President considered a national emergency to exist he could suspend the constitution and rule the country by his own orders (or decrees). There was also an important difference in the method of election used for the Reichstag. This was known as proportional representation and is explained in the following table.

ELECTORATE Each electorate has 100,000 voters	VOTES PER PARTY (Votes counted in thousands)			
	Party A	Party B	Party C	Party D
1	40	36	15	9
2	10	38	40	12
3	10	25	60	5
4	30	30	35	5
5	10	71	10	9
6	10	41	45	4
7	15	35	40	10
8	35	34	10	21
9	15	63	17	5
10	25	27	28	20
TOTAL VOTES PER PARTY	200	400	300	100

SEATS WON BY EACH PARTY

	Party A	Party B	Party C	Party D
(a) Our system (one person elected for each electorate)	2	2	6	0
(b) Proportional representation (each party has seats in proportion to its share of the total votes cast)	2	4	3	1

The democratic system of government as developed in Great Britain ensures that all shades of opinion have the right to be heard but it also ensures that each election is a contest between the different parties because, to win an election, a party has to win the greatest number of electorates. Thus in the above table, Party C has managed to convince the greatest number of voters in six of the ten electorates that its policy is the best so that it is now certain to become the Government. And it is certain that it will be able to operate its policy because it has more seats in Parliament than all the other parties combined. The British system tends to produce strong parties and strong government.

Minority power. When we look at the result under a system of proportional representation we find that Party B has now won the most seats and that Party D, obviously little favoured, is now also represented. But now no party has an overall majority so strong government is impossible and, in fact, minority groups such as Parties A and D may be able to cause considerable upset by swinging support from one party to another. Furthermore, the people in each electorate no longer feel they are represented by their own member of parliament because the seats have been apportioned simply by 'counting heads'. So that although all shades of political opinion are now represented in Parliament this has been achieved at the expense of sound government and by removing the important link between the individual voter and the person who actually represents him in Parliament.

Germany's problems. The Weimar Republic, launched with so much hope, soon found itself sailing in heavy seas as it met economic chaos, physical violence and political instability. To make matters worse the ship itself was not well constructed and the weaknesses in the constitution of the republic exposed it to the full force of the political storms that were sweeping Germany in the early 1920s. And, to complete its problems, even the crew had no real confidence in their ship, as the German people felt keenly the injustices of the Versailles settlement for which they blamed the Government of the new republic. Despite these disadvantages, the ship survived for ten years by which time many of its early problems seemed to have been overcome — or, more correctly, were no longer so obvious. Just as confidence was beginning to develop, the ship foundered on the rock of world economic crisis and all attempts at salvage failed. By 1934 she had been written off by her owners as a total wreck and had already been replaced by a new vessel — the Third Reich. At the helm was captain Adolf Hitler and the course that he steered was planned to lead to world conquest.

HITLER AND THE NAZIS

Among the great mass of small political parties that appeared in Germany after the war was the German Workers' Party. Among its members was a former lance-corporal in the German Army who had won the Iron Cross and who, when the Armistice was signed, lay seriously wounded in hospital — Adolf Hitler. Convinced that the German Army had been defeated by treachery, Hitler left hospital determined to enter politics and to avenge this defeat. By 1920 he had established himself as the leader of this party and, at a great rally in Munich, it adopted his programme for German recovery, renamed itself the National Socialist German Workers' Party, or more familiarly, the Nazis, and adopted as its symbol the swastika.

Hitler's tactics. Hitler blamed all of Germany's problems on the communists, the Jews and the victorious Allies. His active policy appealed to the demobilised, unemployed soldiers and to those who had lost their wealth and their hopes in the postwar economic troubles — especially the middle class. He organised his followers into uniformed bands for street fighting and soon these Stormtroopers (S.A.), or Brownshirts, were greatly feared in the streets of Munich. Around himself he developed his own personal bodyguard, the S.S., or Blackshirts, who later became his devoted and fanatical private army, prepared without question to carry out every command of their Führer (or leader), whether it be sabotage or murder.

Failure. The Nazis' opportunity came with the French occupation of the Ruhr industrial area in 1923. They attempted to overthrow the Government of Bavaria (one of the southern States of Germany with its capital at Munich) preparatory to an attack on Berlin but, at the last moment, their supporters in Bavaria withdrew and left the Nazis to carry out their *putsch* (or organised raid) alone. Following the complete failure of the Munich *putsch,* the Nazi Party was destroyed and Hitler and many other leaders were imprisoned. There were many similar incidents in the difficult days of the early 1920s and, if it had not been for later events, it is doubtful if Hitler and his party would ever have been mentioned in the history books of the mid-twentieth century. Certainly, in the more prosperous days of the later 1920s, little interest was shown in the revived Nazi Party after Hitler's release from prison.

STRESEMANN AND RECOVERY

In 1923 Gustav Stresemann, the only noteworthy statesman of the Weimar Republic, became Chancellor and Foreign Minister. Although Chancellor for only a short time, he remained at the Foreign Office until his death in 1929 and during these six years he was the outstanding figure in Germany. He was largely responsible for the French evacuation of the Ruhr and also for the solution of Germany's money problems by the introduction of a new mark based once more on the gold standard. Stresemann accepted Germany's responsibility to pay the war reparations demanded by the Allies and, in 1924, accepted the Dawes Plan. This allowed Germany a breathing space before payments were resumed and then required increasing payments each year as Germany's ability to pay increased with the recovery of its industry and trade.

Locarno Pact. When the promised Allied evacuation of the Rhineland did not begin in 1925, Stresemann began negotiations which resulted in the signing later in the year of the Locarno Pact. France and Germany recognised as permanent their common frontier established by the Treaty of Versailles and, together with Belgium, promised 'in no case to attack or to invade each other'. This agreement was guaranteed by Italy and Britain. As a result of the improved international relations which followed, the Allies began the evacuation of the Rhineland and, in 1926, Germany was admitted to the League of Nations with a permanent seat on the Council, the executive body of the League (see Chapter 4). So now Germany, within eight years of her humiliation at Versailles, had once more been accepted as an equal and a partner by the other nations of the world. It appeared as if the past would be forgotten and the world could look forward to a new age of peace.

Meanwhile, within Germany, American loans were financing the rebuilding of industry. Tremendous public works programmes were undertaken and the rebuilding of Germany's merchant navy began. Prosperity was steadily returning to the country and by 1929 the standard of living was higher than it had been before the war. The Nazis, Communists and other minority parties still existed but their declining popularity was shown by election returns. In 1928 the Nazis won only twelve of the 490 seats in the Reichstag compared with their thirty-two in 1924. Many of their former supporters discovered a new hope for the future in the remarkable recovery that Germany appeared to be making during the 1920s and had no further use for a party that used violence and extreme methods to gain its ends.

THE BEGINNING OF THE END

But Germany's apparent prosperity was similar to the Biblical house that was built on the sand. It was based largely on foreign loans and, when these suddenly ceased as depression struck the United States of America in 1929, Germany's new-found prosperity was destroyed overnight. Foreign markets could no longer afford to buy German goods and, by 1932, industrial production had been halved. Unemployment and bankruptcy reappeared and the resultant economic distress gave a further opportunity to the Nationalists, Communists and other enemies of the Weimar Republic. Their first chance came when Germany was required to ratify (or accept) the new proposals of the Young Plan which proposed to spread the German reparation payments over the next fifty-nine years. Nationalists (composed mainly of the business interests) and Nazis (drawing support more from the middle and working classes) combined to demand a referendum, or special vote by the whole nation, to decide the question. Although the referendum did not reject the Young Plan, it was ratified by the Reichstag by only two votes.

Nazis advance. At no stage in the history of the Weimar Republic had any party had a majority of the total seats in Parliament[1] and it was now apparent that opponents of the republic were gaining in strength. This was vividly illustrated in the elections of 1930 when the Nazis increased their number of seats from twelve to 107 to become the second largest party in the Reichstag while the Nationalists secured forty-one. Together these parties formed the largest single group in Parliament and controlled over one-quarter of the total seats. Faced with a national economic crisis and the persistent obstructionist tactics of the Nationalists and the Nazis, the German Chancellor, Brüning, asked the President to grant him the emergency powers provided under the constitution (see page 38). For the next two years, while unemployment rose to six million, Brüning used the emergency powers to govern Germany by decree. This meant that Parliament no longer governed the country and that the attempt to introduce democracy to Germany had failed. It was a short step from the decrees of Brüning to the dictatorship of Hitler.

THE NAZI REVIVAL

From the failure of his attempt to seize power by force in 1923, Hitler learned that ballots (i.e. votes) rather than bullets were more likely to bring success. If he was to overthrow the Weimar Republic then he must first win the support of enough German people for the Nazis to dominate the Reichstag. With this purpose in mind he began, while in prison, to write *Mein Kampf* ('My Struggle') which set out the Nazi programme for domination of Germany and for German domination of the world.

Hitler's beliefs. Hitler claimed that the nation should be thought of as one people or *volk:* it was wrong to speak of the upper, middle and lower classes in a country but that the people should all be regarded as belonging to a single nation. Membership of such a nation was decided, said Hitler, purely by race. Now most of the peoples of Europe were descended from the Aryan branch of the human race — as opposed to the Jews who were Semites and the Chinese who were of Mongolian origin, and

[1] Remember the weaknesses of proportional representation discussed on pages 38-9.

so on. Because of intermarriage and migrations there had been a considerable mixing of races in Europe over the centuries but Hitler claimed that, of the European races, those least affected by this and therefore of purest Aryan descent were the Germans. The Germans were a master race, or *herrenvolk*. Finally, he declared, the only way for this great nation to recognise its national unity and to achieve its rightful position in the world was by loyalty to a single leader, the Führer. To support his claims, Hitler twisted and distorted the history of western civilisation but, as one modern historian has said, *Mein Kampf* may have been bad history but it was good prophecy. [1]

Rise of Hitler. Armed with a programme and a philosophy Hitler set out in the years following his Munich failure to revive and reorganise the Nazi Party. Although popular support was limited during this period he was not deterred. Financial help came from many of the big industrialists and the Junkers who feared the growth of communism and were willing to support any party that had as its aim the preservation of private property and the revival of German greatness. Propaganda poured from the party printing presses, and its newspaper, the *Volkischer Beobachter,* had an increasing circulation. Public meetings, while not always well attended, were staged with great show and were always preceded by parades of uniformed Blackshirts and Brownshirts carrying huge banners with swastikas crowned by imperial German eagles and goosestepping to military music.

If the German people did not support the Nazi Party during these years, at least they could not ignore its existence. By 1929 Hitler had welded the Party into a strong and devoted machine ready to follow him without question and willing, indeed eager, to show its strength by outbursts of brutality against the 'enemies of the nation'. Also, by the formation of the Hitler Youth, he had begun to win the support of a new generation of Germans. Boys who were happy to play soldiers in this organisation in the twenties were willing to die for their Führer in the thirties. If the Weimar Republic had failed to win support by educating for democracy, this mistake was not going to be repeated by Hitler who realised that adult support in the future depended on winning the loyalty of the children of the present.

NAZI DICTATORSHIP

Presidential elections were due in 1932. Since 1925 the office had been held by Field Marshal von Hindenburg, one of the greatest

---

[1] C. F. Strong in *Dynamic Europe* (1945) p. 349. Published jointly by Hodder & Stoughton and University of London.

national heroes of World War I. Hindenburg was now in his eighty-fifth year and old age and the strain of the war had sapped much of his vitality. However, he agreed to seek a second term as President and, in an election that proved to be an important trial of strength, he was opposed by three other candidates. In the second ballot that was necessary to ensure that one of the candidates secured an overall majority Hindenburg was re-elected President, winning over nineteen million votes. But, in second place, less than six million votes away, was Adolf Hitler. For him to have risen in the few short years since Munich from obscurity to a position where he had become a serious contender for the highest office in the land seemed nothing less than remarkable. Either he was a genius or else the German people had temporarily lost their reason. Only the future could tell.

Hitler Chancellor. The Presidential elections were followed later in the same year by those for the Reichstag. Increasing unemployment and despair led many to support the Nazi Party, which spoke boldly of a national recovery under its leadership. In a sweeping electoral victory the Nazis won 230 of the 608 seats to become the strongest party in Parliament by almost 100 seats. They still did not have an overall majority and Hindenburg was able to avoid calling on Hitler to become the Chancellor or even to join the Cabinet. The Nazis had a minor setback in the second elections held in the same year but they still remained the largest single party. In January 1933, following a series of compromises and intrigues by the various opposing groups, Hitler was appointed Chancellor. In the struggle for power that was taking place it was expected that he would simply be a puppet whose strings were pulled by his Nationalist backers, the Junkers and the industrialists headed by von Papen who became Vice-Chancellor.

Nazis' triumph. But with total success in sight Hitler was not willing to settle for anything less and immediately called for fresh elections in the hope of winning a complete majority in Parliament. A week before the Germans went once more to the polls the Reichstag building was destroyed by fire. Seizing upon this incident to accuse the communists and to raise the cry of the 'Red Peril', the Nazis began a wave of anti-communist, anti-socialist and anti-Jewish violence. At the same time restrictions were placed on the newspapers, on freedom of speech and other individual liberties. The party won 288 seats in the new Parliament and, with the support of the fifty-three Nationalists, was at last in command of the Reichstag. To make assurance doubly sure Hitler immediately banned the Communist Party so that its eighty-one elected representatives were unable to take their seats.

Suppression of the Communist Party was merely a beginning. A few days later the Reichstag voted Hitler emergency powers to rule for the next four years. In effect the Reichstag had voted itself out of existence and, within three months, other political parties were destroyed and the Nazi Party was declared to be the only legal political party in Germany. Trade unions were also made illegal and were replaced by the Labour Front, which included employers as well as workers. This ensured that workers went where they were directed by their employers or the Government. In this way every organised body that could oppose the new regime was either abolished or silenced, while the Gestapo, the secret police organised by Herman Göring in 1933, terrorised ordinary Germans: any who were even suspected of opposition were killed or imprisoned.

German people 'all one'. Throughout its history Germany had consisted of a number of different States and these had been recognised in the constitution of the German Empire when it was established in 1870. The federal nature of Germany had also been preserved in the Weimar Republic and it was the representatives of *Länder,* the territories which replaced the old States, who had made up the second house of the German Parliament, the Reichsrat. By declaring that the German people were one, undivided nation Hitler was able to destroy the Reichsrat without abolishing it. The disappearance of the *Länder* simply left the building but removed its members!

The Nazi triumph was complete. Every aspect of the national life quickly passed under the control and scrutiny of party officials. Within twelve months almost every opposing voice had been silenced. With returning prosperity, due more to improving world trends than to any actions of Hitler, most people found they were soon better off than they had been since 1918 and so tended to approve the new Government. Only the churches offered resistance. Pastor Martin Niemöller and other church leaders, both Protestant and Roman Catholic, refused to accept Hitler's claim that it was not possible to be both a German and a Christian but, like many of the prophets of old, they tended to be voices crying in the wilderness. Nothing could stop the triumphant progress of the Nazi machine.

THE SUPREME FÜHRER

But the revolution was not yet complete. The Nazi dictatorship was by now assured, though not necessarily the dictatorship of Adolf Hitler. Fearing that his position as leader of the party was threatened, he organised a fearful massacre of his possible rivals or opponents. On June 30, 1934, the infamous 'Night of the Long Knives', more than a hundred Nazis and other leading Germans were murdered by the S.S. and the Gestapo. Only one final step remained to be taken. When President Hindenburg died early in August, Hitler simply announced that, while retaining the position of Chancellor, he would henceforth also be President. His power was now complete. Within Germany he used this power to convert the country into a completely totalitarian State in which every aspect of national life was directly controlled by the Government. The way in which he used his power in the outside world will be examined in the next chapter.

NOTEBOOK SUMMARY
The Growth of Nazi power in Germany to 1934

TREATY OF VERSAILLES
1. Attitude of Allies towards Germany (Note what it was and why. Who represented each of the 'Big Four'?)
   France
   Britain
   U.S.A.
   Italy (Refer to page 26 for Italy's reason for fighting Germany)
   Effect of Allied attitude (Note the basis of the treaty and the way it was presented to the Germans)
2. German territorial losses
   In Europe (Note what was lost and to whom)
   Overseas
   Population losses
3. Safeguards against German aggression
   Note restrictions imposed
4. Reparations
   Their purpose
   French attitude and actions
   How they were paid and the results
5. German reactions (In each case note the German position and attitude)
   War guilt
   Nation States
   League of Nations

POSTWAR GERMANY
1. Unemployment and starvation (Note reasons and results)
2. Collapse of money system
   Reasons
   Effects
3. The Weimar Republic
   Its democratic features

Its constitutional weaknesses (Note Presidential powers, proportional representation)
Attitude of the German people

HITLER AND THE NAZIS
1. Origin of the Nazi Party
Position of Hitler
Party organisation
Sources of support
2. Munich Putsch
Object
Result

GERMANY RECOVERY, 1924-29
1. Importance of Stresemann
In economic recovery
In international acceptance of Germany
2. Results of recovery in Germany
Economic
Political

BEGINNING OF THE END
1. Economic collapse
Reasons
Results (Note how the *economic* results lead to *political* results)
2. Emergency Government (Note its significance)

NAZI REVIVAL
1. Nazi programme (Note its three main features)
2. Financial support (Reason for this)
3. Showmanship (Its effect)
4. Hitler Youth (Its importance)
5. Position by 1929

NAZI DICTATORSHIP
1. Importance of 1932 Presidential election
2. Reichstag elections, 1932
Reasons for Nazi successes
Hitler Chancellor (Reason for appointment. Result)
3. Reichstag fire (Its significance in 1933 elections)
4. Steps to dictatorship
Emergency powers
Removal of opposition (Note restrictions on (a) organised groups, and (b) individuals. Also note attitude of the Churches)
Acceptance by German people (Reasons)

HITLER SUPREME
1. Night of the Long Knives (Significance)
2. Death of Hindenburg (Importance)

WORDS TO KNOW
The following words used in this chapter need to be understood.
Most of them have been explained in the text but all of them should
form part of a history student's vocabulary. Make a list in the back

of your notebook, with meanings, of those words that are new to you. Learn these and use them in your essays:

Abdicate, armistice, diktat, electorate, Führer, Gestapo, herrenvolk, Junkers, Kaiser, mark, Mein Kampf, plebiscite, proportional representation, putsch, ratify, Reichsrat, Reichstag, reparations, Third Reich.

BOOKS TO READ OR CONSULT

Bullock, A. *Hitler, A Study in Tyranny,* Harmondsworth, Penguin, 1963.

Edwards, A. D. *Hitler and Germany 1918–1939,* London, Heinemann Educational Books, 1972.

Elliot, B. J. *Hitler and Germany,* London, Longman, 1966.

Grunberger, R. *Germany, 1918-1945,* London, Batsford, 1964.

King-Hall, S. *Three Dictators,* London, Faber, 1964.

Shirer, W. L. *The Rise and Fall of the Third Reich,* London, Pan, 1964.

QUESTIONS FOR ESSAYS OR DISCUSSION

1. (a) What were the conditions in Germany 1914-33 which made it easier for Hitler to come to power?

   (b) Describe the process by which Hitler achieved power in Germany up to 1934.

2. (a) What were the main terms of the Treaty of Versailles that affected Germany?

   (b) What was the German attitude to the treaty and was this attitude justified?

   (c) What use did Hitler make of the Treaty of Versailles to further his ambitions in Germany up to 1934?

3. (a) What were the weaknesses in the constitution of the Weimar Republic?

   (b) In what ways and with what success did Hitler exploit these weaknesses?

3

FROM WORLD WAR I
TO WORLD WAR II

It has often been said that World War II was simply a continuation of World War I, and indeed it may well have seemed like it to those who lived through or fought in both. In 1914 the most recent war to have involved the whole of Europe on a large scale had been fought more than one hundred years before when Napoleon Bonaparte had cast his shadow over almost the entire continent. Yet within less than half a normal lifetime the world was disrupted by two wars which, for the first time in history, involved not just armies but entire populations.

In 1939, as in 1914, Germany was the strongest military nation in the world and, on each occasion, it was on the side of aggression. World War I was sparked off by the problem of national minority groups in the Balkans — World War II by similar problems in Poland. Both of these wars followed intensive national competition in armaments, in trade and in colonial expansion. In each case there was a steady buildup of international 'incidents' which ultimately led to a position from which retreat seemed impossible and war the only alternative. But it is much too simple an explanation to say that, in 1939, history was merely repeating itself. Although there are similarities between the development of the two wars, a closer examination will show that there are also many differences.

THE PERIOD OF HOPE

With the conclusion of 'the war to end war' in 1919 most people believed that 'the world is now safe for democracy'. Their hopes seemed justified in the next decade as, after an initial period of settling down following the upheaval of four years of war, democracy appeared to be firmly established in most countries and peace seemed assured. In Germany, economic recovery had raised the standard of living above the prewar level, while in the United States of America President Hoover declared in 1928 that, 'We in this country are nearer to the final triumph over poverty than ever before in the history of any land'. If all was not well underneath, at least the surface was not ruffled too much as most countries seemed to be steadily overcoming their problems and improving conditions for their people.

International good will. On the international scene the story was the same. The signing of the Washington Treaty in 1922 seemed to suggest that the rivalries and jealousies of Europe were not going to be transferred to the Pacific. Japan, by accepting an inferior position for its navy, did not appear to have serious colonial ambitions or a desire to become the dominant Power in east Asia.[1] The Nine Power Treaty signed at Washington in the same year guaranteeing the integrity (or preservation) of China and recognising equal trading rights for all seemed further evidence of the spirit of international co-operation that was abroad in the early 1920s.

In Europe the Locarno Pact of 1925 suggested a similar spirit. That France and Germany were able to recognise their common Rhineland frontier and agree never to go to war against each other again seemed a certain safeguard of peace, particularly as the Pact was guaranteed by Britain and Italy. These four nations were the great Powers of Europe and they, more than any others, could make or destroy the peace of Europe. The acceptance of Germany as a member of the League of Nations with a permanent seat on the Council in 1926 presupposed the settlement of earlier antagonisms and pointed the way to increasing international co-operation.

This spirit of optimism reached its highest point with the signing of the Briand-Kellogg Pact, or the Pact of Paris, in 1928. It was originally proposed by the French Foreign Minister, Briand, as a joint Franco-American statement denouncing war to mark the tenth anniversary of American entry into World War I. However, American enthusiasm resulted in the signing of a peace pact by almost all nations, including all the great Powers, in which war was 'unreservedly renounced as an instrument of national policy'. In spite of high sounding aims the Pact provided no guarantees, had no machinery to make it work and, in effect, was not worth the paper it was printed on.

League of Nations. During the 1920s the League of Nations was quietly establishing itself as an international force for peace. No major disputes occurred to test its real effectiveness but numerous small problems were referred to it for settlement. As well as its humanitarian activities — such as assisting with the problems of refugees — and its economic assistance — providing advisers and loans to help reconstruction in Austria, China and

[1]A naval ratio of 5:5:3 was agreed between Britain, the United States and Japan.

other countries — the League was active in military disarmament conferences, the settlement of disputes by arbitration and the safeguarding of the rights of minority racial groups. Apart from the United States (see Chapter 7) and the Soviet Union, admitted in 1934, all the major and most of the smaller nations were members by 1929, when membership totalled fifty-five.

UNDERLYING PROBLEMS

Italy. However, there were signs that all was not right with the world. In Italy economic problems and political unrest had already resulted in the emergence of Mussolini and the beginning of the establishment of a new type of dictatorship — the Fascist totalitarian State such as Hitler was later to create in Germany (see Chapter 2). Italy had failed to secure from the war its fair share of the fruits of victory. Although it recovered small Italian-speaking areas from the Austrian Empire as it was broken up, it did not receive control of any former German or Turkish colonies nor did it gain other territory in Europe that the Allies had promised if Italy joined the war against Germany. It was unlikely that Mussolini, anxious to restore the glory of the ancient Roman Empire, would accept this situation.

Japan. Another dissatisfied victorious nation was Japan. Its part in the Allied victory had been small and, in fact, it had used the war rather as an opportunity to strengthen its position in China. Opposition to Germany had suited the Japanese very well as it had allowed them to seize German trading stations and rights in China without any interference from the nations of Europe. However, the Americans had not been prepared to accept large-scale extension of Japanese interests and control in China and, at the end of the war, had forced the return of at least some of these gains to the Chinese. Furthermore, Japanese acceptance of the restrictions imposed by the Washington Treaty was more of a reluctant recognition of the inevitable than an expression of Japan's peaceful intentions.

Feeling of fear. German dissatisfaction with the Versailles Settlement has already been examined (pages 33-5) but the fact that Germany had not expressed resentment during the greater part of the 1920s did not mean there was none. Like Mussolini in Italy, Hitler was all too soon willing to act to rectify these grievances. Thus, in spite of an apparent air of co-operation and international good will there was an undercurrent of fear and dissatisfaction in the world of the 1920s. This was shown by the failure of most nations to disarm. Although the signatories of the Charter of the League of Nations undertook to reduce their armaments, this promise was never fully carried out. Of all the great nations only Britain made a serious attempt to honour this pledge. Dominated by a fear of a German revival, the French sought every possible safeguard for the European Settlement of 1919. As well as signing military pacts with Poland, Czechoslovakia, Rumania and Yugoslavia in the mid-twenties, France also began to plan the vast line of fortresses, later known as the Maginot Line, along her German frontier from Switzerland to Belgium. Other nations followed her example.

Less noticeable but nevertheless important undercurrents also contributed to international tension. The statesmen at Versailles had set out to practise the principle of self determination whereby every racial group would be able to control its affairs in its own State. As a result new nations such as Poland, Czechoslovakia, Hungary and Yugoslavia appeared on the map of Europe and many boundary adjustments were made in existing States. However, racial groups are so intermingled, especially in eastern Europe, that a perfect solution to this problem was impossible without wholesale mass migrations. So, in spite of the best of intentions, there were still over thirty million Europeans living under foreign flags after the Peace Settlement was finalised. We have already seen that it was a problem of this sort that was the immediate cause of World War I. The problem still remained.

Colonies resented. British and French acquisition of most of the former German and Turkish colonies also aroused resentment. Although they were to be administered on behalf of the League of Nations, many believed that this was just a blind to allow the victorious nations to enjoy the benefits of the colonies without actually seizing them. Thus, underneath all the apparent good will and co-operation there were many thorny problems unsolved and many jealousies and resentments that could easily lead to serious international crises given the right circumstances. These were provided in 1929.

THE PERIOD OF DOUBTS

Although there were a number of underlying problems, the twenties remained a period of optimism. President Hoover captured the spirit of the times in his inaugural address in March 1929 when he said, 'I have no fears for the future of this country. It is bright with hope.' But, in October of the same year, hope rapidly changed to doubt as a serious financial crisis developed on the Stock Exchange in Wall Street, New York. Panic followed and investors hastened to sell their shares before their values fell any further. Literally millions of shares changed hands in a few days as public confidence continued to decline. Shortly the effects of this were being felt in almost every country in the world. American statesmen urged that 'prosperity was just around the corner', but it was not until world industry and agriculture had again to gear themselves for war ten years later that anything like normal conditions of employment and economic expansion returned. What caused this depression that was to have such a serious effect on international relations?

Overproduction. Throughout the western world farmers in the postwar decade faced the problem of overproduction. New methods, the increased use of machinery and the revival of European farming meant that the bread-eating world could not use all the wheat being produced. Consequently prices fell so sharply that, in 1929, wheat was cheaper than it had been at any time since the reign of King Henry VIII in England 400 years earlier. Coffee growers, cotton planters and farmers generally found that increasing agricultural production was not being matched by increasing consumption. Millions of farmers were faced with ruin. The climax came with the industrial depression in the early thirties when city dwellers, faced with smaller pay packets and reduced incomes, had less money to spend on food and clothing. For millions of farmers the prospect of ruin suddenly became a reality.

In the industrial world the situation was similar although not so obvious at first. In the postwar decade the tremendous growth of the motor car, radio, motion picture and other new industries led to great industrial development. There was an increased demand for rubber, oil, iron and other raw materials and new employment opportunities were created in a host of related industries. While the whole world shared in this growth and prosperity it was most evident in the United States, which had emerged from the war as the wealthiest nation in the world. But the prosperity was not shared by all sections of the nation. Wages did not increase as rapidly as prices and, while the big businessmen increased their wealth, millions of wage earners faced difficult times. Although mass production allowed great increases in the quantity of goods available for sale, low wages for factory and other city workers and low farm incomes resulted in many of these remaining unsold.

Trade restrictions. Therefore, in both agriculture and industry, the western world was suffering from overproduction while the hungry and underprivileged people of Asia were too poor to buy its surplus food and goods. To solve this problem, most nations, by the end of the twenties, had imposed restrictions on foreign trade. These were designed to protect their own industries and to prevent other countries 'dumping' their surplus products at low prices. These restrictions greatly reduced world trade and unemployment began to increase as industries were forced to reduce production. Rather than solve the problem, the restrictions on trade simply intensified it. Now nations with surpluses of goods which they could not sell on their home markets found it increasingly difficult to sell them overseas. More and more people faced the prospect of being out of work.

Investment of Savings. Much of the industrial growth in the twenties had been financed by borrowed money. When times are prosperous, people are usually willing to lend or invest their money. While one common way of investing money in this country, especially for the person with limited savings, is by depositing it in a Post Office savings account from which it is borrowed by the Government, this is not by any means the only method available. Many people invest their savings in industry or commerce by buying shares in a company producing or distributing goods for sale. These may range from cars to table knives and from woollen blankets to nylon stockings. Whatever the product, the factory in which it is made or the shop in which it is sold requires finance. This is usually provided by the sale of 'shares', which are available for purchase on the Stock Exchange. The purchasers of these shares not only share the risks involved in the making and selling of goods but also have the chance of sharing in the profits if the business is successful.

It is loan money of this type that provides a large amount of the money necessary to finance the development of industry. Most people who invest their money in this way are happy to see it increased by the annual dividends which accrue if the company is making a profit. However, some investors try to buy shares which they expect to rise in price in the hopes of selling them at a profit. Such investors, known as speculators, aim to make money not by the normal process of industrial expansion but by gambling in shares. Similar speculations are often made with real estate (especially building sections), antique furniture and works of art. The effect of such speculation is usually to force the value of the articles concerned to an artificially high level not related to their real worth. This was what happened on the Stock Exchanges in the United States in the 1920s.

Share values forced. In the period of great confidence that followed World War I in America millions of ordinary people invested life savings in expanding industry. Big business was ready to gobble up vast numbers of dollars and paid handsome dividends on such investments. The inability of customers to pay for the vast array of new washing machines, furniture and cars was not of immediate importance. Within the United States 'time payment' was introduced, while overseas countries were provided with increasingly large American loans to enable them to buy American goods.

Meanwhile, encouraged by the general air of confidence, speculators were active on the Stock Exchange forcing up share values as they bought and sold in the hope of making quick fortunes. Too often they worked with borrowed money, advanced by the banks and the share-brokers, and they only paid for their shares when they had managed to sell them at a profit.

The 1929 crash. It was this bubble of false optimism that burst with such suddenness in October 1929. Throughout the twenties share prices had fluctuated as there were occasional moments of doubt. They had always recovered and prosperity had seemed even more assured than before. But in 1929, following a particularly wild period of speculation, panic broke out. As share prices fell, the bankers and brokers who had lent money to speculators demanded repayment of their loans and, failing to get it, sold their clients' shares for whatever prices they could get. Share prices continued to fall and millions who had begun the month of October with fortunes ended it in debt.

If the effects within the United States were serious, overseas they were disastrous. For more than a decade American dollars had been 'priming the pump' of European industrial recovery. Without warning the flow was reduced to a trickle and then ceased altogether. Confidence was destroyed, industries closed down, unemployment figures soared and widespread poverty returned. The twenties, which after a shaky start had promised so much, ended on a note of doubt that was to have serious results in the next ten years.

While the democratic nations of the world tried to grapple with the problems of unemployment by various types of State action such as public works schemes and unemployment benefits, other countries found a different solution. In Germany, Italy and Japan public distraction was provided by employment in the armament factories and the armed forces and, especially in Germany, in the building of great autobahnen (motorways) with a military as well as a peaceful purpose. At the same time these nations diverted attention from their internal problems by beginning policies of aggression overseas. The international co-operation of the twenties was rapidly replaced by a new age of aggressive nationalism with each nation striving to achieve its own interests with little consideration for the interests of others.

Dictatorships. Meanwhile in eastern Europe many of the new States formed after the war found the pressure of events was too great for their recently established democratic institutions to survive. Faced with the economic problems caused by the depression or the racial problems caused by the amalgamation of different groups, and presented with the examples of apparently successful dictatorships in Germany, Italy and Russia, many of them soon followed suit. Before the end of the thirties Austria, Hungary, Yugoslavia, Rumania, Bulgaria, Albania, Turkey, Greece, Poland, Latvia, Lithuania, Estonia, Portugal and Spain had all become dictatorships. Only Czechoslovakia remained unaffected but, even there, increasing Nazi pressure made the task of government very difficult. Democracy appeared to have failed.

It was not to their elected representatives that people looked to solve their problems but rather to strong leaders who did not hesitate to use force to achieve their ends and who promised greater prosperity and national glory in return for unquestioning obedience. Democratic governments such as our own depend for their success on their individual citizens. It is their aim and purpose to safeguard the rights and liberties of every individual, no matter what his race, religion or political beliefs. In return they expect to receive the loyalty and support of the citizens who make up their nations.

All-powerful State. The new dictatorships of the thirties subordinated the rights of the individual to the needs of the State. Supported by vast propaganda campaigns and loyal troops the national leaders were able to convince their people, either by persuasion or by fear, that national glory and national prestige were the highest goals that they could seek. If the rights of the individual as we understand them clashed with the needs of the nation there was no doubt as to which would triumph. A new generation of children grew up in these countries believing that their greatest privilege was to fight and, if need be, die for their country. These were to become the soldiers who would follow their leaders with fanatical loyalty in the belief that it was for the honour and glory of their fatherland.

INTERNATIONAL AGGRESSION

One of the countries most seriously affected by the depression was Japan. Between 1929 and 1931 her export trade was halved and some solution had to be found to her increasing economic troubles. Directly across the Yellow Sea lay the Chinese province of Manchuria. Since the beginning of the twentieth century Japan had been actively interested in Manchuria which had many of the raw materials she herself lacked. Most of the factories and railways there had been developed with Japanese money and the region had proved important in the development of Japanese industry. It seemed to provide the obvious solution to Japan's economic problems.

However, Manchuria was part of China and its rich agricultural lands were becoming increasingly important in a land where famine was common. It was unlikely that China would agree to unlimited Japanese influence there, but the situation was similar to that in nineteenth century Africa where the native rulers had been powerless to stop the advance of the more powerful European nations. So, when Japanese soldiers staged a bomb incident at the important railway town of Mukden on the night of September 18, 1931, they were quickly able to defeat local Chinese troops and over-run the whole province. Chinese appeals to the League of Nations produced an investigating committee but no action.

Lesson for others. To Americans and Europeans who lived thousands of miles away the affair seemed of little importance but they were mistaken. Japan had successfully used force to gain its ends. The lesson for any nation that wished to follow its example was obvious. Japan followed its initial success in Manchuria with attacks on Shanghai. In 1932 the League of Nations, meeting in Geneva, condemned the Japanese action in invading Manchuria and refused to recognise the newly created State of Manchukuo which it claimed was simply a 'puppet State' under direct Japanese control. The Japanese reply was to resign its membership of the League in 1933 and, at the same time, to expand its influence on the mainland by invading the neighbouring Chinese province of Jehol immediately north of the Great Wall. The western nations, seeing no threat to themselves and possibly hoping that Japan might come into increasing competition with the Soviet Union, still took no action (map, page 131).

FADING HOPES FOR PEACE

The repercussions of Japanese aggression in Asia were not immediately felt in Europe where, shortly after the invasion of Manchuria began, a great disarmament conference opened. The League of Nations had been planning the conference for some years and it was finally held in 1932. However, although it met at intervals for the next two years, it was a dismal failure. When other nations refused to reduce their military strength to the level that had been imposed on Germany by the Treaty of Versailles (see page 35), Hitler, who had just come to power in Germany, withdrew from the conference and soon afterwards Germany resigned from the League of Nations.

Germany rearms. In January 1935 a plebiscite (a special vote by the people) was held to decide the future of the Saar industrial area which, since the end of the war, had been administered by the League of Nations. Control of this area was vital to Hitler's plans. Encouraged by the overwhelming vote for reunion with Germany and freed from international commitments by his withdrawal from the League, Hitler began to rearm Germany. In March he announced that the German air force, the Luftwaffe, had been re-established and that military conscription was to be reintroduced. This was followed in April by the news that Germany had a fleet of submarines. The rearmament that had been started in secret now proceeded openly.

Stresa front. Hitler's assurances that German rearmament was purely for defence were not well received by the other nations of Europe, and in April 1935 the Prime Ministers of Britain and France met Mussolini at Stresa in Italy to discuss the possible German threat to European peace. The Stresa Front that was established as a result of this meeting was simply a statement by the three nations supporting the League of Nations and the Pact of Paris and an agreement to act together to oppose any nation that attempted to alter the provisions of the Treaty of Versailles if this endangered the peace of Europe. But although German rearmament had already broken one of the terms of the treaty and appeared to be a threat to the peace, no action was considered. The weakness of the Stresa Front became obvious when, next month, Germany announced a programme of full-scale rearmament. When this was followed in June by an agreement between Britain and Germany which recognised Germany's right to rebuild her navy up to one-third of the size of the British navy, it was apparent that the Stresa Front was a dead letter. This was confirmed by Mussolini's invasion of Abyssinia in October.

ITALIAN AMBITIONS

Until 1935 Mussolini appeared to be an important force for peace in Europe and the mobilisation of Italian forces on the Austrian border in 1934 had prevented Germany's seizure of that country. However, as Italy became more tightly gripped by the depression, an overseas distraction became necessary. This would provide employment in the forces and in the armament factories and could also help to restore Italian national pride. Abyssinia (see map, page 17) lying as it did between the Italian colonies of Eritrea and Somaliland, had long attracted the attention of Italy. In 1889 an Italian protectorate had been established but an attempt, in 1896, to increase control over the territory had resulted in a humiliating defeat for Italian troops at Adowa. Eager to avenge this humiliation and to establish Italy as an important imperial nation, Mussolini determined to conquer Abyssinia. Spears and other primitive native weapons proved of little avail against the modern equipment of the Italian army and air force and, despite heroic resistance, the country was quickly at the mercy of the invaders when the Italian attack began in October 1935.

Again no action. Once again the aggression was condemned by the League of Nations but no action was taken. It was proposed that sanctions (or trade restrictions) should be imposed on Italy and, in particular, that her oil supplies should be cut off. To be effective, sanctions had to be all embracing but once again national self-interest prevailed. France regarded Mussolini as a powerful counter-balance to the probable German revival under Hitler; Britain was anxious to find a peaceful solution; and in the United States, untroubled by membership of the League of Nations, businessmen found considerable profit to be gained by selling to Italy the munitions she needed. Aggression had again triumphed but this time it was much closer to Europe and involved one of the great European Powers. The few sanctions imposed had only caused resentment and in 1936 Italy followed Japan and Germany out of the League of Nations.

THE AGGRESSORS COMBINE

Japan and Italy had now shown their hands. Germany was quick to follow. While the League of Nations debated and condemned Italian annexation of Abyssinia, Hitler boldly marched his troops into the demilitarised Rhineland. Although his action was in direct defiance of both the Locarno Pact and the Treaty of Versailles it produced nothing more than protests from France and Britain. Indeed, many people in Britain believed that Germany was simply regaining territory that was rightfully hers. In spite of the admission of the Soviet Union to the League of Nations in 1934 it was still communism rather than fascism that was most feared by the people of western Europe.

Events in Spain. Meanwhile, events in Spain momentarily attracted Europe's attention. Since a military *coup d'etat* (or seizure of the Government) in 1923 Spain had had an unhappy history, culminating in the abdication of King Alphonso XIII and the establishment of a republic in 1931. Internal difficulties continued until, in July 1936, General Franco, commander of the Spanish forces in Morocco, landed with his troops in the south and a civil war broke out. The importance of this war for Europe lay not so much in the successful establishment of a dictatorship by Franco, but in the support that was offered to the opposing sides by major European Powers. The Republicans, who opposed Franco, were supported to some extent by the Soviet Union but Franco received considerable help in men and weapons from both Germany and Italy.

Fascist alliance. Before the Spanish Civil War, Hitler and Mussolini had already seen advantages in closer co-operation. Drawn closer by their intervention in support of Franco, the two dictators agreed in October 1936 to work together in foreign policy. Thus was born the Rome-Berlin Axis. A month later Germany signed an Anti-Comintern Pact with Japan for their mutual protection against Russian aggression. It only remained for Italy to join this Pact in 1937 to complete the alliance of the Fascist States. Although there were no definite promises of military assistance in these agreements they foreshadowed future events. Each of these States had already openly defied the League of Nations. Together, their confidence in their ability to act in their own interests without fear of the consequences was immeasureably increased.

FAILURE OF COLLECTIVE SECURITY

Since 1918 France had been greatly concerned for its safety. Although on the victorious side Frenchmen had not forgotten that German armies had fought on French soil three times in the past hundred years. France had always lacked faith in the League of Nations as a powerful enough force to prevent further attacks by Germany and, as we have seen earlier in this chapter (pages 50-52), had been active in the creation of additional safeguards. Specific pacts aimed at preserving peace had been signed with Poland and the Little Entente nations (Czechoslovakia, Yugoslavia and Rumania). The Locarno Pact and the Pact of Paris had been signed by all the important European Powers. By the end of the twenties French safety, on paper at any rate, seemed assured.

Pact with Poland. But by 1934 German rearmament, although not openly admitted, was common knowledge in Europe. In the same year Hitler gained a notable diplomatic victory by signing a ten-year, non-aggression pact with Poland which greatly weakened the defence system that France had been developing so carefully. Faced with this double danger the French Foreign Minister, Barthou, set out to increase precautions against the possibility of a German attack and began negotiations with the Soviet Union to develop an Eastern European defence agreement. France was chiefly responsible for the admission of the Soviet to the League of Nations in 1934 and, by the start of 1936, had settled its differences with Italy and signed a pact with Russia in which each agreed to provide immediate assistance if the other was attacked. At last it appeared that Germany was contained.

Turning point in history. However, the Franco-Russian agreement had unforeseen consequences resulting as it did in the immediate German reoccupation of the Rhineland. This proved to be a turning point in European history. It was a direct breach of both the Treaty of Versailles and the Locarno Pact and military action against Germany would therefore have been quite justifiable. Yet, distracted by the Abyssinian crisis, Britain and France took no action. Thereafter it was too late. From 1936 onwards German annual expenditure on armaments was more than double the combined spending of Britain and France. The nations of the world had failed to act together to stop the aggression of Japan, Italy or Germany. Collective security had failed.

Appeasement. Neither Britain nor America shared France's fear of Germany, but there were other reasons that prevented these nations from taking a stand against aggression. The British people sincerely wanted peace and there was a strong pacifist or anti-war spirit in the country. As in France, almost every British family had lost at least one relative in the Great War and there was a strong body of public opinion determined that Britain would never again be involved in war, whatever was at stake. This opinion was reflected in the politicians of the 1930s; Prime Ministers Baldwin and Chamberlain believed that peace could be preserved by discussion. When Neville Chamberlain became Prime Minister in 1937 he was anxious to meet Hitler and Mussolini and to reach agreement on the problems of the times. Unfortunately, while Chamberlain believed that the promises made at these meetings were made to be kept, Hitler believed that they were made to be broken — when the time was right.

Voices of warning. Of all the British politicians of the 1930s, the only one to raise his voice in warning against the Fascist dictators was Winston Churchill, at that time out of favour with his party and regarded as a warmonger. Few people took him seriously when he said in the mid-thirties: 'Each one hopes that if he feeds the crocodile last the crocodile will eat him last. All of them hope that the storm will pass before their turn comes to be devoured. But I fear, I fear greatly, the storm will not pass. It will rage and it will roar, ever more loudly, ever more widely. It will spread to the south. It will spread to the north.'

As the decade progressed, his warnings began to assume a note of prophecy.

Across the Atlantic another lone voice was raised against the threat of Fascist aggression as President F. D. Roosevelt warned of the dangers for America and the entire free world if aggression continued unchecked. But Americans continued to cling to the isolationist outlook which had been typical of their thinking for more than a century. It had been with considerable reluctance that America had entered World War I and it had been quick to shake the dust of Europe from its feet at the close. The refusal to sign the Treaty of Versailles or to join the League of Nations typified the belief that Americans should not allow themselves to become involved in the problems of the Old World. A series of Neutrality Acts in the middle thirties indicated this determination not to be caught up in European affairs again. There seemed little to hinder Hitler from proceeding with his plans.

PRELUDE TO WAR

In 1937 Japan, encouraged by its previous success and by the failure of the League to take a firm stand against aggression elsewhere, began an undeclared war on China (see Chapter 6). In Europe, Hitler sensing the time was right, invaded Austria in 1938 to complete the *Anschluss,* or union with Germany. Although this was a deliberate breach of the Treaty of Versailles there were many who were prepared to accept Hitler's claim that he was simply righting a serious wrong. If the Treaty of Versailles had recognised the right of other people of the same nationality and language to rule themselves, then, said Hitler, it was only proper that this right should also apply to Germans.

Success in Austria was followed by a campaign to recover the 'lost Germans' who, as a result of the Versailles Settlement, had become minority groups in foreign countries. The two largest of these groups were to be found in Czechoslovakia and Poland. Czechoslovakia had been much the most successful of the new nations created in 1919 and there was no truth in the Nazi claim that the German minority were being oppressed by the Czech Government. But in September 1938 Hitler declared that, 'Three and a half million Germans are being oppressed in the Czech State. They too are the creatures of God. The Almighty did not create them that they should be surrendered by Versailles to a

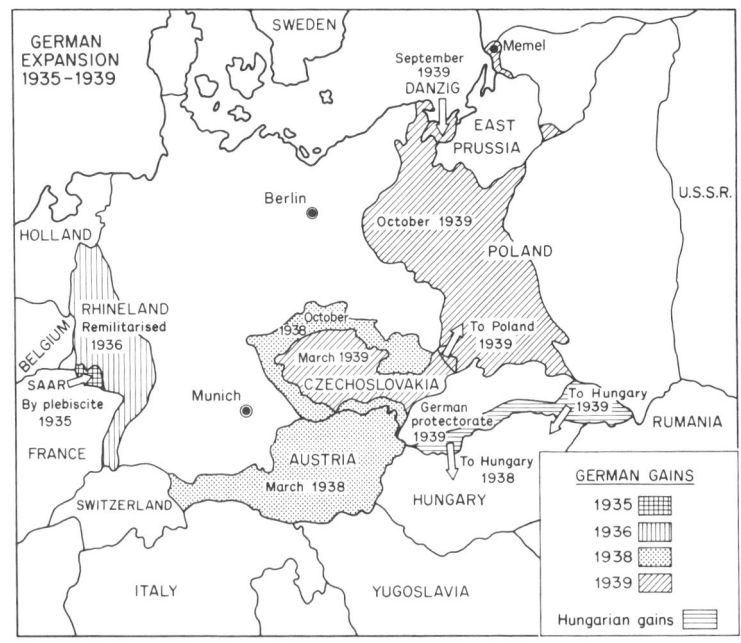

FIG. 10

FIG. 11 — The German occupation of Sudetenland, 1938.

foreign Power which is hateful to them. I say that if these tortured souls cannot obtain rights and help by themselves, they can obtain them from us!'

Failure at Munich. The following day Prime Minister Chamberlain asked Hitler to meet him as soon as possible to discuss the situation in Czechoslovakia. The meeting took place at Munich on September 15, 1938.

For a fortnight proposals and counter-proposals were discussed in the capital cities of Europe while Hitler, losing patience at the refusal to grant his 'last territorial claim in Europe', mobilised his forces ready to invade Czechoslovakia in order to seize the predominantly German Sudetenland. A last-minute intervention by Mussolini persuaded Hitler to meet Chamberlain, Mussolini and Daladier (the French Prime Minister) at Munich. Without consulting Czech wishes, the four leaders agreed that the Sudetenland was to be evacuated immediately and united with Germany. Chamberlain returned to London claiming that he had brought the British 'peace in our time', but in the House of Commons Churchill argued that Britain had 'suffered a total and unmitigated defeat'.

Within six months Churchill was proved to be right as, in March 1939, Hitler completed his occupation of Czechoslovakia. With its easily defended mountain frontiers, its highly developed armament works at Skoda, and its efficient heavy industries, Czechoslovakia was the one strong State in eastern Europe apart from the Soviet Union. Its absorption not only greatly increased the military and industrial strength of Germany, but completely destroyed the French system of alliances that had been developed so painstakingly during the previous twenty years. French safety was now seriously threatened and British pacifism and American isolationism had suffered a severe shock. It was doubtful if Hitler would be allowed to proceed unopposed with his plans for the conquest of Europe.

Invasion of Poland. Convinced that Britain and France were prepared to talk but not to act, Hitler seized Memel from Lithuania, demanded the return of Danzig and the right to build a railway line across the Polish Corridor (see map, page 63). He was little concerned by an Anglo-French guarantee that they would not allow Poland to suffer the same fate as Czechoslovakia but, as a safeguard, signed a non-aggression pact with the Soviet Union in August 1939. This included a secret agreement to divide Poland between them — the bribe that probably won Russian support. Hitler, reinforced by the knowledge that he need no longer fear a war on two fronts, invaded Poland on September

1, 1939. Two days later Britain and France declared war on Germany. World War II had begun.

Meanwhile, anxious not to be outdone by the German Führer, Mussolini had seized Albania and was preparing to turn the Adriatic Sea into an Italian lake. When the collapse of France was imminent Italy hastily declared war in the hopes of sharing the spoils. Hitler's refusal to permit the entry of Italian troops to France turned Mussolini's attention to Africa and the Middle East where he was initially successful. Having overrun France Hitler prepared for the invasion of the British Isles but his failure to win command of the air in the Battle of Britain in 1940 forced him to postpone his attempt. Now that he was supreme on the continent he turned against Russia with whom his peace pact had only been a convenient agreement until he was ready to attack.

Pearl Harbour attack. Further east, the third aggressor, Japan, anxious to extend its influence over the whole of Asia, suddenly attacked the American naval base at Pearl Harbour in Hawaii on December 7, 1941. The resultant American declaration of war meant that virtually the whole world was now at war. The high hopes of 1919 had been destroyed and many men who had survived World War I lived to see their sons killed in the second world conflict.

NOTEBOOK SUMMARY
Between the wars

THE PERIOD OF HOPE

1. Internal recovery
2. International co-operation
   Washington Treaty (Date, Signatories, Terms)
   Nine Power Treaty (Date, Terms)
   Locarno Pact (Date, Signatories, Terms)
   Germany in League of Nations (Date, Significance)
   Pact of Paris (Date, Proposers, Importance)
   League of Nations (Membership, Successes)

UNDERLYING PROBLEMS

1. Italy (Note reasons)
2. Japan (Note reasons)
3. Germany (Note reasons)
4. Other problems
   Disarmament
   Alliances
   Racial minorities
   Enemy colonies

THE PERIOD OF DOUBTS

1. Agricultural problems

2. Industrial problems
3. Trade problems
4. Financial problems
   Reasons (Note borrowed money and speculation)
   Results (Wall Street crash and its effects)
5. Depression (Note differing solutions in democracies and Fascist States)
6. Dictatorships
   Where
   Reasons for formation
   Chief features (compare with democracy)
   Results for international relations

INTERNATIONAL AGGRESSION

1. Japan
   Reasons for aggression
   Where
   Significance (i.e. Importance for international relations)
2. Disarmament failure
   Disarmament conference
   German attitude
   German rearmament (Note steps)
3. Stresa Front
   Members
   Decisions
   Weakness (Note reasons)
4. Italy
   Reasons for aggression
   Why Abyssinia?
   Significance (i.e. Importance for international relations)
5. Germany
   Reasons for aggression
   Where and when
   Significance (i.e. Importance for international relations)

THE AGGRESSORS COMBINE

1. Spain (Importance of civil war for Europe)
2. Rome-Berlin Axis (When? Terms)
3. Anti-Comintern Pact (When? Terms)
4. Alliances completed
5. Significance for peace

FAILURE OF COLLECTIVE SECURITY

1. Attitude of France
   Dominant feature
   Action taken up to 1936
2. Rhineland reoccupation (Note its significance)
3. Attitude of Britain
   Dominant feature
   Methods adopted
   Churchill

4. Attitude of U.S.A.
   Dominant feature
   Action taken
   Roosevelt

PRELUDE TO WAR (In each case note the reason, the event, action taken by other nations and the significance)
1. Japan
2. Austria
3. Czechoslovakia
4. Poland
5. World War II (Note steps by which whole world became involved)

WORDS TO KNOW

The following words used in this chapter need to be understood. Most of them have been explained in the text but all of them should form part of a history student's vocabulary. Make a list in the back of your notebook, with meanings, of those words that are new to you. Learn these and use them in your essays:
   Abdication, Anschluss, appeasement, arbitration, collective security, Fascist, humanitarian, isolationism, Luftwaffe, pacifism, plebiscite, referendum, sanctions, stocks and shares, totalitarian.

BOOKS TO READ OR CONSULT

Carr, E. H. *International Relations Between The Two World Wars, 1919-39,* London, Macmillan, 1947.
Chambers, F. P. *This Age of Conflict,* New York, Harcourt, Brace & World, 1962, Parts 2-4.
King-Hall, S. *Three Dictators,* London, Faber, 1964.
Priestly & Betts, *Momentous Years, 1919-58,* London, Dent, 1960 (Rev. Ed.).
Stone, R. *The Drift to War,* London, Heinemann Educational Books, 1975.
Thomson, D. *Europe Since Napoleon,* London, Longmans, 1962, Chs. 25, 26, 28.

QUESTIONS FOR ESSAYS OR DISCUSSION

1. Describe the chief features of international relations in the 1920s and account for the sudden change in the early 1930s.
2. What were the main causes of World War II?
3. (a) What do you understand by the term appeasement?
   (b) Why did Britain and France follow this policy from 1931-38?
   (c) Illustrate THREE occasions on which appeasement operated.
4. Describe the main events from 1933 onwards that led to the outbreak of a world war in 1939.
5. Do you agree that, 'The most important cause of World War II was the peace settlement which ended World War I?' Give reasons.

Fig. 12 — A street tea party in London on Peace Day, July 1919.

Fig. 13 — The United Nations Security Council in 1971.

4

TOWARDS WORLD PEACE

Ever since history began man has been a fighter. The earliest cave drawings show man as a hunter and fighter of animals but very early in the period of written history are to be found accounts of men fighting against other men. And the violence of modern warfare can be matched by that of earlier times — as in the *Destruction of Sennacherib* when 'The Assyrian came down like a wolf on the fold', or by the Mongolian warriors of the Middle Ages who used to pile the heads of their victims into huge pyramids as a warning to others who might be preparing to oppose them.

Nevertheless, as civilisation advances, man should be both more willing and more able to live at peace with his fellow man. The experiments of the League of Nations and the United Nations suggest that he may be more willing but the two terrible wars of the first half of the twentieth century certainly cast serious doubts as to whether he is more able. With the terrifying destructiveness of modern weapons as a constant reminder of the consequences of another failure, twentieth century man must make every effort to learn from the mistakes of the League of Nations and ensure that the United Nations succeeds in its objective of preserving world peace.

The keeping of peace. The idea of a world organisation to maintain peace is largely a product of our own age. In earlier times peace was usually kept by a system known as the 'balance of power', in which nations were expected to be strong enough to keep what possessions they had but not to be able to attack and conquer other nations. If one nation became too strong the others would unite against it, as, for instance, when Europe combined against Napoleon Bonaparte at the beginning of the nineteenth century. Although an attempt was made after the Napoleonic Wars by the great nations to work together to preserve peace it lasted for only a short time. Other attempts at international co-operation before 1918 included the submitting of disputes to arbitration and a number of disarmament conferences, especially those at The Hague in 1899 and 1907.

THE LEAGUE OF NATIONS

It was believed by many that the year 1919 ushered in a new age in international understanding and co-operation. Much of the idealism at Versailles, where the peace conferences were held, was brought by President Woodrow Wilson of the United States. Although many of the ideals included in his Fourteen Points were sacrificed in the hard bargaining that followed the Armistice, he secured the acceptance of the last, which stated that 'A general association of nations must be formed for the purpose of affording mutual guarantees of political independence and territorial integrity to great and small States alike'. The Covenant (or solemn agreement) of this new League of Nations was included in all the treaties signed by the Allies and the defeated nations. Thus, by signing these treaties, a nation accepted the idea of an international body whose purpose was to maintain peace.

Different attitudes. While agreement was reached on the need for an international body to provide a guarantee of world peace, it was not so easy to reach agreement on the way in which this would be achieved. France saw the League of Nations as the answer to her fears for security and the French expected it to be a strong body that was prepared to act to defend the interests and frontiers of its members. This implied that nations were willing to act to protect other members even when they themselves were not in danger. But there was no certainty on this point. Great Britain had always believed in international consultation and had strongly supported the idea of settling disputes by discussion. This was very different from being prepared to send troops anywhere that danger threatened another nation. British interests were largely outside of Europe and Britain had always been reluctant to send an army to Europe unless her own safety appeared to be at stake. The United States went even further and refused to have anything to do with the body that had been created at the insistence of its own President. [1] Apparently certain that it would gain nothing but trouble by joining the League, the United States returned to its policy of isolation after having made a separate peace with Germany. So there was no guarantee that members of the League would be prepared to act against a future troublemaker.

The defection of the United States was a serious weakness from the outset, but in spite of this forty-two nations had already joined when the League held its first meeting in Geneva in 1920. As all except the defeated States and the Soviet Union were

[1] The reasons are discussed more fully in Chapter 7 (page 153).

eligible to join, this seemed a most promising beginning. Limitations on membership were later removed so that by the time the League moved into its fine new buildings in the Palace of Nations in Geneva in 1936, over sixty nations were members. Although membership fluctuated as new members were admitted and others withdrew, the only nation of consequence that was not, at one time, a member of the League of Nations was the United States of America.

League never strong. However, although its membership was large, the League of Nations was never a strong body. When war broke out in 1939 Japan, Germany and Italy had all resigned their membership after the League had criticised their actions (see Chapter 3) and Russia had been expelled because of its attack on Finland. The only important and powerful members remaining were Great Britain and France and even they were unable to agree on when action should be taken. Besides, strength does not depend on size alone and the loose association of nations in the League meant that it had little power to act in an emergency, as we shall see later.

Hitler's attitude. Another feature which reduced the effectiveness of the League was its association with the peace treaties. In the minds of many people the League, because it was part of the peace settlement, became associated with the preservation of the boundaries and decisions made by the peace treaties. Support of the League seemed to imply acceptance of the 1919 settlement. How could a nation that resented the Treaty of Versailles support the League with any real enthusiasm? It was an easy matter for Hitler to persuade the German people that the League was simply the instrument of the victorious Allies to prevent the German nation from regaining territory that rightly belonged to it. If Hitler succeeded in tearing up the Treaty of Versailles there seemed little likelihood that the League of Nations would survive.

AIMS AND PROMISES

The League of Nations was formed in the belief that all nations wanted peace, which, after four years of war, was probably a reasonable assumption. However, it was not possible to predict whether all nations would continue to want peace or whether they would be willing to honour the promises they made on becoming members. Any society depends to a large extent on the good will of its members. In our own country, for instance, we can safely assume that the majority of our citizens are loyal and law abiding. International society is in a similar position. Whereas we have a police force to protect us against those who are not, there is no international army to control lawlessness among nations.

Disarmament. On joining the League each nation made solemn promises which were included in the Covenant but, because there was no international police force, the preservation of peace relied almost entirely on the good will of the members to keep their promises rather than on the strength of the League to enforce them. By signing the Covenant, nations agreed to disarm 'to the lowest point consistent with national safety and the enforcement by common action of international obligations'. But what did this mean? In our own country we do not hesitate to walk on our streets after dark but in some South African cities Europeans dare not go out of doors at night unless they are armed. Similarly a nation that did not feel itself threatened by a powerful neighbour could afford to keep its promises to disarm while a nation in the opposite position would be most reluctant to reduce the size and strength of its forces. All previous disarmament conferences had failed to reach agreement but, in the spirit of optimism that prevailed at Versailles, the onus was put on member nations to act in good faith.

Two other promises. Members also guaranteed the territory and independence of fellow members and promised not to resort to war over any matter until a peaceful settlement had been tried first. While this appeared to many of the new nations on the map of Europe as a guarantee of their continued existence, it could be interpreted by others as a denial of their national rights. Thus, while the existence of the League allowed Czechoslovakia and Poland to feel safe Germany could later object that Germans were forced to live under foreign flags. Furthermore, if any member nation ignored its obligations in this respect, the others promised to boycott it by refusing to trade or have any other dealings with the offender.

It is apparent that the primary aim of the League was to preserve peace. All the promises that we have examined from the Covenant refer to matters which, in the past, had been contributory causes of war. There were, however, many other causes of friction and tension which could be removed by international co-operation. Anything which causes misery or unhappiness for large numbers of people can produce dissatisfaction and resentment and these provide the foundations on which unscrupulous leaders can build dictatorships. Promises to solve such problems are usually linked with talk of national glory and foreign conquests. Thus the problems of health, working conditions, racial minorities and a host of similar matters can have an important bearing on world peace. Also, by working together in such matters which are generally non-controversial it was hoped that nations would acquire the habit of international co-operation that would stand the test of exposure to more dangerous issues.

ORGANISATION AND WORK

The Assembly. As the war had been a victory for democracy, it is not surprising that the League was modelled on democratic institutions. The general representative body of the League was the Assembly which met annually although it could be summoned for a special session in times of emergency. Here each nation was represented by a delegation of up to three but had only one vote. This recognised the democratic principle of the equality of States whether large or small. The Assembly was seldom called on to act in the physical sense of the word but it provided the main opportunity for nations to air their grievances and to discuss their problems. Its power was moral rather than physical because the voice of world opinion could often prove a powerful force for peace.

As all decisions of major importance had to be unanimous, every nation had both the right and the opportunity to interfere with the wishes of the majority. This underlying weakness in the structure of the League was to be an important reason for its failure and illustrates the unwillingness of nations to allow decisions affecting them to be made by other States. In other words, nationalism was still stronger than internationalism.

The Council. While it was important to protect the interests of the smaller States, it was also necessary to recognise the greater responsibilities of the larger nations. This was achieved in the Council or Executive, which met at least three times a year. In the original constitution of the League there were eight members of the Council, four of whom represented Britain, France, Italy and Japan and had permanent seats in recognition of their importance as world leaders. The remaining four seats, later increased to eleven, were held by smaller nations in rotation. As unanimous decisions were necessary before any action could be taken this meant that the interests of the major nations were protected. It was the task of the Council to make plans for disarmament, to advise on the protection of members, to mediate in international disputes and to deal with urgent matters between meetings of the Assembly. It was the Council's responsibility to recommend the imposition of sanctions (i.e. a trade boycott) or the use of force against an aggressor. The only occasion on which sanctions were imposed was against Italy when it attacked

Abyssinia in 1935 but they were too few and too late and caused Italy no real concern. (See page 59). The use of military force was never recommended.

The Secretariat. Just as a national government requires permanent officials to attend to the details of administration, so does an international body. An international civil service, or Secretariat, was established at Geneva under the control of the Secretary-General to conduct the day to day business of the League. Its staff came from many of the member countries and it provided the interpreters, recorders, secretaries, and other personnel needed to conduct the League's business. It was also a fact-finding body with the responsibility for collecting and recording information on any subject under inquiry by the League. Such matters included health and social problems, disarmament, racial minorities and the control of former enemy colonies.

International Labour Organisation. Two other important bodies were developed in conjunction with the League of Nations. The first of these was the International Labour Organisation (ILO) which also had its headquarters at Geneva. Representatives of governments, workers and employers met annually to share information and to seek to improve working conditions and living standards by promoting new laws to assist the great mass of the world's population who depended on industrial employment for their livelihood. It was the task of the International Labour Office to give the annual conference all the information it needed to make decisions. Such decisions became international standards which delegates would attempt to persuade their own governments to adopt. Examples of the standards adopted included the recognition of an eight-hour day and forty-eight-hour week with paid annual holidays as the right of all workers; the right of workers to form trade unions; the prevention of the employment of children under the age of fifteen years; and prevention of the use of white lead, which is poisonous, in paint manufacture. Although all countries did not adopt all standards they became an international yardstick against which each nation could measure its progress in improving working conditions.

International Court. In 1900 an international Arbitration Court had been established at the Hague but few nations had gone to it. If Austria had made use of this court to investigate the murder at Sarajevo in 1914 the history of the world may have been changed. However, a start had been made, and the peacemakers were able to develop the idea and establish, in 1922, the first Permanent Court of International Justice, also at The

Hague. Like its predecessor it had limited powers and could neither compel a State to appear before it nor enforce its decisions when they were reached. In spite of these limitations it achieved a remarkable degree of success. By 1939 its fifteen judges had been asked to consider almost seventy cases while over 400 international treaties contained provisions for referring disputes to the Court for its jurisdiction or legal settlement.

Work of commissions. Some of the most important work of the League was achieved by its various commissions which were established to deal with special problems. The Mandates Commission was set up to oversee the former enemy colonies which were administered on behalf of the League by various nations, notably France, Britain and members of the British Empire. It was the duty of the mandatory Powers to assist in the development of their territories towards self-government and eventual independence and they had to promise not to use them as military bases. Tanganyika (German East Africa) and Palestine came under British control, Syria and the Cameroons under French, and Western Samoa became the responsibility of New Zealand. Although the Mandates Commission received annual reports from the controlling Powers and could offer advice, it had no real authority over these territories. This lack of authority has been demonstrated by South Africa's refusal to hand over to the United Nations its mandate for German South-west Africa which South Africa now treats as part of its own territory. Other commissions dealt with health, the drug traffic, the position of women, and other social and economic problems too widespread for individual nations to deal with effectively.

THE FAILURE OF THE LEAGUE

Fundamentally, the League of Nations failed because the Great Powers bypassed or rejected it. The United States never joined it and most of the successful diplomacy involving important nations, such as the Locarno Pact, the Washington Treaty, the Pact of Paris and the Dawes and Young Plans dealing with reparations, was achieved apart from the League.[1] It suited Great Power interests to settle matters themselves rather than refer them to the League. Furthermore, there were instances when small nations were unfairly treated because major Powers with whom they had disputes ignored the League and used their greater strength to gain their ends. Thus when Italian soldiers were murdered on the Greek island of Corfu in 1923 the Greeks were forced to pay a large sum to Italy in compensation but they, in

[1] See Chapter 3, page 50.

return, received no compensation for the naval bombardment of the island by Italian warships.

Weaknesses shown. The League survived the 1920s and even achieved some successes but the events of the 1930s quickly exposed its weaknesses and brought about its fall. All efforts by the League to persuade nations to co-operate to overcome the economic crisis of 1929 and the world Depression that followed ended in failure. Co-operation was rejected in preference for national self-interest and trade restrictions intensified rather than solved the problem. The Depression also gave the dictators the opportunities they needed and it had hardly begun before Japan launched her attack on Manchuria. This was the first real test case because it involved aggression by a major Power — one of the Big Four. The failure of the League to do more than condemn the action was disastrous. Japan was not even expelled. It was Japan who chose to withdraw. Similarly, the Depression encouraged aggressive nations to provide employment in the munitions factories with the result that the League's Disarmament Conference from 1932 to 1934 was foredoomed.

If non-intervention in affairs in the Far East could be excused or at least passed off as being of little concern to the western world, the same could not be said of the events that followed. First Hitler withdrew from the League over the question of German rearmament, then Mussolini invaded Abyssinia. As we saw in Chapter 3 (see page 59) sanctions when applied were too little and too late. Germany invaded the Rhineland; civil war broke out in Spain in which European nations intervened, even if unofficially; Japan attacked China: in none of these instances was the League able to take any effective action.

League unable to act. It was obvious that the League either could not or would not act so that the success of Hitler's invasions of Austria and Czechoslovakia was almost a foregone conclusion. The Munich Agreement was made without reference to the League and it was only when the invasion of Poland posed an immediate threat to the safety of the Great Powers of Europe that they were prepared to act, and even then it was as a result of individual agreements and not through the League of Nations.

Lacking military power, dominated by a desire for peace at almost any price and restricted in its actions by lack of support from the Great Powers and the need for unanimous decisions, the League was seriously hampered from the outset. It had been hoped that collective security would prevent further war but, when the pressure was applied by aggressive Powers in the 1930s, this proved to be a vain hope. While it was able to control small

TOWARDS INTERNATIONAL CO-OPERATION

FROM LEAGUE OF NATIONS

TO UNITED NATIONS

ARBITRATION

International Court of Justice: Meets at The Hague. Fifteen members appointed for nine years. Gives rulings on problems and disputes submitted to it

League: Voluntary acceptance of decisions

United Nations: Decisions must be accepted

WELFARE

League: I.L.O. and some special commissions (e.g.: health, race, position of women)

Economic and Social Council: Works for peace by improving social and economic conditions. Co-ordinates the work of many specialised agencies and commissions (e.g.: World Health Organisation, Food and Agriculture Organisation, Children's Emergency Fund, Universal Postal Union)

A WORLD PARLIAMENT

League Assembly: GENEVA
U.N. General Assembly: NEW YORK
A *forum* for international discussion
Exerts the force of *world opinion*
All members have only one vote
Prepares the annual budget
Admits new members
U.N. General Assembly can *act for peace* if Security Council cannot agree

CIVIL SERVICE

Secretariat: Collects information, registers treaties, provides secretaries and interpreters. Its work has been greatly expanded in the United Nations

Secretary-General: In charge of the Secretariat. In U.N. he can act himself or recommend Security Council action to preserve peace

THE EXECUTIVE

Council: 'Big Four' plus ten. Met three times a year. Unanimous decisions. *Planned* disarmament. *Advised* on protection. *Mediated* in disputes. Could *recommend* action

Security Council: 'Big Five' plus ten. In permanent session. 9/15 decisions. Veto. Responsible for disarmament and world peace. Power to *act* and to use *force*

TRUST CONTROL

Mandates Commission: Eleven independent experts. Former enemy possessions. *Advised* on administration and problems. Eventual goal self-government

Trusteeship Council: 'Big Five' plus six. Former mandates. *Ensures* sound administration. *Supervises* and *inspects*. Most trust territories now independent

nations and settle their disputes the League never felt sufficiently confident to take a firm stand with important and powerful members. Unless a Great Power was prepared to co-operate by its own choice, the League of Nations seemed powerless to act against it. The machinery was available but the great nations of the world were not yet ready or willing to use it and put their faith in it. It was not until the world had been shocked by another war that a more effective international body was established.

SUCCESSES OF THE LEAGUE

Though the League of Nations was clearly a failure, it would be wrong to ignore the successes achieved by the League. One prominent modern historian [1] has suggested that possibly the greatest importance of the League and its related bodies was that they existed at all. They would not have been formed unless a large number of nations had believed in the idea of internationalism. This does not mean that they favoured a single world government, a sort of 'super-State', but that they believed that governments could work together to achieve world peace. While the Great Powers accepted and promoted the ideas of internationalism the future looked bright — as it did for the greater part of the 1920s. But when they openly abandoned these principles or were not prepared to defend them when they were challenged, failure was almost certain. This was the tragedy from which recovery proved impossible.

Achievements. Apart from its actual existence what then did the League achieve? We have already noted the successes of the International Labour Organisation, the World Court and the various special commissions. Apart from these the League was successful in dealing with over thirty political disputes arising from World War I. For instance it settled differences over boundaries between Yugoslavia and Albania and between Greece and Bulgaria, both of which could have led to wars in the Balkans. It arranged the return of prisoners of war and the settlement of refugees, a field in which the famous Norwegian Arctic explorer, Dr Nansen, played an important part. If its failures paved the way for World War II, its successes, especially in the humanitarian field, prepared the way for an extension of its work by the United Nations.

THE UNITED NATIONS

President Wilson's Fourteen Points had their counterpart in the Atlantic Charter issued in August 1941 by Prime Minister Win-

[1] Thomson, D., *Europe Since Napoleon*, p. 607.

ston Churchill and President F. D. Roosevelt following their dramatic and secret meeting aboard a British battleship 'somewhere in the Atlantic'. Although this Charter, which stated both the war aims and the peace aims of the two countries, made no mention of a postwar international organisation, this was most certainly implied. When the Charter promised the achievement of both individual and national liberty and the 'securing to all peoples of security from aggression and foreign domination' this could obviously be best guaranteed by international co-operation.

Historic conference. The United Nations really began as a wartime alliance and was established at the start of 1942 shortly after America entered the war when the twenty-six countries involved in the war against Germany and her allies agreed at Washington to accept the Atlantic Charter. It was not until November 1943 that the first talks to discuss a peacetime international organisation were held in Moscow, where Churchill, Roosevelt, Stalin and Chiang Kai-shek agreed that such a body, 'based on the principle of the equality of all peace-loving States, and open to membership by all such States, large and small, for the maintenance of international peace and security', should be established as soon as possible. This historic conference took place at the turning point of the war. In Africa the decisive battle of El Alamein had been fought and Montgomery and the famous Eighth Army had started to drive Rommel and his Africa Corps out of Africa. Also an Anglo-American army under Eisenhower had landed in Morocco and Algeria. Meanwhile, in Russia, plans were well advanced for the Battle of Stalingrad which began later in the same month and which not only stopped the German advance into Russia but proved to be the start of a Russian advance into Germany which did not end until Berlin itself had been occupied.

Once the principle had been agreed to by the 'Big Four', progress in the development of the United Nations was rapid. A further conference of these Powers at Dumbarton Oaks, near Washington, in November 1944 established the basic framework and, at their last conference together at Yalta early the following year, Churchill, Stalin and Roosevelt confirmed the Charter for the United Nations. One month before the unconditional surrender of Germany in May 1945, the representatives of fifty-one nations assembled at San Francisco to approve this Charter, which came into effect on October 24, 1945 — known since as United Nations Day. The world had once more staked its hopes for future peace on an international organisation. Time alone would tell whether the lessons of past failures had been learned.

Comparison with League. Certain differences from the membership of the League of Nations are immediately apparent. From the outset the membership of the United Nations included both Russia and the United States, the two strongest Powers in the world, and all the other major world Powers together with the great majority of smaller nations. In fact, by the start of 1965, the original membership had more than doubled to reach 115 and, as more former colonies gain their independence, membership should continue to grow. The most significant result of this growth has been the increase in the number of African and Asian States that belong to the United Nations. This increase has been so marked that the Afro-Asian group (or bloc) is now in a majority and can thus outvote the larger members on important issues affecting world peace. The importance of this will become more apparent when we examine the working of the General Assembly.

Non-members. However, certain features of membership, or rather non-membership, give cause for concern. There are only a few nations who have so far shown no interest in becoming members of the United Nations and, apart from Switzerland, these are mainly very small States with populations of less than a quarter of a million. But there are other large and important nations who have had requests for admission rejected or who have not applied for membership because they have known that they would not be admitted. In each case these are countries which have been divided politically and in which one part of the country is supported by western nations and the other by those of the communist bloc.

The largest and most important of these were Communist China and Germany while the others were the northern and southern parts of Korea and Vietnam. When the United Nations was formed China became a charter (or foundation) member but the revolution of 1948 resulted in the formation of two Chinas, neither of which recognises the other. But as Nationalist China (Taiwan) was already a member and was supported by a group of Western nations led by the United States, it was able to prevent the admission of Communist China until in 1971 the Americans abstained and a sufficient majority voted for Communist admission. In 1973 another important advance came with the admission of East and West Germany. The other four major states, North and South Vietnam and North and South Korea, have proved a more difficult problem. When both Vietnams applied for membership after the Vietnam War the United States refused to agree unless the Korean question was considered at the same time. China refused this so all four remain excluded. There have been other controversies over membership with moves by the Afro-Asian block to exclude South Africa and extend some sort of recognition to the Palestine Liberation Organisation, despite Israel's opposition.

Encouraging record. Until 1965 the United Nations could look back on a period of twenty years' growth without any resignations, a feat that was much more encouraging than the record of the League in the same period. It is true that there had been occasions when nations had withdrawn their representatives as a protest against some action of which they disapproved. In 1950 the Soviet representatives walked out after the first refusal to admit Communist China, while in 1958 France took a similar action when its policy in Algeria was criticised in the General Assembly. Also disapproval of South Africa's racial policy led to talk of expelling that country from the United Nations but despite these and similar incidents membership remained intact until January 1965. In that month Indonesia resigned its membership as a protest against the appointment of Malaysia, a country whose existence it did not recognise, to a seat on the Security Council. However, Indonesia retained its membership of the Specialised Agencies and rejoined after the overthrow of Sukarno. Although the United Nations does not include all nations, it can still claim to be an almost totally representative international body.

The need for a permanent headquarters for the new body had to be faced as soon as peace was assured. Because Geneva had unfortunate associations with the failure of the League, the first meeting of the General Assembly was held in London in January 1946. After many offers had been investigated it was decided, by a narrow margin, to establish the permanent headquarters in New York. But where in this densely populated city of skyscrapers would there be room to erect buildings large enough to provide for the thousands of employees and representatives who would need to be accommodated? A sudden and unexpected solution was found to this problem by the gift of a valuable site in the heart of the city from one of the best known and wealthiest families in America, the Rockefellers. It is on this site that the familiar buildings now stand. Most photographed is the thirty-nine storeyed headquarters of the Secretariat constructed in glass and marble. Beside it stand the low, curving building in which the Security Council meets and the domed building which houses the General Assembly. It is in these buildings that decisions affecting the future peace and welfare of the world are made.

AIMS AND PROMISES

Our studies in previous chapters have shown us that fear is the main cause of international tension. We have seen that, when a nation feared attack from a more powerful neighbour, it sought protection by making an alliance with another nation. This in turn often produced another alliance directed against the first so that, often quickly, Europe was divided into two groups based on fear. It was in this way that the Triple Alliance and the Triple Entente emerged to face each other before World War I (see Chapter 1) and that France built up a series of alliances against Germany in the 1920s and 1930s. This has been the typical method of preserving peace throughout modern history and it has always ended in war. Even the League of Nations was not strong enough to stop the growth of rival alliances aimed at preserving what historians call 'the balance of power'. It was the aim of the founders of the United Nations to learn from the past and so produce an organisation capable of sufficient strength and unity that 'collective security', or the combined strength of all members, would succeed where the balance of power had failed.

Twofold purpose. Extracts from the Charter make clear the twofold purpose of the United Nations:

We, the peoples of the United Nations, determined to save succeeding generations from the scourge of war . . . and to reaffirm faith in fundamental human rights, in the dignity and worth of the human person, in the equal rights of men and women and of nations large and small, and to establish conditions under which justice and respect for obligations . . . can be maintained, and to promote social progress and better standards of living, *and for these ends,* to practise tolerance and live together in peace . . . to unite our strength to maintain international peace, and to ensure . . . that armed force shall not be used, save in the common interest, and to employ international machinery for the promotion of the economic and social advancement of all peoples, *have resolved to combine our efforts to accomplish these aims.*

Thus, like the League before it, the United Nations had both the political objective of keeping world peace and the social and economic goal of increasing human happiness.

It is easy to agree with the New Zealand historian, Dr Desmond Crowley, [1] when he suggests that whereas the League was founded in a spirit of idealism, the United Nations reflects the realism that followed an international failure and six years of war. The

[1] *The Background to Current Affairs,* p. 113.

emphasis on equality hindered the working of the League and, when it came to the point, its members were not prepared to put many of the high ideals of the Covenant into practice. Disarmament is an example of this. On the other hand the Charter of the United Nations does not set out any aim that it is impossible to achieve. It concentrates on those areas in which international co-operation has the greatest chance of success. While it agrees to examine the whole question of disarmament it does not require impossible or unrealistic promises in this direction from those who sign it. Meanwhile, it places a great emphasis on the welfare of the underprivileged people of the world and in this sphere it has achieved remarkable success. As food, health and education are brought within the reach of more and more people, this may well prove the most important contribution that any international organisation can make towards the cause of world peace.

ORGANISATION AND WORK

General Assembly. Though generally similar, the United Nations and the League have also important differences designed to make the new body more effective. (See chart, page 77.) All nations are still represented in the General Assembly, now by a delegation of up to five, with only one vote irrespective of their size. But the former need for unanimous decisions has been replaced by a simple majority in most cases and a two-thirds majority for important matters. The General Assembly continues to be a forum or meeting place for the expression of world opinion and has to approve the annual budget and the admission of new member States.

Its functions have been extended in one important direction. Because of the repeated deadlocks in the Security Council it has been possible, since 1950, for the Assembly to take over the responsibility for maintaining peace. If nine of the fifteen members of the Security Council support a proposal vetoed by one of the permanent members, the matter is referred to the General Assembly which, in such circumstances, can be called to meet within twenty-four hours. If a two-thirds majority can be gained, then the United Nations is able to act to preserve peace.

Security Council. The greatest changes that have taken place are in the executive — known as the Security Council to emphasise its main function. Here the five principal allies from World War II (U.S.A., U.S.S.R., Britain, France and China) were given permanent seats and the remaining six places were filled by other nations elected by the General Assembly for two-year terms.

Because of the very greatly increased membership of the United Nations, the Charter was amended in 1963 to increase the number of non-permanent members from six to ten. However, because changes to the Charter must be ratified, or approved, by the members, the alteration did not take effect until January 1, 1966. Under the new provisions five of the elected seats are held by the nations of Africa and Asia, two by the Latin American States, one by the countries of eastern Europe, and the remaining two by 'west European and other States'. In this way the seats are filled without a major political struggle between the rival power blocks. Communist China replaced Nationalist China in 1971.

Right of veto. Unlike its League counterpart, the Security Council is in permanent session in New York. Its decisions are not just recommendations but are made on behalf of the United Nations and are binding on its members. In recognition of the important role of the permanent members each has the right of veto, which allows any one of the 'Big Five' to stop action by voting against a proposal. The only course open in such cases is to refer the matter to a special meeting of the General Assembly as we described earlier. Although the veto was originally intended to be used as a last resort, this has not been the case. It has been used most by the Soviet Union (over 100 times) although other Great Powers have used it on occasions when their own interests have been directly involved. While the inclusion of the veto has been criticised as preventing action in many serious cases, it can also be argued that it is simply a recognition that the Great Powers will not support action against their own interests — veto or no veto. The small nations may be able to command a majority in the debates of the General Assembly, but if the scene is changed from the political to the military arena it is the armies and armaments of the major Powers which will still prove most powerful. In other words, the position has not changed and the continuation of world peace still depends largely on the willingness of the Great Powers to co-operate.

Secretariat. The Secretariat has been enlarged and its duties extended in the United Nations. Although its headquarters are in New York where a staff of over 4,000 is employed, there is also a European office at Geneva employing over 1,000 people. The Secretary-General has a most important and demanding role. He can ask the Security Council to act to preserve peace and he is also empowered to take certain measures himself. It was while engaged on a mission of this nature to the Congo in 1961 that Swedish Secretary-General Dag Hammarskjöld (pronounced Dāg Hammershield) was killed in an air crash. In the eight years since he had succeeded the first Secretary-General, Norwegian Trygve Lie, his name had become linked with world peace. His successor was U Thant from Burma. In 1971 U Thant was succeeded by Kurt Waldheim of Austria. At various times all these men have come under criticism from the big powers but they have generally maintained their independent peace-keeping role.

Trusteeship Council. Another body whose responsibility has been increased is the Trusteeship Council which replaces the Mandates Commission. The 'Big Five' and six other States, balanced between trust and non-trust nations, make up its membership. It is no longer merely an advisory body but also has the responsibility for ensuring that the trust territories, the former enemy colonies and the mandates from the League of Nations, are administered in the interests of their inhabitants. This involves regular visits to the trusts to inspect progress and to hear the views of local people, as well as the receipt of reports from the countries responsible for their care. Most former trust territories have now become independent, the most recent being Papua-New Guinea in 1975. The one major exception is Namibia or South West Africa which South Africa has so far refused to relinquish. The powers of the International Court of Justice have also been extended so that nations appealing to it now have to agree to accept its decisions as binding. Failure to do so can mean that the decision will be enforced by the Security Council.

Social, economic fields. Perhaps the greatest change in international affairs has taken place in the social and economic fields. The Economic and Social Council (ECOSOC) undertakes a vast extension of the similar work of the League of Nations. It works through a large number of specialised agencies and commissions whose work it co-ordinates. Among the best known and most important from the point of view of reducing human suffering and so increasing happiness are the World Health Organisation (WHO), the Food and Agricultural Organisation (FAO), the Educational, Scientific and Cultural Organisation (UNESCO), the International Children's Emergency Fund (UNICEF) and the International Labour Office whose work has continued.

In this book, space does not permit a detailed treatment of their work and a few examples will have to suffice. However, there are an increasing number of excellent films and books available which tell the exciting stories of their work.[1] When we remember that half of the children in the world can neither read nor write and that almost three-quarters of the world's people still have little opportunity of reaching a doctor when they are ill and much less

[1] Some examples of these are given on page 91.

chance of visiting a dentist, we begin to appreciate the magnitude of the task that faces these specialised agencies.

And yet already the progress made has been little short of fantastic. In 1949 WHO used thirty tons of vaccine to prevent a cholera epidemic in Egypt. Similar campaigns have been mounted against two of the most deadly killers — tuberculosis and malaria — which together kill almost eight million people each year and incapacitate a further 350 million! Projects undertaken by FAO, often in combination with UNICEF, have included the combating of locusts in South America, the introduction of school meals in Greece, the development of irrigation and improved farming techniques in South-East Asia and the introduction, in 1961, of an experimental world food programme to deal with chronic malnutrition (or permanent suffering from undernourishment) .and food emergencies.

UNESCO aims to establish a minimum world standard of education which would include knowledge about agriculture, handicrafts, health, citizenship and world affairs as well as the basic reading, writing and number skills. Meanwhile, through exchange scholarships and cultural collections (e.g. art) it is working towards fostering international understanding. At the same time a vast seientific project in the Amazon valley will be of benefit to all people living in underdeveloped tropical rainforest areas.

Other branches of ECOSOC range over matters as diversified as telecommunications, trade, human rights, finance, weather forecasting and civil aviation. Whatever their function, these agencies are all contributing to increased international understanding and co-operation and so have their part to play in the safeguarding of world peace.

PROBLEMS OF UNITED NATIONS

The most obvious and the most serious failure of the United Nations has been the breach between East and West, commonly referred to as the Cold War and the subject of Chapter 9. The creation of regional defence pacts such as the North Atlantic Treaty Organisation (NATO), the South-East Asia Treaty Organisation (SEATO) and the communist Warsaw Pact suggests that collective security has not been completely successful so that nations have fallen back on the old system of forming alliances and rival alliances for their protection. Whether these groups create respect for their strength or suspicions of their intentions is an open question.

Palestine. In the thirty years following the war the United Nations was faced with four local wars in the Middle East, each of which could have spread to include large areas of the world. In Palestine, war between the Jews and the surrounding Arab nations in 1948 produced broken United Nations truces, the murder of their mediator Count Bernadotte of Sweden, and a final solution in the creation of Israel following the military success of the Jews. Almost ever since United Nations observers have had to patrol the frontiers to try to prevent any further outbreaks of fighting (see pages 210–15).

Korea. Intervention in Korea to check North Korean aggression in 1950 was only possible by the temporary absence from the Security Council of the Soviet Union (see page 81). Although United Nations troops were successful here, the ultimate result was to increase the division between East and West. This is not to suggest that no action should have been taken but rather to explain that an apparent victory for the authority of the Security Council was not as significant as it might at first appear.

Suez and Hungary. War between the Arabs and the Jews was renewed in 1956 and Britain and France intervened to protect their interests in the Suez Canal Zone. Immediate action by the General Assembly and the willingness of Britain and France to withdraw in favour of a United Nations force again appeared an important success. But the United Nations took no action when President Nasser of Egypt broke his promise and took complete control of the Suez Canal soon after this. Nor did it act when, in the same month, the Soviet Union crushed a revolt in Hungary, a supposedly independent nation, and refused to admit a team of UN investigators led by a New Zealander, Sir Leslie Munro. These incidents taken together showed that when great Powers were co-operative the United Nations could succeed most convincingly in stopping fighting, and equally that when they refused to co-operate the United Nations was powerless.

The Congo. Finally, when Belgium hastily left the Congo in 1960, leaving the area almost totally unprepared for independence, a violent civil war broke out. United Nations intervention to restore law and order was greatly hampered by the attitude of Russia which accused the western members of 'imperialism' or, in other words, of trying to extend their influence into a newly independent African State. When United Nations forces eventually withdrew in August 1964 after an occupation which had cost 235 lives and over £100 million, the problem had not been solved. Rebellions were still occurring and immediately following the withdrawal of troops Tshombe, the leader of the revolting Katanga province who had been forcibly removed by United Nations troops twelve months earlier, became for a time Prime Minister of the Congo.

Kashmir trouble. Apart from these major troubles involving United Nations troops there has also been intervention in a number of other incidents with varying degrees of success. Following the granting of independence to India and Pakistan in 1947 a dispute developed over the future of Kashmir, whose Hindu ruler was most unpopular with his predominantly Moslem subjects. Both sides intervened and by 1964, although the United Nations had secured a ceasefire over fifteen years earlier, a final solution had not been found. The partition of the area was not acceptable either to India or Pakistan and further fighting broke out in August 1965. Only the determined intervention of the Security Council and the appointment of a ten-nation border patrol restored peace in September — without any better prospect of a permanent solution. However, through the mediation of Soviet Prime Minister Kosygin in January 1966, the two countries pledged to renounce the use of force to settle their disputes. But this agreement was reached *outside* the United Nations. Moreover the United Nations was unable to play a major role in one of the worst postwar crises — in South-East Asia — and only a secondary role in the Middle East.

In the dispute between Indonesia and the Netherlands the United Nations was more successful. United Nations assistance secured the recognition of the independence of Indonesia (all of former Dutch East Indies except New Guinea) in 1949 and again, in 1962, effected the peaceful transfer of West New Guinea to Indonesia.

Disarmament. Apart from actual physical intervention in disputes, the United Nations has been faced with other serious problems, one of the most important being the question of disarmament. This has become of even greater concern for world peace since the development of the atomic and hydrogen bombs and the large-scale production of guided missiles (or flying bombs) armed with nuclear warheads. It is a frightening thought that one Polaris submarine is armed with sufficient missiles to cause more damage and destruction than all the bombs dropped by both sides in World War II — including the atomic bombs. Each Polaris missile is one thousand times more destructive than the atomic bomb dropped on Nagasaki! For these reasons alone, the international control of armaments has become a more pressing question than ever before as man's inventiveness has now made it possible for him to blow himself out of existence.

The Security Council is specially responsible for disarmament. Also the Atomic Energy Commission was established in 1946 to work towards the international control of atomic energy. Little real progress has been made in either direction. The test-ban treaty signed by Britain, America and Russia in 1963 banned all except underground nuclear tests. Although this was a promising step towards peace, it included only three nations and, since it was signed, France, China and India have conducted tests and a large number of other countries, including some in the Middle East, have the technical ability to join the 'nuclear club'.

Money troubles. The most recent problem to embarrass the United Nations has been finance. Peace-keeping operations and the work of the UN specialised agencies cost millions of pounds and the failure of some nations to meet their financial obligations has increased international tension. The general costs of the United Nations, apart from additional peace-keeping expenses, amount to over £4,000,000 each month, and while over one-quarter of this is provided by the United States it is important that all nations pay their share regularly. Throughout recent years many nations including Russia and France have fallen behind with their payments. Although the Charter provides that any nation which is two years behind in its payments is to be denied a vote in the General Assembly, the enforcement of this rule would increase rather than decrease world tension. Russia has maintained that it will not support the cost of United Nations forces in the Congo or the Middle East because it did not approve of the use of them in either case. Increasingly in the 1970s the Third World countries have used their numerical superiority to secure their own ends in the organisation to the anger of the U.S. and other Western Powers who pay most of the costs.

Much achieved. But in spite of all the unsolved problems that face the members of the United Nations a considerable amount has been achieved in the years since 1945. Local wars which could so easily have spread have been isolated and the influence of the small nations of the world for peace has been amply demonstrated. In human affairs the success has been remarkable and international co-operation has resulted in a significant progress against the great enemies of mankind — hunger, disease and illiteracy. Finally, and by no means of least importance, the United Nations has survived in a world still divided by fear, suspicion and jealousy and, in doing so, has become a much more truly international body than the League of Nations. So long as it continues in this way there must at least be a reasonable hope of world peace.

NOTEBOOK SUMMARY
Towards World Peace

Take a double page of your exercise book and head one side 'League of Nations' and the other 'United Nations'.

LEAGUE OF NATIONS

ORIGIN
1. Ideas of Wilson
2. Attitudes of:
   France
   Britain
   U.S.A.
3. Initial weaknesses — in each case note reasons
   Membership
   Loose organisation
   Association with peace treaties
4. Headquarters

AIMS AND PROMISES
1. Promises
   Disarmament — note reasons for failure
   Territory and independence of members — different attitudes
   Others
2. Aims
   Peace
   Welfare — note significance for peace

ORGANISATION AND WORK
Note the main features, functions and weaknesses of the separate parts of the League. Include examples where possible.
1. Assembly
2. Council
3. Secretariat
4. Mandates Commission
5. World Court
6. Social and Welfare Work
   ILO
   Commissions

UNITED NATIONS

ORIGIN
1. Ideas of Churchill and Roosevelt
2. Wartime conferences
   Washington
   Moscow
   Dumbarton Oaks
   Yalta
   San Francisco
3. Membership
   Who can join?
   Strengths and weaknesses
   Influence of Afro-Asia
   Withdrawals
4. Headquarters

AIMS AND PROMISES
1. Aims
   Collective security — note difference from 'balance of power'
   Social and economic aims
2. Promises — make a comparison with the League.

ORGANISATION AND WORK
Treat as for the League but take special note of attempts to make the machinery more effective.
1. General Assembly
2. Security Council
3. Secretariat
4. Trusteeship Council
5. World Court
6. Economic and Social Council — note the aims and work of the principal specialised agencies (see books below).

FAILURE OF LEAGUE
Note with examples the effects of
1. Attitudes of the Great Powers
2. Depression
3. Failure to act against aggression
   Japan, Italy, Germany.
4. Other weaknesses

SUCCESSES
1. Existence
2. Special Agencies
   Court, ILO, Commissions

PROBLEMS OF UN
1. Cold War — result
2. Local wars — reasons, solutions, influence of UN Palestine, Korea, Suez and Hungary (make a comparison), Congo, Kashmir, Indonesia, Cuba.
3. Disarmament
4. Finance

SUCCESSES
1. Existence
2. Welfare — significance
3. Peace

WORDS TO KNOW

The following words used in this chapter need to be understood. Most of them have been explained in the text but all of them should form part of a history student's vocabulary. Make a list in the back of your notebook, with meanings, of those words that are new to you. Learn these and use them in your essays.

Arbitration, bloc, boycott, collective security, consultation, covenant, dictatorship, forum, guided missile, internationalism, mandate, mediate, nuclear, refugee, sanctions, Secretariat, territorial integrity, trust territory, veto.

BOOKS TO READ OR CONSULT

Faris, D. K. *To Plough With Hope,* London, Gollancz, 1958.
Henderson, J. *World Co-operation,* London, Faber, 1968.
Hornby, J. *The United Nations* (Picture Pageant Series: 1), London, Macmillan, 1963.
Savage, K. *The United Nations* (Today is History Series), London, Blond, 1964.

QUESTIONS FOR ESSAYS OR DISCUSSION

1. Compare and contrast the purpose, organisation, and effectiveness of the League of Nations and the United Nations.
2. Write an account of the ways by which the United Nations works to maintain world peace.
3. (a) Write an account of the structure and work of the Security Council of the United Nations.
   (b) What has the Security Council achieved?
   (c) In what ways has the Security Council failed?
4. 'The United Nations is in many ways the same as, and in certain ways different from, the League of Nations.' Discuss this statement.

FIG. 14 — Russian soldiers leaving for the front during World War I.

FIG. 15 — A modern factory in the Soviet Union.

5

FROM TSARIST RUSSIA
TO SOVIET UNION

'Russia is a riddle wrapped in a mystery inside an enigma', said Winston Churchill in the 1930s. Through his masterly powers of expression he succeeded in summarising our knowledge and understanding of this vast country. There are many reasons both for our lack of knowledge and for the apparent contradictions that are typical of Russia, and some of the most important of these are concerned with geography. Although almost three-quarters of the people of Russia live west of the Urals and therefore in Europe, a glance at the map shows that an even larger fraction of Russian territory lies in Asia. For geographic reasons then, Russia has interests in both Asia and Europe, and is literally pulled in two directions at once. Another important influence that geography has had on Russian history can be seen in the lack of warm-water ports, because in spite of its vast size Russia has few ports that are ice-free for the whole year.

East or West? The history of Russia is full of examples of the influences of these geographic factors. The concentration of population in the west has been determined largely by climate — the north is too cold and the east too dry for intensive settlement. Thus Russia tends to look west and since the reign of Peter the Great over 250 years ago it has taken its place as one of the great Powers of Europe. But because of its isolation and inaccessibility, contact with other European nations has been extremely limited. At the same time there has been strong influence from Asia, especially since the Mongol conquest in the thirteenth century gave the country an eastern outlook which made understanding of western ideas more difficult. Then again, the search for a sea coast has directed Russia's interests towards the Black Sea, the Baltic and the Pacific Ocean. But in every case it has met opposition from other nations which has often resulted in wars. Finally, because of the diverse or widely different origins of its people, Russia has been slow to develop a feeling of national unity such as has been common in most of the nations of western Europe for at least a century and often for much longer.

The Russian enigma. The conflicts that are taking place today in Africa and South-East Asia where new nations are being established and where European or western ideas and methods clash with traditional cultures, are typical of the problems that have faced Russia for centuries. As a result, Russia has become an intricate mixture of east and west, neither wholly understood nor trusted by western nations and, for her part, unsure and often suspicious of them. This mutual feeling of uncertainty and distrust is not a new development in our own times but was already firmly established at the start of the twentieth century.[1] Understanding of this situation is necessary in any attempt to understand the development and policies of the Soviet Union.

OPENING OF TWENTIETH CENTURY

Although parliamentary democracy as we know it in this country had developed strongly in Britain, France and other western countries by 1900, Russia was still an autocracy in which the Tsar was a dictator who ruled without any form of national parliament. When Alexander III became Tsar in 1881 he said, 'The voice of God orders us to stand firm at the helm of government with faith in the strength and truth of the autocratic power which we are called to strengthen and preserve for the good of the people'. When the unfortunate and tragic Nicholas II succeeded his father to become the last of the Tsars in 1894, he clung to this belief and declared, 'Let it be known to all that I, devoting all my strength to the pursuit of the good of my people, will maintain the principle of autocracy as firmly and steadfastly as did my late father'.

Whereas Britain and other western nations had had extensive experience in the development of government by a parliament gradually representing more and more sections of the population, Russia entered the twentieth century with a system of government more suited to the conditions of the Middle Ages. The people of Russia had never had any real experience of sharing in the government of their country.

Economic backwardness. In the field of economics there were also important differences. The industrial and agricultural revolutions, which had begun in Britain over a century earlier, had swept across Europe and North America during the nineteenth century. The use of machinery on farms had not only increased food production but had also released additional labour to operate

[1] Illustrations of this may be found in Chapter 1 where Russia's relations with other European Powers before 1914 were discussed.

the machines in the factories in the new industrial towns which rapidly began to appear on the coalfields. These developments created great wealth for farmers and factory owners who used it to develop further industries and to extend trade to the undeveloped parts of the world. At the same time unhealthy and overcrowded living and working conditions created serious social problems in these industrial towns and led to the growth of an important new voice in the affairs of these countries, that of the town workers or *proletariat* as they are often called.

But these changes had scarcely reached Russia where, even by 1914, eighty per cent of the people were still engaged in agriculture and lived as desperately poor peasants on the millions of small farms that were typical of Russia. Men rather than machines still planted and harvested the crops on these farms. However, aided by French loans following the Franco-Russian alliance of 1894 (see page 23), industry was beginning to develop by 1900. Its chief features were that it was confined to a few important towns and that the factories that developed were generally very large. Thus, in spite of general economic backwardness, similar social conditions to those already described above appeared in Russia in a number of large and important cities, where a dissatisfied town working class emerged ready to demand improved living and working conditions.

Political feeling. Absence of a parliament in Russia was not to suggest that there was no political feeling in the country. There had always been dissatisfied groups in Russia but, because of the difficulties of winning support in a country where towns were few, communications difficult, and most people could neither read nor write, they had achieved little success. Their risings had been easily suppressed and their leaders either shot or deported to work in the Siberian salt mines — a fate far worse than transportation to the Australian convict settlements from early nineteenth century England.

But new developments in Russia encouraged the growth of new political groups and of these the most important to appear at the end of the nineteenth century was the Social Democrat Party, or 'Cadets', which based its policy on the beliefs of the mid-nineteenth century German socialist, Karl Marx. Although the party existed as a secret society and was forced to hold its meetings outside Russia, it was to have a tremendous influence on the future of the country. For the first time in modern Russian history there were available, at the same time, leaders, followers and a revolutionary doctrine. These were to provide the starting point for the revolution of 1917.

MARX AND MODERN COMMUNISM

Modern communism, especially as it is practised in Russia, has developed largely from the writings of Karl Marx who spent most of his life as an exile from his native Germany. In Paris, Brussels and London he saw many of the worst social effects of the nineteenth-century industrial revolution and met leading socialists from other countries. From his experiences, discussions and reading he developed a theory of history which he expounded in a number of books, the most important being the now famous *Communist Manifesto*, the foundation of Russian communism, and *Das Kapital*, commonly called the communist 'bible', in which he attacked the evils and forecast the decline of capitalism.

Marx's doctrine. Marx claimed that the only true basis of wealth was human labour but that this required land and capital (or money for investment, usually in industry) before it could produce anything. Because land and capital belonged, in a capitalist society, to only one class, the *bourgeoisie* or moneyed class, he argued that the desire to make a profit became the most important aim and that, as a result, those who had 'nothing to sell but their labour' received low wages and had to live and work in poor conditions. He called this the 'exploitation of labour' and there was plenty of evidence to support his claims in the factory towns of mid-nineteenth century England.

But Marx did not stop here and in fact he saw the struggle between the worker and his employer as part of the vast cycle of history. In ancient Egypt and ancient Rome it was the struggle between slave and slave owner. In the Middle Ages it became a struggle between serfs and lords. Now in the nineteenth century it was the proletariat against the capitalists. The ultimate result was to be a great revolution. The workers would overthrow and destroy their employers and create a new society in which every person would work 'according to his ability' and would be provided for 'according to his needs'. Marx who, because of his wanderings, had little feeling of belonging to any country, saw this as a worldwide revolution, and so the idea of international communism was born.

Communism or Welfare State? It is important for us to remember that one of the features that distinguish Marxian communism from other forms of socialism is that Marx believed that the only way in which his aims could be achieved was by a revolution. In this belief he concluded his *Communist Manifesto* with a rousing call to action: 'The workers have nothing to lose in this revolution but their chains. They have a world to gain. Workers of the world unite!' From our mid-twentieth century viewpoint it is obvious that Karl Marx did not ever envisage the development of the Welfare State in which there is room for private enterprise (or individual ownership of business and property) and also for the State to act to protect the welfare and security of its citizens. Nor did Marx provide a detailed blueprint for the development of Communism in non-industrialised societies. As a result there has been increasing ideological divergence amongst the various Communist parties. Some still hold that revolution is the only way forward whilst the large Communist parties in France and Italy believe that they can progress through participation in democratic elections to parliament. The greatest disagreement about Marxism has been between the Russians and the Chinese (see pages 190–1).

THE REVOLUTION OF 1917

We have already seen some important political, social and economic reasons for the growth of discontent in Russia in the early twentieth century. But none of these in itself, nor, for that matter, even a combination of them, would have been sufficient to start a revolution. National discontent was brought to a head at the start of the century with the defeat by Japan in 1905. This defeat not only exposed the weakness of Russia's military power but also completely discredited the Tsar and his Government. During the war, workers who marched to the Tsar's palace to ask for his help were shot down by his troops. The long-held belief in the Tsar as a 'Little Father', died with them.

Revolt of 1905. One historian has claimed that Nicholas II lacked the ability to control a village let alone to govern Russia and the disasters of 1904-5 seemed to prove this. As a result a revolution occurred in 1905 which won some concessions such as the calling of a national Parliament or Duma, freedom of speech and of meeting and reduced press censorship. However, these gains were shortlived and, although parliaments continued to meet periodically until 1917, Tsarist autocratic rule was rapidly restored and personal liberties again disappeared. This was the situation in Russia when war broke out in 1914.

War. The year 1914 offered the Tsar a last chance to redeem the failure of 1905. Victory would have resulted in greatly increased prestige and would possibly have allowed a continuation of his personal rule. Defeat proved disastrous. Although the declaration of war was accompanied by an outburst of patriotism this was only a passing phase. The Russian armies were poorly equipped, Russian industry could not supply their needs in sufficient quantities, and the railways were so little developed that they could not transport the goods that were available to the soldiers at the front. Allied efforts to supply Russia by the opening of a route through the Balkans were thwarted when the Gallipoli campaign failed to dislodge the Turks from their strongholds guarding the entrance to the Black Sea. In September 1915, as if to complete the disaster, the Tsar left his capital at Petrograd [1] and took personal command of his armies.

Home front suffering. Meanwhile, on the home front, conditions were steadily deteriorating. The peasants suffered most as their horses and crops were commandeered to supply the needs of the army and their sons were conscripted to fill its ranks. In the cities conditions were almost unbearable and strikes became increasingly common. Morale fell as defeat followed defeat and refugees flooded into the main cities. In Petrograd a typhus epidemic broke out.

With the departure of the Tsar to the front the Government was virtually left in the hands of the Tsarina. However, she was largely under the influence of a self-styled monk, Rasputin, who had become established at the court after his hypnotic methods had apparently assisted the sickly son of Nicholas and Alexandra. The murder of Rasputin in December 1916 was followed by wild rumours that the Tsar would abdicate but he refused to consider any concessions.

March Revolution. As city conditions became even more unbearable food riots broke out in Petrograd in March 1917 and quickly turned into a revolution. Such an uprising, lacking in leaders, aims or plans, had no right to succeed and should have been easily suppressed. But the troops refused to fire on the crowds, the police fled, and within a week the Russian capital and a number of other important cities had renounced the Tsar and set up their own local governments. In attempting to return to his capital the Tsar was captured and, with the rest of the royal family, was placed under arrest. Before the end of the month he was forced to renounce his throne by signing his abdication.

Tsardom had ended but what was to take its place? No one was prepared and the Duma in Petrograd hastily set up a Provisional Government to control the country until more permanent plans could be made. At the same time soldiers, peasants and town workers began to elect their own local committees, or 'soviets'. The most important and powerful of these was the Petrograd Soviet which quickly assumed the leadership of this new movement.

Two systems. Russia now had two systems of government — the Provisional Government and the soviets. For the next six

[1] The Russian name had replaced the German, St Petersburg, in 1914.

months the key figure in Russia was Alexander Kerensky who held important positions in both. In July he became the leader of the Provisional Government and announced that Russia was now a republic. Lacking any positive programme for improving conditions in Russia, the Provisional Government aimed to continue the war on the side of the Allies and promised land and labour reforms as soon as a new government was elected by the people. But the Russian people were not prepared to wait. They were sick and tired of war, hunger and misery. They wanted action and they wanted it immediately. The time was ripe for the Bolsheviks to act.

Emergence of Lenin. When the Social Democrat Party (see page 95) met for its second congress in London in 1903 it was largely dominated by the personality of Vladimir Ulyanov, better known in history by his revolutionary name — Lenin. Although his father was a Russian noble, Lenin was engaged in revolutionary activity from an early age. In 1886, at the age of sixteen, he left his parents' comfortable home in Simbirsk (now called Ulyanovsk in his honour) on the banks of the Volga River to attend the university at Kazan about one hundred miles to the north. However, within twelve months he was expelled for attending a revolutionary meeting. Although he was able to return two years later he had, by then, begun to study Marxism. The execution of his elder brother for taking part in an unsuccessful plot to assassinate the Tsar determined Lenin on a course of illegal revolutionary activity which ended, temporarily, with his exile to Siberia in 1895. Following his part in the unsuccessful revolution in 1905, Lenin was again exiled and settled in Switzerland where he busied himself writing pamphlets and organising the Social Democratic Party.

Lenin's policy. Although Russia was an industrially backward country and the conditions needed for a Marxist revolution did not appear to exist (see page 96) Lenin saw the war as an opportunity for the workers to overthrow the Tsar and his Government. He believed that a strong and highly organised revolutionary party, with the support of the peasants as well as the industrial workers, could overthrow the Government, seize power and establish a socialist society. By persuading the Bolsheviks (or, literally, 'the majority men') to accept his views at the 1903 congress, Lenin became the principal figure in the formation of modern Russia. However, the Mensheviks (or 'minority men') were still an extremely strong group and it was their ideas, favouring the gradual establishment of a socialist society after a long period of industrialisation and parliamentary government, that dominated the Provisional Government set up in March.

Return of Lenin. When the March Revolution occurred Lenin made haste to return to Russia from Switzerland. The Germans, knowing he was anxious for peace and certain that he would create even greater confusion in Russia, allowed Lenin to cross Europe in a sealed train and he arrived in Petrograd in April. Meanwhile Stalin had already arrived from Siberia, where he had been serving his fifth sentence for political crimes, and Trotsky, the best known of the Russian revolutionaries, quickly returned from the United States where he had been on a lecture tour. The principal actors were now assembled, the stage was set and the curtain almost due to rise on the greatest drama in the history of Russia.

'Peace, land and bread' and 'All power to the Soviets' became the slogans with which the Bolsheviks hoped to win the support of the mass of the workers and peasants for the overthrow of the Provisional Government. Continued German victories with heavy Russian casualties at the front and desperate food shortages in the cities rapidly increased Bolshevik support.

Hardly any food. The picture was vividly captured by an American journalist, John Reed, in his book *Ten Days That Shook The World*. 'September and October are the worst months of the Russian year — especially the Petrograd year. Under dull grey skies, in the shortening days, the rain fell drenching, incessant. Week by week food became scarcer. The daily allowance of bread fell from a pound and a half to a pound, then to a three-quarters of a pound, to half a pound, to a quarter of a pound. Towards the end there was a week without any bread at all. Sugar one was entitled to at the rate of two pounds a month — if one could get it at all, which was seldom. There was milk for about half the babies in the city; most hotels and private homes never saw it for months . . . Meanwhile, the ladies of the minor bureaucratic set (i.e. wives of Government officials) took tea with each other in the afternoon, carrying each her little gold or silver or jewelled sugar box, and half a loaf of bread in her muff and wished that the Tsar were back, or that the Germans would come, or anything that would solve the servant problem.' [1]

John Reed travelled extensively in Russia in 1917 and also visited the battlefields. 'At the Front the soldiers fought out their fight with the officers and learned self-government through their committees. In the factories, these unique Russian organisations, the Factory-Shop Committees, gained experience and strength . . .

[1] Reed, J. *Ten Days That Shook The World*, Frome, Lawrence and Wishart, 1961, page 9 (first published 1926).

All Russia was learning to read and *reading* . . . We came down
to the Front of the 12th Army, back of Riga, where gaunt and
bootless men sickened in the mud of desperate trenches; and when
they saw us they started up, with their pinched faces and the flesh
showing blue through their torn clothing, demanding eagerly, "Did
you bring anything to read?" . . . It was against this background
of a whole nation in ferment and disintegration that the pageant
of the Rising of the Russian Masses unrolled . . .'

The industrial workers were seizing control of the factories,
the peasants were seizing control of the land and the soldiers at
the front were deserting in their thousands. It was time for the
Bolsheviks to seize control of the government for, said Lenin,
'History will not forgive us if we do not assume power now.'

November Revolution. The actual revolution of November 1917
was almost an anti-climax to the events that have just been
described. On the morning of November 7 troops occupied key
points in Petrograd, Kerensky fled, a brief resistance in the
Winter Palace (the headquarters of the Provisional Government)
was soon overcome and, by nightfall, the city was in the hands
of the Bolsheviks. Immediately the Provisional Government was
abolished and the soviets were declared the true government of
the country. Within little more than a week similar *coups* (or
seizures of power) had occurred in most of the principal cities
of Russia. It had been almost too easy for the Bolsheviks to seize
power but their real success could only be judged by their
handling of the vast task that lay ahead of them. Would they be
able to hold it?

LENIN AND THE SOVIET UNION

'The chief hero of this remarkable chapter of history', wrote one
Russian observer, 'was the chairman of the Petrograd Soviet and
the organiser of the Red Army — Leon Trotsky'. But the man
most responsible for the Bolshevik seizure of power and therefore
the man with greatest prestige in Russia in 1917 was Lenin and,
on the day following the Revolution, he was elected Chairman
of the Council of People's Commissars (representatives) which
was to be the new Government of Russia. For the next seven
years he was the dominant figure in Russia and, when he died in
1924, the impossible seemed to have been achieved. Not only
had there been an almost miraculous economic recovery but the
Bolsheviks had also overcome all their opponents and were the
undisputed rulers of the country. In his honour Petrograd was
renamed Leningrad and, after an impressive State funeral, his
embalmed body was finally placed in a glass-topped tomb in the

Red Square in Moscow to become a centre of pilgrimage for communists throughout the world.

Civil war. In 1917 the immediate problem facing the Communist Government (as the Bolsheviks now became known) was the defeat of their enemies. Peace was quickly made with Germany by the Treaty of Brest-Litovsk in March 1918. Its terms made the later Treaty of Versailles seem almost humane. Russia lost over one-quarter of its land area and population and over three-quarters of its iron and coal deposits and once again it was rumoured that Lenin was a German spy. Freed from the fear of the enemy without, the communists were now able to concentrate on the enemy within. During the next three years a ferocious civil war was waged in Russia. Under the inspired direction of Trotsky the Red Army literally destroyed all opposition, even although the Whites, as their Russian opponents were called, could count on assistance from British, French and Japanese troops sent to keep Russia in the war and to check the expansion of communism. The penalty for losing was death and, in the massacres that followed, priests and businessmen, landowners and nobles, died in their thousands. Among the first to be put to death were the Tsar and all members of the royal family. The prophecy of Marx was being fulfilled.

Famine. By 1920 the internal enemies of the Soviet Union had been silenced but an even more serious danger remained to threaten the young republic — famine. The civil war had placed unbearable demands on the peasants. Their crops had been confiscated to feed the Red Army and the city workers. Their labour had been conscripted to build roads and railways. And, as if this was not enough, the money they received in exchange for their goods and their labour was worthless. As in Germany, so in Russia (see pages 36-7). The Government solved its financial problems by using the printing press. The peasants replied by reducing production to provide only for their own needs and this, combined with the serious crop failures in the wheatlands of the Ukraine in 1921, produced a famine in which more than four million people are believed to have died.

Lenin's economic policy. The genius of Lenin became apparent in the economic crisis that now faced the country. From Moscow, now restored as the Russian capital, he announced the New Economic Policy in 1921. He realised that the success of communism in Russia, where the peasants and not the industrial workers made up the bulk of the population, depended on an alliance between these two groups. The New Economic Policy had as its basic aim the regaining of peasant support which had been won by the promise of land in 1917 and lost in the years that had followed by the seizure of their crops. Under the new policy the peasants, after giving a portion of their crops to the Government (really a tax in kind), were allowed to sell the remainder as they wished. In the cities private shops and factories reopened. The value of the rouble was restored and Russia resumed trade with foreign countries.

Overseas observers began to breathe more easily as the threat of world communism declined. It appeared to many as if communism had been tried and had failed and that Russia would move quietly but steadily towards the type of parliamentary democracy and capitalist economy (i.e. with considerable private ownership of industry and agriculture) that was by now firmly established in the major nations of western Europe and North America.

But the adoption of the New Economic Policy was not an admission of failure. It simply recognised that the time was not ripe for a complete communist State and was a temporary measure to give the country a breathing space and the Party an opportunity to reorganise. Large-scale industry and foreign trade remained a State monopoly and Lenin made it clear that the original Bolshevik aims had not been rejected. A vast programme of education was introduced in schools, in factories and in the Red Army to teach acceptance and to win support for the new order. Youth organisations, notably the Young Pioneers and the Young Communists, were formed to train future members of the party. Years before Hitler came to power in Germany the Russian communists had perfected similar methods of winning and keeping the support of the masses (see page 43). The communists also saw the Christian Church as a threat to their success and anti-religious instruction was given in schools. Even the sale of Christmas trees was prohibited.

Party dictatorship. At the same time a new system of government was developed. In 1922 the Russian Republic was combined with the other provinces of Tsarist Russia to form the Union of Soviet Socialist Republics. As in this country, local government was placed in the hands of elected councils or soviets. In contrast to our central government at Westminster which is *directly* elected by adult citizens voting individually, the All Union Congress of Soviets in Russia was elected *indirectly* by the local soviets. The All Union Congress met only once a year and appointed the real government of the country, the Central Executive Committee. As the Communist Party was the only official political party and chose all candidates at elections, it can readily be seen that it was assured of permanent control. Perhaps the chief difference between the dictatorship of the Tsar and that of the Communists was that the latter was more efficient!

THE EMERGENCE OF STALIN

When Lenin died in 1924 his logical successor seemed to be Leon Davidovitch Bronstein who, since his escape from exile in Siberia in 1902, had been known by his assumed name of Trotsky. He had first met Lenin in London and after the revolution in 1917 had become the first Foreign Minister of the new State. Trotsky was a firm believer in the 'world revolution' for the establishment of communism and was closely associated with the Communist International (or Comintern) formed in Moscow in 1919 to plan for this event.

Clash with Trotsky. Among the other possible successors to Lenin was Joseph Djugashvili — better known as Stalin, 'the man of steel' — who, in 1922, became the first General Secretary of the Communist Party. The conflict between these two men was foreseen by Lenin who had always distrusted Stalin and was anxious to take steps to remove him before he became too powerful. However, Lenin died and Trotsky's attempt to defeat Stalin was too late. After the failure of communist revolutions in Hungary and Germany in 1919 there was more support for Stalin's aim of concentrating first on 'socialism in one country' than for Trotsky's belief in world revolution.

Triumph of Stalin. In the struggle for power that lasted from 1924 to 1927 Trotsky was finally outmanoeuvred by Stalin and was banished from Russia in 1929. After moving from country to country he eventually settled in Mexico where he was murdered in 1940.

Living as we do in a country where we not only expect there to be opposition to and criticism of the Government but where we actually elect and pay members of Parliament for this very purpose, we may find it difficult to understand such conflicts as the struggle between Stalin and Trotsky. We must remember, however, that in communist doctrine (or belief) there can be only one correct policy. Once this has been decided opponents must either accept it or be silenced. There is not room for two leaders with different interpretations. Furthermore, a dictator feels safer when he has removed his opponents.

THE DICTATORSHIP OF STALIN

For almost twenty-five years, from 1929 until his death from a heart attack at the age of seventy-four in 1953, Joseph Stalin was the unchallenged ruler of Russia. Like both Lenin and Trotsky he had been involved in revolutionary activities from his youth. He came from a poor working class family in the province of Georgia in southern Russia and his deeply religious mother wanted him to become a priest in the Greek Orthodox Church. He was expelled from the seminary at the age of sixteen for criticising the Tsar, and between 1902 and 1913 he was arrested five times for his part in a number of bank robberies to raise funds for revolutionary purposes. When the Provisional Government released all political prisoners in March 1917 he returned to Petrograd from Siberia and joined the Bolsheviks.

Rule by terror. Stalin's opportunity for personal power came with the death of Lenin and he was quick to seize it. Following the defeat and exile of Trotsky he made himself a more powerful dictator in Russia than any Tsar had ever been. His methods were similar to those used by Hitler in Germany. We have already seen that the Communist Party ruled Russia and in the same way Stalin ruled the Communist Party. Just as the party dominated every aspect of national life through its control of education, the newspapers, broadcasting, industry and agriculture, so Stalin dominated the party by ensuring that people of his own choosing were in all the important positions. In the 1930s a vast campaign of terror removed thousands upon thousands of Russians to the isolated wasteland of Siberia. At the same time, within the party itself, a great purge took place of all who could possibly be considered by Stalin as opponents of his personal power.

While his opponents were being removed by the Moscow Trials, Stalin presented the nation with a new and apparently more democratic constitution in 1936. This introduced a federal system of government similar in organisation to that of the United States and Australia. Each of the separate republics was represented in the Council of Nationalities (corresponding to the American Senate) by four members while the Council of the Union (like the American House of Representatives) was elected in proportion to the population of the member states.

The real Government. But here the similarity ends because these two houses which make up the Supreme Soviet meet only twice a year in order to elect the Presidium and the Council of Ministers which are the real Government of the country. Although the vote was given to all over the age of eighteen years the Soviet Union was no more of a democracy than it had ever been. Behind the whole structure of Government stood the Communist Party and behind the party stood Stalin. In the background, silent and efficient, were the political secret police. Although the name

FIG. 16 — Lenin (1870–1924).

FIG. 17 — Stalin (1879–1953).

altered (from Cheka to OGPU to NKVD to MVD) the function remained the same; to seize, try and punish any who were suspected of opposition to either the party or to the personal rule of Stalin.

THE FIVE-YEAR PLANS

By 1928 Stalin believed the New Economic Policy had served its purpose and that it was time to begin the next stage of the communist revolution. He introduced the first Five-year Plan which aimed to establish complete State control of industry, agriculture, and the cultural life of the nation. In its simplest terms this was an attempt by the Soviet Union, 'to overtake and surpass, by her own unaided energies, the most advanced countries of the capitalist west', so that Russia would become a 'social paradise' and the envy of all other workers throughout the world. They, inspired by the Russian example, would also rise and overthrow their capitalist masters and so world communism would be achieved not directly but indirectly. The first plan was declared to have been completed in 1932, only four years after its announcement and it was followed by further Five-year Plans each setting higher goals and demanding greater sacrifices from the Russian people.

Popular support. In the field of industrial development the success of the plans was staggering. The Russian people had never enjoyed the high standard of living that we accept without question. Hardship and shortages, lack of personal freedom and obedience to authority were not introduced by the Communists. They had always been characteristics of life in Russia. But now, encouraged by hopes of a better future that could be gained only in a communist society, they willingly accepted the misery and poverty of the 1930s and strove to meet the quotas set in factories and mines. Shock brigades of devoted and highly trained Communists moved from factory to factory to set the pace and to encourage others to work harder. So successful was the propaganda campaign that many devoted their day off each week to voluntary labour on Government projects. In this way much of Moscow's underground railway system was built. Russia was transformed from an industrially backward nation to an important world Power in a little over a decade, and this without the assistance of any foreign loans.

Success in industry was not matched by success in agriculture. The peasants who had so recently gained control of their own land were not at all willing to part with it. Under the New Economic Policy many former peasants, the kulaks, had become prosperous and efficient farmers and simply rejected the invitation to join the new collective farms. But private ownership could not be allowed to continue in the countryside when it had been abolished in the towns. Moreover, who but the peasants could provide the enormous amount of labour required in the factories, mines and forests if Russian industry was to advance?

Collectives. In 1929 the forcible development of collective farms began. The peasants replied by burning their crops and slaughtering their livestock but they were no match for a determined and unscrupulous Government. Thousands of peasants were rounded up by the Red Army and shot, while whole village populations were transported to the labour camps of the northern forests or forced to become miners or construction workers in Siberia or central Asia.

By 1939 Stalin could claim that virtually the entire farmlands of Russia had been collectivised. On these new State-owned farms former peasants worked as agricultural labourers tilling the soil they had so recently owned. In theory these large farms, often up to 10,000 acres (an enormous size compared with farms in Great Britain), were provided with machinery, but in practice there were seldom sufficient machines available and much of the work had to be done by labour gangs. Politically, the collective farms have achieved their objective by removing the one remaining capitalist class, the private farmers. However, in spite of increased use of machinery, the introduction of better methods and the development of marginal lands, agriculture has remained the greatest single problem in Soviet Russia right up to the present day.

Position in 1939. By 1939 Stalin had largely achieved his aim of creating 'socialism in one country'. The Russian economy and society had been completely reshaped. Russian industry was among the most modern in the world and industrial production was almost ten times as great as it had been in 1914, although it still lagged well behind that of the United States. There were over four million tractors in use on Soviet farms (there had been none in 1928) and almost all the land had been collectivised. Two-thirds of the population were under the age of thirty and had spent almost their entire lives under communist rule, and ninety-five per cent of the adult population were wage workers in State factories or co-operative stores, or were members of agricultural collectives. Almost all the children were at school learning the skills necessary to make them good workers and the beliefs that would make them good communists. There was little fear of another revolution in Russia. But there was no relaxation of

Stalin's dictatorship which, if anything, became even more rigid as Russia prepared to meet the threat from Germany which exploded into war in 1941.

RUSSIAN FOREIGN POLICY

As we saw at the start of the chapter (see page 93) Russia has for long been suspicious of the West and in return has never been completely trusted by western nations. This mutual distrust has had an important influence on the relations between the two; not just in this century, but at least since the time of Peter the Great. We have also seen that, following the revolution of 1917, Britain, France and Japan intervened in Russia to support the enemies of the new Communist Government. Faced with this refusal to accept or recognise its position as the new Government of Russia, the Communist Party refused to have any dealings with other nations for some years. In fact it even fostered and encouraged revolutionary attempts in a number of countries, notably in Hungary and Germany.

Search for security. The failure of foreign communist revolutions and the emergence of Stalin with his policy of first establishing 'socialism in one country' saw a change in the Russian attitude towards other countries. In 1922 the nations of western Europe and the United States were dumbfounded when Russia and Germany signed a treaty of friendship which led to an increase of trade between the two. However, the rise of Hitler altered matters and drove the Soviet Union to seek protection from the German threat in the collective security of the League of Nations (see page 61). Believing that the Munich agreement showed that Britain and France were not prepared to fight against Hitler, the Soviet Union once again changed sides in 1939 and signed a non-aggression pact with Hitler in which each promised that it would not attack the other and in which they also agreed to share Poland between them.

Western frontier. These apparent contradictions in Russian foreign policy are not nearly as confusing as they would appear at first sight. They represent the simple and unchanging aim of Russia for centuries — to keep its western borders safe from attack by the important nations of Europe. The events between the wars show that Russia used whatever means seemed most likely to succeed at the moment, so that it was prepared to ally with Germany at one time and against it at another, depending on which seemed safer. Also Stalin set out to further increase security by building up a system of 'buffer States' between Russia and Germany. Poland was part of this system, which also included territory (Bessarabia) seized from Rumania and the small Baltic States of Latvia, Lithuania and Estonia which had recovered their independence in 1919 (see map opposite).

War with Germany. Stalin's hope of remaining neutral while Germany and its opponents fought to a standstill was rudely shattered when, without warning, the German invasion of Russia began in June 1941. For the next four years Russia was an ally of the West, and British and American convoys carried food and military supplies along the hazardous route to Archangel and Murmansk on the Arctic coast. Despite this assistance and the tremendous development of its industry, Russia suffered staggering losses. Although some of these were caused by the advancing Germans, others were the result of the 'scorched earth' policy adopted by the retreating Russians. These tactics of burning and destroying everything of possible use to the enemy had been used with success against Napoleon Bonaparte more than a century earlier and once again, in combination with the severity of the Russian winter, proved an important factor in the defeat of Russia's enemies. The counter-offensive which finally began from the ruins of Stalingrad in October 1942 did not end until victorious Russian armies marched into Berlin two and a half years later.

Satellite States. In keeping with the policy of security in the west Russia occupied many eastern European countries as her armies advanced towards Berlin. Whether they were 'freed' from Nazi control like Hungary and Czechoslovakia or captured as German allies like Bulgaria, the result was the same. Many of the countries that had received their independence following World War I lost it following World War II. Their names still appeared on the map of Europe but they became communist 'satellite' States under Russian control (see map opposite).

Within the Soviet Union a new series of Five-year Plans was introduced to restore the damage caused by the war. Considering the magnitude of its losses, Russian recovery was remarkable. At the same time as industrial and agricultural production was restored an army of almost four million men was developed and large sums of money were devoted to nuclear research. In 1949 Russia exploded its first atomic bomb and this, together with its large army, rapid economic recovery and greatly increased territory, has made it one of the two most important nations in world affairs in the mid-twentieth century.

KRUSHCHEV AND PEACEFUL CO-EXISTENCE

When Stalin died in 1953 the usual struggle to find a successor took place. From it, in 1956, emerged Nikita Krushchev. Like

RUSSIAN GAINS FROM
WORLD WAR TWO

Territory
seized

1 Finland
2 East Prussia
3 Poland
4 Czechoslovakia
5 Bessarabia
(Rumania)

Soviet
satellites

Independent
communist
states

ARCTIC OCEAN

Murmansk

Archangel

FINLAND

U.
S.
S.
R.

BALTIC
SEA

Leningrad

ESTONIA

LATVIA

Moscow

LITHUANIA

Berlin

WEST   EAST   POLAND

Brest-Litovsk

Bonn

GERMANY

CZECHOSLOVAKIA

AUSTRIA

HUNGARY

RUMANIA

YUGOSLAVIA

BLACK SEA

ALBANIA

BULGARIA

Fig. 18

Stalin he was of humble origin, being the son of a miner in the rich wheatlands of the Ukraine. As a young man of twenty-three he had fought in the Red Army in 1917 and during World War II he had been an important guerilla leader in fighting against the Germans. Like Stalin also, he had risen to prominence as Secretary of the Communist Party. Here, the resemblance ended. Unlike the harshness usually associated with the 'man of steel' it is more common to think of Krushchev as a pleasant and happy person with a ready smile. But beneath this pleasant exterior there was an iron will and great ability. When he replaced Marshal Bulganin as Prime Minister in 1958 he held the two most important positions in the country. As his opponents had been either executed or disgraced in the years following Stalin's death his power was complete.

Stalin disgraced. However, he did not stop here. Since 1953 he had been steadily increasing his control over the party. Then, at the first party congress after the death of Stalin, he launched a great anti-Stalinist campaign. He told the people of Russia that Stalin had been a tyrant who had relied on terror to keep himself in power and he promised that such methods would never again be used. He accused Stalin of having developed what he called the 'cult of the individual' by which he twisted and distorted facts to show himself as the great and heroic leader of the Russian people. To complete Stalin's disgrace, his body was removed from its place of honour beside that of Lenin and reburied in an unmarked grave inside the walls of the Kremlin.

Economic policy. By 1956 the effects of the war on Russia had been largely overcome. Krushchev announced that the next goal was to overtake American production and living standards by 1970. This involved a greater emphasis on the production of consumer goods and of food for, although the Russian standard of living had been steadily rising, it was still far short of that enjoyed by most people in the western world. But many problems remained to be overcome before these goals could be achieved. Food production continued to increase at a very slow rate compared with increases in population and industry. A poor harvest in 1963 forced the Government to import wheat for the first time since the Revolution. At the same time large-scale spending on armaments and the space research programme restricted the amount of money and equipment available for increasing the supply of cars, refrigerators, radios, shoes, clothing, processed foods and many other goods which Krushchev had promised the Russian people to match the living standards of the West.

Attack on religion. The Christian Church has always been one of the strongest and most outspoken opponents of communism both in Russia and in other countries. Throughout its long history Christianity has thrived on persecution and all attempts in Russia to destroy the Church have failed. In recent years the Soviet Government has adopted a new approach in its campaign against religion by trying to popularise atheist holidays and ceremonies. Quite elaborate wedding ceremonies take place in many cities in a 'Palace of Happiness', often a luxuriously re-furnished villa once owned by a Tsarist noble. In some cities parents are encouraged to 'register' their children in a special ceremony designed to replace the normal religious service of baptism. It is even suggested that baptism is an unhealthy prac-tice, and a survey of one Russian town claimed that skin diseases were three times as frequent among baptised babies as among the non-baptised! Yet in spite of these and other attempts, and even although the Russian Eastern Orthodox Church is very much under Government control, recent evidence suggests that a strong religious revival is taking place, at least in some parts of Russia.

Foreign policy. Krushchev's policy of raising the standard of living had important effects on Russia's relations with other countries. We have already seen that Russian suspicion of the West was longstanding (see page 93) and, although the Soviet Union was an ally of the western nations in World War II, this suspicion continued. The Cold War, or the war of nerves, which began with the defeat of Germany, will be discussed in Chapter 9. For the moment it is sufficient to note that, under the leader-ship of Krushchev, the Soviet Union adopted a less hostile foreign policy and appeared hopeful of winning converts to communism by example rather than by force. This is the policy that has been called 'peaceful co-existence'.

BREZHNEV, KOSYGIN AND THE FUTURE

Despite his apparently unassailable position, Krushchev was suddenly replaced as both First Secretary of the Communist Party and as Prime Minister in October 1964. He and Stalin had shown clearly that, when these two positions were held by the same man, his position was all-powerful. To prevent a repetition of this situation Krushchev was replaced by two men — Mr Alexi Kosygin as Prime Minister and Mr Leonid Brezhnev as First Secretary of the Communist Party. As First Secretary, Mr Brezhnev became the most powerful person in Russian politics, although it was not until twelve months later that he received any official position in the Government. His appointment to the Presidium of the Supreme Soviet (see page 105) in October

1965 was seen as a significant consolidation of his personal power.

Mr Brezhnev's background was similar to that of Mr Krushchev. He, too, was from the heavy industrial area of the Ukraine where he grew up as a steelworker. When the Revolution came in 1917 he was a boy of eleven years so that, in the following years, he was able to benefit from the new educational opportunities available in Russia and become a qualified surveyor. His rise in the Communist Party was rapid and in the years after 1956 it became apparent that he was being trained as the successor for Mr Krushchev.

Of immediate concern to the outside world was the effect that the change of leadership would have on Russian foreign policy.

In fact the main themes of Krushchev's policy continued. The Russians while continuing to maintain massive conventional and nuclear forces sought some form of arms limitation and a long-term detente with the United States (see below).

THE SOVIET UNION TODAY

The Soviet Union today is a very different country from that ruled by Stalin. After the fall of Beria the power of the secret police was curbed and the days of Stalin's mass and arbitrary killings were gone. The country opened its door at least a little to outsiders — indeed the Intourist organisation exists in order to encourage controlled tourism from the Western world — and it is a little easier for some Russians to travel overseas. Cultural and trade exchanges between Russia and the West have steadily increased in recent years. On the other hand Russia remains a one-party state. The interlocking party and government systems control all aspects of industry and agriculture, radio and press, television and education, the arts and religious practice.

Although the worst aspects of the police system under Stalin have disappeared, labour camps remain, the secret police still act as a powerful coercive force on the party's behalf, and, though opponents of the regime are unlikely to be shot out of hand, they may be subject to more subtle but terrifying pressures such as consignment to mental institutions. Particular victims of the system have been Jews who have sought permission to emigrate to Israel, fundamentalist Christians such as the Baptists, and racial groups such as the Tartars who were suspected of being disloyal to Russia during World War II. There has also been a persistent group of writers, scientists and artists who, while remaining patriotic Russians, have criticised the regime. They have all in consequence suffered from pressures from the system, frequently being silenced through imprisonment or, as in the case of the Nobel prize-winning novelist Solzhenitsyn, sent into exile.

Economic strength. For the majority of Russians the dissidents and their underground opposition writings are of little interest. For them, especially if they live in the cities, life has improved enormously since the war. With one-sixth of the total land surface and the third largest population in the world the Soviet Union stands out as one of the two economic and technological giants of the age. Despite its geographic disadvantages and its great industrial backwardness at the beginning of the century, the hardships of the early five-year plans and the huge investment in basic industrial growth at the expense of consumer goods has now paid off. There has been much criticism, even in Russia, of waste and inefficiency within the bureaucratic state-run industries, but their achievements cannot be denied. Latterly the Government has returned to some extent to economic competition between individual factories to make them more efficient and has had to pay incentive bonuses to workers. On the other hand the Soviet system has avoided, by its system of controls, the mass unemployment and spiralling inflation from which the capitalist economies have suffered so much in the 1970s.

A very high proportion of Russia's economic investment continues to go into heavy industry and in particular into defence expenditure. By a huge diversion of effort the country caught up with the Americans in terms of nuclear power and actually beat them by a few months in the race to put a man into space. On the other hand there has been a steady improvement in the range and quality of consumer goods available to the ordinary Russian. His standard of living in terms of housing, consumer goods and car ownership would seem rather poor by Western standards, but it represents very great progress in Russia. Moreover the average Russian is compensated to some extent by relatively cheap public transport and holiday facilities, by a good health system, and wide-scale provision of higher education.

Economic and social problems. The problems of inefficiency in industry are much less significant than the persistent failure of the agricultural system. The collectivisation of the 1930s did not produce the hoped for results. The peasants seemed to lack incentive under the new system and before World War II there were frequent shortages and even famines. This problem has remained, so that despite the huge numbers involved in agricultural production (ten times as many as in the United States), and the huge areas of land available, the country has never managed to be regularly self-sufficient in food. Krushchev tried to beat the problem by a huge investment in the development of the 'virgin lands' — areas of Central Asia which had previously not been cultivated but success there was short lived and in 1963 the Soviet Union had to buy large quantities of grain from America and Canada. There was some improvement in the late 1960s but adverse climatic conditions in 1971-2 brought a disastrously low grain harvest and the Russians were seeking to buy American grain again in 1975 after the worst harvest for ten years.

The problem of agriculture is not simply an economic one. The countryside is much less well served than the town in terms of education and health services and the contrast between the city dweller and the peasant which was a feature of Tsarist Russia is far from having disappeared.

Military strength. As we have seen, much of the economic development of the Soviet Union has been directed towards the creation of military strength. Its army of over two million is second in size only to that of China and is equipped with much more sophisticated weapons. There is compulsory military service so all Russian men have had considerable military training. The air force matches that of the United States and the country's nuclear force of bombs and rockets has the capability for world-wide destruction. Most recently the Soviet Union has very rapidly developed its naval power and has fleets in the Atlantic, Pacific and Indian Oceans shadowing the naval forces of the United States and her allies. Russia still maintains large forces in Eastern Europe but the greatest concentration of military might is along her border with China. There have been attempts by Russia and America to reach agreement on arms limitation, but these have generally foundered over the difficulty of mutual inspection. In 1975 Russia played a leading part in the European Security talks in Helsinki. On the face of it this appeared to herald a further thaw in East-West relations, but the Soviet Union is still committed to the aim of world-wide Communist ascendancy under Russian direction. What her leaders appear to have decided is that this can be better achieved by peaceful means in certain parts of the world than by open warfare and revolutionary uprisings. The Russian leadership is also deeply concerned not to be involved in confrontations with both the Western world and the Chinese at the same time.

World Communism. In its original form Marxism was supposed to be a truly international movement. Some early leaders, notably Trotsky, saw Russia as the starting point for a Communist revolution which would sweep across the world and create a new society in which governments as we know them would simply wither away. Writing in 1917, Lenin envisaged 'a federation of voluntary organisations in which there will be a new heaven and a new earth' where people would 'voluntarily work according to their ability . . . and each will take freely according to his needs.' During the inter-war period Russia was very isolated, world revolution had not followed the

Russian Revolution and she was the only Communist state. After the war Russia's power was enormously increased and progressively Communist control was established over Eastern Europe. But the East European people's democracies were clearly satellites subservient to Russian interests. Even at this stage Russian overlordship in the Communist world was not entirely unchallenged as Tito effectively asserted the independence of his Communist regime in Yugoslavia. However until the death of Stalin this was very much the exception and the communist parties in both the satellites and in the Western democracies acknowledged Moscow's leadership.

The death of Stalin led to a gradual shift. Russia was to remain overwhelmingly more powerful than the European satellites, but her new leaders could not command the same sort of authority as Stalin and gradually national interests reasserted themselves against Russian control. In East Germany there were riots in 1953 which led to some reforms in the regime. In 1956, the year in which Krushchev denounced Stalin at the Party conference, a revolt in Poland led to the reinstatement of Gomulka, the popular nationalist Communist leader to control of the party from which Stalin had deposed him. The Russian leadership were alarmed, but accepted limited Polish self-government since the country was clearly still committed to remain firmly in the Soviet bloc. A revolt in Hungary later in the year against the unpopular Rakosi regime went much further. Not only did it restore a popular national leader, Nagy, but it threatened to establish a multi-party state outside the Communist bloc and this was more than Russia could allow. Troops were sent in and the new regime toppled, but even so Russian control had to be loosened. Over the following decade the monolithic nature of the Eastern European Communist bloc was fractured in many ways. As these countries recovered from the war and began to prosper so they inevitably developed more trade links with the West. And they were no longer content to remain subservient to Russia's economic plans. For instance, Rumania, whilst remaining an orthodox Communist state, refused to follow Russia's directions in economic development.

A new challenge to Soviet control in Eastern Europe came in 1968 when liberal Communist leaders in Czechoslovakia tried to establish a less rigid and nationally independent form of socialism. For a while it seemed that the party secretary Dubcek and his allies might be able to maintain the delicate balance between allaying Russian fears and fulfilling the hopes of the Czech people which had been awoken by the 'Prague Spring', but in August the Russian troops moved in and Dubcek and his allies were progressively removed from all positions of power. Yet even the defeat of the Czech liberals could not turn the clock back altogether and the Russian intervention provoked a degree of criticism from Communist parties and their supporters in Western Europe that would have been inconceivable in the days of Stalin.

The greatest split in the world movement, however, was between the Soviet Union and China. Even in Stalin's time the relationship between the two giants of the Communist world had not been easy. After 1949 Russia did provide technical and economic aid, but always at quite a high price. With the death of Stalin, Mao Tse-tung was clearly the most senior Communist leader in the bloc. The events of 1956 deeply disturbed the Chinese. They were not happy about Krushchev's denunciation of Stalin at the twentieth party conference nor with his handling of the Polish and Hungarian troubles. For their part the Russian leaders were unwilling to support the Chinese in their general revolutionary plans in Asia especially against India, while the Chinese bitterly opposed Krushchev's first attempts to defuse the Cold War through his meetings with President Eisenhower.

In 1960 all Russian technical and economic aid was withdrawn from China at a time when that country was facing particularly difficult economic circumstances and the bad relations between the two countries came out into the open. More and more they became rivals rather than partners in their relationships with neutral states around the world. The Chinese were deeply critical of Krushchev's Cuban policy (see page 217) and even more so of his subsequent efforts at detente with Kennedy. The dismissal of Krushchev did nothing to abate the vilification of the Russian leadership by the Chinese who forged close links with the Albanians and encouraged other East European countries to challenge Russian predominance. In return the Russians sought to establish good relations with both the North Vietnamese and the North Koreans as a counterweight to Chinese influence. From the late 1960s onwards both countries were attempting to reach a limited settlement with the West, and with America in particular, in competition with each other.

The quarrel between the two great Communist powers is partly a matter of ideological disagreement — a dispute over the way in which the world Communist movement should advance both against its capitalist enemies and in terms of internal social and economic policy. It is also the result of much older fears and rivalries between the two countries — quarrels for instance over territories in Central and North-East Asia which have been in dispute for centuries. It is the resurgence of this rivalry which has produced a much more complicated pattern in international power politics than the old East–West split in the early days of the Cold War and has meant that Russia's foreign policy is no longer simply geared to matching the world influence of the United States.

NOTEBOOK SUMMARY
From Tsarist Russia to Soviet Union

INFLUENCES OF GEOGRAPHY
1. Size and population distribution
2. Ports
3. Climate
4. Eastern invasions
5. People
6. Results: Russian outlook — Attitude to others — Attitude of others

POSITION IN 1900
1. Autocratic government — note particularly the *attitude* of the Tsar
2. Economic backwardness — note the situation, changes occurring and their effects
3. Political feeling — note results of earlier dissatisfaction and new trends

MARX AND MODERN COMMUNISM
1. Marx's doctrine: Attitude to labour — Attitude to capitalists — Theory of the class struggle — Ultimate results
2. Communism or Welfare State?
   Difference between communism and socialism
   Result of emergence of Welfare State

REVOLUTION OF 1917
1. Background causes (note their significance): War with Japan — Palace massacre — Character of Tsar — Failure of Dumas
2. World War I: Opportunity for Tsar — Military failure — Home front
3. March Revolution: Reasons and success — Provisional Government (organisation and aims) — The soviets (organisation and reasons for support)
4. Emergence of Lenin
   Career — brief outline
   Policy — Bolsheviks v. Mensheviks
   Return to Russia — policy
5. Conditions in Russia, 1917
   Social and economic conditions — Attitude of the people
6. November Revolution: Main events and immediate results

LENIN AND THE SOVIET UNION
1. His position and importance
2. Civil war: Peace with Germany — Work of Trotsky (What enemies were there?) — Result of civil war
3. Economic position, 1920
4. 'New Economic Policy': Reasons for it — Chief features — Foreign opinions — Temporary nature (note the safeguards for the future)
5. Party dictatorship: Chief features of new government — Comparison with Great Britain — Comparison with Tsardom

THE DICTATORSHIP OF STALIN
1. Trotsky: Early career and beliefs — Clash with Stalin (note reasons) — Defeat and fate
2. Emergence of Stalin: Early career — Methods of gaining and keeping power — His control of Russia
3. The Five-Year Plans   Results in industry
   Reasons for introduction   in agriculture
   Reasons for popular support
   (Note development of collectives and their significance)
   Achievements by 1939: in industry — in agriculture — social revolution in education

FOREIGN POLICY
1. Relations with the West
2. Search for security — note particularly the changing attitude towards Germany and the establishment of 'buffer States'
3. War with Germany: Attitude to war — Effect of war — Western frontier (note development of satellites) — Postwar recovery

PEACEFUL CO-EXISTENCE
1. Emergence of Krushchev: Early career — Rise to power — Disgrace of Stalin
2. Economic policy
3. Attack on religion
4. Foreign policy

AFTER KRUSHCHEV
1. Defeat of Krushchev
2. Emergency of Brezhnev
3. Foreign policy

THE SOVIET UNION TODAY
1. Party dictatorship — chief features
2. Economic strength — chief features
3. Economic problems — possible solutions?
4. Military strength — note effect on international relations
5. World communism
   Main features of Russian policy since 1917 — note changing emphasis
   Competition with China
   Russia's problems

WORDS TO KNOW

The following words used in this chapter need to be understood. Most of them have been explained in the text but all of them should form part of a history student's vocabulary. Make a list in the back of your notebook, with meanings, of those words that are new to you. Learn these and use them in your essays:

Abdication, autocracy, Bolsheviks, bourgeoisie, capitalist economy, Cold War, collective, communism, coup d'etat, Duma, kulak, laissez-faire, Mensheviks, nuclear weapons, party line, peaceful coexistence, Presidium, private enterprise, proletariat, satellite State, socialism, soviet, totalitarian, Welfare State.

BOOKS TO READ OR CONSULT

Bruce Lockhart, R. H. *The Two Revolutions,* London, Phoenix House, 1957.

Catchpole, B. *A Map History of Russia,* London, Heinemann Educational Books, 1974.

Conquest, R. *Common Sense About Russia,* London, Gollancz, 1960.

Footman, D. *The Russian Revolution,* London, Faber, 1964.

King-Hall, S. *Three Dictators,* London, Faber, 1964.

Lee, P. and Bearman, G. *Russia in Revolution,* London, Heinemann Educational Books, 1974.

Sturley, D. *A Short History of Russia,* London, Longman, 1964.

QUESTIONS FOR ESSAYS OR DISCUSSION

1. (a) Why was the Tsarist Government in Russia overthrown so easily in 1917?

   (b) Why did the Provisional Government fail in Russia in 1917?

   (c) Describe the steps the Bolsheviks took to establish themselves under the leadership of Lenin till 1924.

2. (a) What problems faced the Bolsheviks in Russia between 1917 and 1920?

   (b) What measures were used to solve these problems and how successful were they?

3. Make a survey of the internal history of Russia since 1917 under each of the following headings:

   (a) The main leaders and their policies;

   (b) Industrial growth;

   (c) The changing pattern of agriculture.

4. Discuss the contributions of Lenin, Trotsky, and Stalin to the history of Soviet Russia.

5. (a) What have been the basic aims of Russian foreign policy since 1917?

   (b) How and with what success did Stalin seek to achieve these aims up to 1953?

   (c) How and with what success did Krushchev and his successors seek to achieve these aims between 1956 and 1965?

6

JAPAN SINCE 1870

The early history of Japan, like that of most eastern countries, is still much of a closed book. However, we do know that before Alfred the Great was born in England in the mid-ninth century the Buddhist religion and many other ideas from China were strongly established in Japan. The first European influence was felt in Japan with the arrival of Portuguese and Spanish traders and missionaries in the mid-sixteenth century about the time when Elizabeth I became Queen of England.

The closed door. Fear that this was the beginning of foreign conquest led the Japanese rulers to ban all Europeans from Japan in 1640 and to forbid any Japanese to travel abroad. Any who did so and returned to Japan were liable to be put to death. For the next 200 years the only Japanese contact with the western world was through the Dutch who were allowed to send one ship each year to trade with the port of Nagasaki.

The Perry expedition. As the need for foreign markets and raw materials increased in Europe following the industrial development of the early nineteenth century, interest in Asia was renewed. At the same time Americans began crossing the Pacific to trade with China from the ports of California. Because Japanese ports would be convenient for obtaining provisions, American traders asked their Government to request Japan to open its ports to foreign ships. With this intention, Commodore Perry sailed into Tokyo Bay in 1853. Impressed by his model railway and over-awed by the demonstration of his naval strength the Japanese had little alternative but to agree.

Although the Japanese made only limited concessions at this stage, the way was now open for increased western influence and other nations were quick to follow the American lead. By 1870, Britain, France, the Netherlands and Russia had secured similar privileges which gave their nationals the right to trade with and settle in Japan. All these treaties included 'extra territorial' clauses which required crimes committed by foreigners in Japan to be tried in their own countries under their own laws. While this protection was originally considered essential, it later became a serious point of difference between Japan and other nations because the Japanese regarded it as an insult which caused them to 'lose face', a most important concern for all eastern peoples. **Internal changes.** Within Japan the arrival of the foreigner produced important changes. For 250 years the Government of Japan had been in the hands of a military dictator, or *shogun.* He ruled the country from Tokyo while the Emperor, in the ancient capital of Kyoto, had lived in complete seclusion and had taken no part in government. This system of two Governments was not acceptable to the western nations, who quickly recognised the Emperor as the real leader of the country. In 1867 the old Emperor died. He had been completely opposed to the opening up of Japan but he was followed by a fourteen-year-old boy who, under the influence of new advisers, grew up to accept the ideals of the new age. Meanwhile the *Shogun,* realising his failure, resigned in the same year. Thus by 1870, Japanese isolation had been destroyed; after 800 years, the Emperor was once again the official ruler of the country, and preparations had begun to meet the changed conditions in which Japan now found itself.

'ENLIGHTENED RULE', 1867-94

It is customary in Japan to refer to a period not by the name of the Emperor (as we speak of the 'Victorian Age') but rather by a name that is symbolic of his reign. That the reign of Emperor Mutsuhito should be known as the *Meiji,* or 'period of enlightened rule', is a significant reminder of the tremendous changes that took place in Japan in the latter half of the nineteenth century. Japan has sometimes been called 'the Britain of the East', because of its island position on the edge of a great continent and because, from small beginnings, it became the leader of new developments and the centre of a great empire. But whereas in Britain this ascendancy was gradually developed over many centuries, in Japan it was achieved in little more than half a century. For this reason alone there were many differences in the methods by which it was accomplished.

The end of feudalism. Japan began the new age still in the grip of a feudal system similar in many ways to that which had been imposed on England by William the Conqueror in the eleventh century. There were almost three hundred local feudal lords, each with his own private army of professional soldiers and his own hereditary or family estate. In 1869 four of the most important and powerful of these *daimyos* (feudal lords) voluntarily surrendered their properties to the Emperor. They were followed by almost all of the *daimyos* in a demonstration of the type of loyalty that is a marked feature of the Japanese people. In 1871 feudalism was officially abolished.

Meanwhile many of the *samurai,* or professional soldiers, had followed the lead of their feudal masters. By ceasing to wear their swords, their official badge of rank, they surrendered the privileged positions that their class had enjoyed for centuries. A further law in 1876 forced all remaining *samurai* to do likewise. As a result all Japanese subjects of the Emperor were now on an equal footing and the way was open for a new central government modelled on European lines.

Central Government. An important feature of the changes that took place in Japan was the influence of western ideas. Many of the ablest young men in Japan were sent overseas to study methods of government, education and defence. German influence was most apparent in the new central system of government that was developed. In complete contrast to the British method of locally elected councils controlling matters of local importance, all local government in Japan was in the hands of officials appointed by and responsible to the central Government in Tokyo, which had become the new imperial capital in 1868. These positions were at first filled by former *samurai* but, as education developed, they were later open to those who were successful in competitive examinations.

Constitution of 1889. Some of the Emperor's advisers were anxious to see the introduction of a limited constitutional monarchy on the British model. This would have meant that the power of the Emperor would have been carefully controlled or limited by a constitution which would have ensured that his ministers were responsible to an elected parliament. Others preferred the German system where the constitution provided for an elected parliament but left the ministers free from its control because they were appointed by and responsible to the Emperor. The British system limited the power of the King in favour of Parliament but the German system limited the power of Parliament in favour of the Emperor. The one was democratic, the other autocratic.

When the Constitution was announced in 1889 it was obvious that the German model had been preferred. The preamble or introduction to the Constitution showed that the position of the Emperor was to be preserved when it stated that, 'The rights of sovereignty (i.e. control) of the State We have inherited from Our ancestors, and We shall bequeath them to Our descendants'. Although the Constitution provided for a parliament it was by no means democratic and the right to vote was restricted to less than half a million voters and was based on the ownership of land. At that time Japan had a population of fifty million. In spite of its limitations the Constitution was still a great advance. It was the first constitution granted to his people by any monarch in east Asia. But it was very much the gift of the Emperor to his people and appeared to place few restrictions on his power. Like most of the changes that took place in Japan, it was part of a revolution from above which made it a direct contrast with the Russian Revolution (see page 97) which came from below. In practice, the new Constitution placed the main power in the hands of the Emperor's advisers who rapidly became the real rulers of the country.

Prince Ito. Of the young men who went overseas to study during the early years of the *Meiji,* the most important was Ito Hirobumi, a former *samurai* of the important Chosu province in the southwest of Japan. In 1863, risking punishment by death, he smuggled himself out of Japan to Shanghai and worked his passage to London. After studying in London and America he returned to Japan, at the risk of his life, and quickly became an important leader in the new Japan. Originally opposed to the extension of foreign influence in Japan, he was now determined that Japan must modernise and become a great nation. He believed strong government was essential if Japan was to succeed in this aim and, when he was sent overseas in 1882 by the Emperor to study western systems of government, he went directly to Berlin. He returned to Japan convinced that the German system gave the leaders of the nation the greatest power. Under his guidance the constitution was planned and introduced and, in 1890, he became the first Prime Minister under the new constitution. For the last twenty years of the nineteenth century he was the dominant figure in the country and may well be regarded as the architect of the new Japan.

Economic development. Trade developed rapidly after 1853 but it was usually the foreigners rather than the Japanese who became rich as a result. With a growing demand for imported goods and little to offer in return, Japan quickly found itself in difficulties. To make matters worse trading rights and customs duties had been fixed by treaties which the Japanese could not alter without the agreement of the foreign nations. As they were benefiting from the trade, this agreement was not likely to be forthcoming.

To solve these economic problems, the Japanese began to modernise their industry, agriculture, transport and banking.

Western experts were called in to give advice. The Bank of Japan was established to control the nation's finances, a merchant navy was developed, the first railway was opened in 1872, and postal and telegraph services were introduced. Although the industrial revolution was just beginning, there were over 200 steam factories in Japan by 1890. In all of these developments the Government played a leading role. The State had always directed and controlled many aspects of national life and now it was the only body with sufficient finance and the organisation available to direct the rapid and large-scale development that was essential if Japan was to overtake the industrial nations of Europe and America.

Wealthy families. One of the distinctive features of Japanese industry as it emerged during this period was the concentration of wealth and control in the hands of a few families. Just as the United States in the same period produced its Rockefellers, Carnegies and Morgans, so did Japan have its Mitsuis and Mitsubishis. But whereas in America the financial giants succeeded by their own efforts, often directed against Government interests, the reverse was true in Japan. The *zaibatsu,* as the group of rich families was called, worked in close co-operation with the Government which gave the group every support. By offering bribes it was even able to 'buy' some of the political parties and so be sure of their votes in Parliament.

Changes in education. The Japanese were quick to realise that the foundation of a successful modern State was a sound education system. As early as 1872 a start was made towards compulsory primary schooling and a complete education programme was soon developed. The University of Tokyo, established in 1877, became the first of the important centres of higher education that were steadily established. Many of the teachers in these new schools and colleges were foreigners while an increasing number of Japanese went overseas to study. In these ways western ideas and technical developments were quickly absorbed and adapted to suit Japanese needs.

From the outset the education programme was planned to produce loyal citizens. Children were taught to accept, without question, the authority of their seniors. Although many of the ideas and methods which underlay the new Japanese education came from France and Germany, there was also a typically eastern influence which emphasised respect, loyalty and obedience as the greatest of the virtues. These were the foundations on which later Japanese militarism was built.

A modern nation. By 1894 the period of transition had ended. The Japan of 1853, and even the Japan of 1870, was no longer recognisable. Feudalism had been replaced by a central system of government and the great majority of Japanese children were at school. Trade and industry were rapidly expanding and Japan was ready to extend its influence beyond its own shores and to take its place as one of the great nations of the world. All of this progress was in marked contrast to developments in India, where modernisation was almost entirely the work of the British administration, and in China where a proud and ancient civilisation seemed to be crumbling and unable to adapt itself to the impact of the West. Japan had provided an example, if not an inspiration, for other Asian nations and was soon to be given the opportunity to prove to them that the East could more than hold its own with its rivals from the West.

PROBLEMS AND AMBITIONS

Japan suffers from two serious geographic disadvantages. Many parts of the British Isles are considered to be quite unsuitable for farming but problems caused by relief are not nearly as serious in this country as they are in Japan. Although Japan is almost half as large again as Great Britain, a much greater area is useless for agriculture. In fact, whereas no county in Britain is wholly unsuitable for either agricultural or pastoral farming, this is possible on less than a fifth of Japan.[1]

Therefore, with a steadily increasing population in the late nineteenth century, Japan was faced with the problem of feeding and employing its people. This problem has been solved in many countries by the development of large industrial cities to provide employment for many and to produce goods which can be sold abroad in exchange for food. Britain is a good example of this type of development but Japan, on the other hand, is poorly supplied with the minerals necessary for the establishment of large-scale industry. Apart from some deposits of copper ore and low-grade coal the country has no important mineral resources. If the Japanese programme of modernisation and industrialisation was to succeed it was imperative that solutions be found to the twin problems of providing the people with food and the factories with raw materials.

The need for markets. The cost of modernisation is always high. In most western countries such as Britain and the United States it is borne by industry so that, as markets expand and profits increase, more capital is available to invest in industrial expan-

[1] See comparative maps in *Oxford School Atlas*, p. 54-5, O.U.P., London.

sion. But Japan, being late in the industrial race, was competing with the clock because other nations had already established a substantial lead. This meant that money had to be borrowed and equipment imported to allow for the more rapid development of industry. It also meant that markets were necessary so that the profits from trade could be used to repay foreign loans.

Because its industries developed late Japan found that the best markets were already taken. If it was to compete in these areas it was necessary to keep production costs low and this in turn meant low wages for Japanese factory workers. However, because they were poorly paid, these workers were unable to afford to buy many Japanese goods so manufacturers had problems selling sufficient goods on the home market as well as overseas. Meanwhile, imports continued to be larger than exports which meant that Japan had an unfavourable balance of trade. There did not appear to be an easy solution to this problem of steadily increasing indebtedness to other nations.

Imperialism. The problems that faced Japan were by no means new. They had been faced to a greater or lesser extent by most western nations that had industrialised. Other nations had sought a solution to these problems by establishing overseas empires and, in the 1890s, Japan began to seek a similar solution. Trade had been established with Korea, the nearest part of mainland Asia, in 1875 but the country was under the nominal control of China. Increasing Chinese weakness encouraged the Japanese to hope that Korea might become a Japanese possession and thus a source of rice and a market for Japanese goods.

Another Chinese possession close to Japan was Manchuria. Although it had been part of the Chinese Empire for over two hundred years its rich mineral, timber and agricultural resources had never been fully developed. China approached the end of the nineteenth century under increasing foreign domination and appeared to be in no condition to extend its influence in Manchuria. However, Japanese eyes were not the only ones that were turned in this direction: the Russians who, in 1892, had started to build the Trans-Siberian Railway to link up with the Pacific port of Vladivostok, also saw Manchuria as a likely addition to their Empire.

Militarism. The increasing discontent within Japan from poorly paid industrial workers could not be ignored, even though they had no vote. Once again western nations provided a model for Japan to copy. Prussian armies had recently completed the unification of Germany, and British and French armies in India and Indo-China were showing what powerful and determined nations could achieve. To many Japanese leaders the military conquest of Korea and Manchuria appeared to offer an obvious solution to all of the nation's problems. Not only would these areas provide markets and raw materials but their acquisition would bring glory to Japan and would distract attention from the problems at home.

EXPANSION AND EQUALITY, 1894-1914

Those who favoured a warlike policy had advantages on their side. For centuries the noblest occupation in Japan had been that of the soldier. Whereas in China it had been the mandarin or scholar who had been revered, in Japan it had been the samurai class. Although this class no longer existed officially (see page 124) the ancient traditions still continued. The cult of *Bushido*, 'the way of the warrior', remained an important feature of Japanese life. This belief placed loyalty as the greatest virtue and the true follower of the *Bushido* creed had to be prepared to sacrifice his life and his family in the service of his superiors. Self-control when in pain was regarded as one of the greatest tests of character and this had its culmination in *hara-kiri*, a ceremonial form of suicide in which the victim disembowelled himself.

Shinto. Another important influence on Japanese life was the religion of Shintoism. Literally Shinto means, 'the way of the gods', but because the Japanese regarded their Emperors as being descended from the Sun Goddess the religion came to include respect and reverence for the Emperor and all those in authority. As the descendant of the gods, the Japanese Emperor could do no wrong. When he spoke the nation obeyed. It is difficult for western minds to understand this eastern belief in a semi-divine ruler but, having accepted its existence, it is easy to appreciate the powerful position of those who advised the Emperor and spoke in his name. By the early 1890s Japan had both the incentives to expand and the national heritage that would accept and approve the revival of its military traditions.

When a rebellion broke out in Korea in 1894, both China and Japan sent troops to quell it. Believing that Japan was not ready to undertake a full-scale war and anxious to prevent any further increase of Japanese influence in the peninsula, China provoked a quarrel which led to war. In a few months the bulk of the Chinese navy was sunk or captured and Japanese troops had seized Formosa and Wei-hai-wei (the chief port of the Shantung Peninsula) and were also threatening Mukden, the capital of Manchuria. China was forced to sue for peace.

Japan gets Formosa. By the Treaty of Shimonoseki in 1895, China surrendered the island of Formosa to Japan (see map opposite) and agreed to pay a large indemnity as compensation for damages suffered by Japan. But Japanese ambitions on mainland Asia were thwarted by the western Powers who now saw Japan as a possible rival to their own schemes in this area. The eastern David had defeated its eastern Goliath but was not yet ready to challenge the combined strength of the west. Therefore, Japan reluctantly gave up its claim to the Liaotung Peninsula in southern Manchuria, including the valuable harbour of Port Arthur, and had to be content with forcing China to recognise the independence of Korea. In the following year China allowed the extension of the Trans-Siberian Railway across Manchuria to Vladivostok and Port Arthur, granting the lease of the latter to Russia. Japan's chief opponent had now declared itself. Other western Powers were quick to secure similar privileges, much to the annoyance of Japan.

Manchuria. The Boxer Rebellion in 1900 (see page 170) gave Japan the opportunity to join the western Powers in Chinese affairs. The failure of Russia to withdraw its troops from Manchuria after the rebellion had been suppressed gave Japan the excuse it needed to intervene there. In 1902 an alliance with Britain (see page 24) gave Japan the confidence to undertake a war against Russia aimed at establishing influence on mainland Asia. Japan seized the initiative and attacked Russia without a formal declaration of war in 1904.

Hampered by the distance of the battlefield from Europe and by the inefficiency of its Government, Russia was no match for Japan. The Russian armies retreated steadily as first Port Arthur and then Mukden fell to the Japanese. Meanwhile the Russian Pacific fleet had been either destroyed or captured and a similar fate awaited the Baltic fleet when, after a journey around the Cape of Good Hope lasting more than six months, it arrived in the Sea of Japan in May 1905. By the Treaty of Portsmouth, Russia was forced to evacuate Manchuria and to recognise Japan's special interests in Korea. Also the southern half of the island of Sakhalin, Russia's railways and mines in southern Manchuria, and her lease of Port Arthur were transferred to Japan.

Equality with the West. By its victory in this first important war between a European and an Asian nation, Japan had clearly demonstrated that it was a force to be reckoned with in world affairs. The annexation of Korea which followed in 1910 raised scarcely a protest from the nations of Europe. China, on the verge

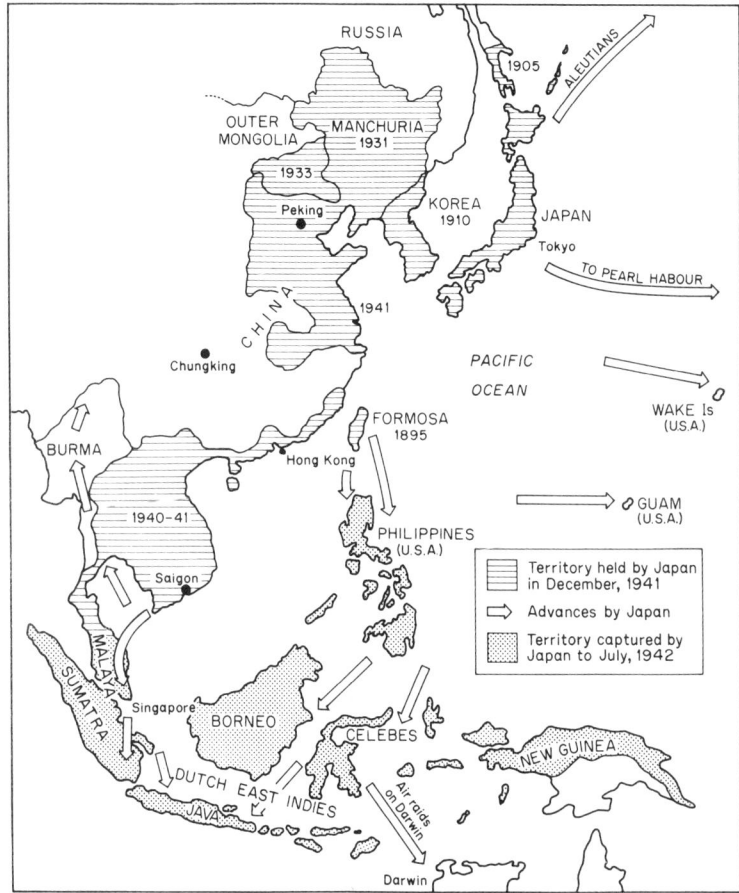

FIG. 19

of revolution, was resentful but powerless (see page 171). Meanwhile, Japan had been pressing for the removal of the irksome restrictions which prevented it from claiming complete equality with the West. In 1899, after numerous representations, other nations followed the lead of Great Britain and the United States and recognised Japanese laws as applying to their nationals residing in Japan. This abandonment of extraterritorial rights was soon followed by the restoration of Japanese control of their own trade (see page 125). For the first time in history an Asian nation could now claim to be equal with the nations of the West. Furthermore, and of even greater significance, this claim was recognised by western nations who now accepted Japan as a modern nation.

THE EASTERN GIANT, 1914-41

Japanese interests in Asia and the Pacific received an unexpected stimulus when war broke out in 1914. As Britain's ally in the east Japan was able to occupy the German trading cities of Kiaochow and Tsingtao (see map, page 131) on the Shantung Peninsula and so become installed in China proper. At the same time the Japanese navy seized the German islands in the north Pacific. These islands, the Marshalls, Marianas and Carolines, were later to prove of considerable strategic value.

The Twenty-one Demands. Taking advantage of European preoccupation, Japan decided to use the opportunity to increase its influence in China at the expense of its western rivals. In 1915 China was presented with a set of demands which would have effectively turned it into a province of Japan. Had it not been for American intervention this fate may have been unavoidable, for China, at this time, was in the grip of civil war. But American influence was still not strong enough to prevent Japan making considerable gains in China and establishing itself as the most powerful force in that unfortunate country. Not only had the Japanese thwarted western ambitions in their own country but they were now ready to challenge them in other parts of Asia.

The Twenty-one Demands fall naturally into five main groups. By the first of these China was forced to recognise virtual Japanese control of the Shantung Peninsula, while the second extended Japanese rights in southern Manchuria and Inner Mongolia. These two groups together placed Japan in an extremely strong position in north China. Japan's shortage of raw materials was illustrated by the third group which gave it a controlling interest in the principal iron and coal industries of China. These, together with the fourth group of demands that China should not cede or lease further ports to any Power other than Japan, were finally agreed to by China, but American intervention prevented the enforcement of the fifth group, which would have forced China to accept Japanese 'advisers' in military, political and economic matters. Even so, the paramount position of Japan could not be questioned.

Washington Conference, 1922. Japanese gains from World War I had been largely recognised in the Treaty of Versailles, which gave Japan the former German North Pacific islands as mandates of the League of Nations (see page 75). The United States, seeing the acquisition of Pacific islands and the growth of Japanese naval power as a possible future threat, took the initiative and called a conference at Washington in 1922. The main results of this conference have already been examined (see page 50) and, together with Japan's agreement to evacuate the Shantung Peninsula, they suggested that there was little to cause concern in this area. However, Japan had invested considerable money in China, and especially in Manchuria, and held a strong economic position in the country which it was determined to exploit for its own advantage.

The Japanese acquisition of Manchuria has already been described in Chapter 3 (see pages 56-7) but the underlying reasons for it require closer attention. As well as the economic gains that would follow the annexation of Manchuria, there were also important political and military advantages to be considered. Manchuria offered the solution to a number of problems which had become more serious during the 1920s.

Nationalism. Although the struggle for equality with the West appeared to have been won before the outbreak of World War I, events in the 1920s suggested that a final solution had not been reached. In spite of a Japanese plea no statement was included in the Treaty of Versailles or the Covenant of the League of Nations recognising the equality of all people irrespective of their race, colour or religious beliefs. To the Japanese, the continuing existence of inequalities seemed to be apparent. In 1922 and again in 1930 the British and the Americans refused to agree to naval equality for Japan. Again, in 1924 American immigration restrictions virtually excluded any further Japanese from settling in the United States where considerable numbers had migrated in the previous fifty years, especially to California. When it is remembered that such apparent injustices are regarded by orientals as causing an embarrassing 'loss of face', it becomes easy to understand why those who advocated aggressive nationalism quickly found favour with many Japanese.

Democracy? World War I was a victory for the democratic nations, with the result that those in Japan who favoured autocratic government on the German model (see page 124) found little support in the immediate postwar years. In 1925 the right to vote was extended to include all adult men and during the twenties the Ministers were chosen from the important political parties in Parliament. Although, on the surface, Japan was moving towards democracy the real power in the country remained in the hands of the privileged few — especially the *zaibatsu*. Ministers may have been chosen from the Parliament but they remained responsible to the Emperor.

Militarism. The combination of a growing national opposition to unfair treatment by western nations and the serious economic effects of the world slump provided the opportunity for those who were anxious to return to a more aggressive policy in world affairs. In 1931 this group, led largely by army officers, organised the invasion of Manchuria in defiance of the Cabinet. The success of the war in Manchuria greatly increased the prestige of the army which began to exert more and more influence on the civil Government. Since 1898 the Ministers of the army and the navy had been serving officers and the only Ministers with direct access to the Emperor. They now used their position to ensure that only laws acceptable to the armed forces were introduced. In fact, if not in name, the country was almost a military dictatorship.

The China Incident, 1937. After an uneasy peace which had lasted since 1932, fighting again broke out in China in 1937 following an incident staged by the Japanese at the Marco Polo Bridge, an important rail centre close to the former Chinese capital of Peking. From the outset the struggle was an unequal one. The large and well equipped Japanese force swept through northern China while the Japanese navy bombarded the coastal cities. All attempts to restore peace proved fruitless and the relentless Japanese advance forced the Chinese to retreat steadily. Before the end of 1937 most of the coastal areas, including the capital at Nanking, were in Japanese hands and a new provisional government had been established in China. Under the leadership of General Chiang Kai-shek the Chinese refused to surrender, and established a temporary capital at Chungking in the well protected Szechwan Basin. By 1939 the war had reached a stalemate, with Japanese forces in control of the coast and the northern provinces and the Chinese defending the interior.

World War II offered Japan the same opportunities for increasing its influence in Asia that had been provided in World War I. In 1940 Germany, Italy and Japan signed an alliance in which they agreed to establish 'a New Order in Europe and Greater East Asia' and to help each other 'with all political, economic and military means' if any one of them was 'attacked by a Power at present not involved in the European War or in the Chinese-Japanese conflict'. Japan had no intention of allowing American intervention to interfere with her plans on a second occasion (see page 132).[1] The New Order envisaged Japan as the manufac-

[1] Although specifically excluded the U.S.S.R. remained suspicious that the alliance was directed against it.

FIG. 20 — Japanese 'Victory March' in Shanghai, 1937.

turing heart of a great Asian Empire which would include Manchuria, China and South-East Asia. Tin, rubber, iron, coal and other raw materials would flow into Japan from China. Malaya and the East Indies in return for the products of Japanese factories. In 1940 Japan became a one-party dictatorship and was ready to launch the next stage of its programme to dominate eastern Asia.

Pearl Harbour, 1941. During the early part of 1941 Japanese forces occupied the French possessions in Indo-China, whereupon Britain, the United States and the Netherlands imposed on Japan a trade embargo (or suspension). As these three nations provided almost two-thirds of Japan's imports, including the bulk of the raw materials for its industry, and took a similar proportion of its exports these restrictions on trade placed Japan in an impossible situation. Either it must withdraw from Indo-China, with a consequent loss of face, or it must expand into the rest of southeastern Asia and seize the raw materials that were essential for its factories. When a military Government led by General Tojo took office in October 1941 events began to move rapidly towards a climax. A surprise attack on the American naval base at Pearl Harbour on December 7 before any declaration of war had been made gave the Japanese an initial advantage which they were quick to appreciate.

Greater Japan. Within weeks Japanese forces had overrun Hong Kong, Malaya, Singapore, Burma, the Dutch East Indies, Borneo and the Philippines. China, which had depended for supplies on the tortuous Burma Road, was now restricted to reliance on the difficult air route 'over the hump' of the Himalayas from India. The Japanese navy sailed unchallenged into the Pacific and Indian Oceans and Japanese bombers raided the city of Darwin in northern Australia. To New Zealanders and Australians whose armies were fighting in the North African desert the war assumed a new urgency. Road blocks were set up on all major highways, air raid wardens were appointed to enforce a blackout and residents of coastal cities dug air raid shelters in their gardens. By mid-1942 Japanese conquests extended from the Aleutian Islands in the north to the East Indies and the Solomons in the south, and from Burma in the west to the Marshalls and Wake Island in mid-Pacific (see map, page 131).

DEFEAT OF JAPAN

Although the initial advantage lay with Japan, it could not expect to hold it indefinitely. By mid-1942 American troops, planes and ships were arriving in the Pacific in ever increasing numbers. In May a decisive battle was fought in the Coral Sea to the immediate northeast of Australia where planes from the American carrier fleet checked the Japanese advance. In the following month a further victory was won in the battle for Midway Island. Although it was not realised at the time, the Japanese had reached the limit of their advance.

These victories were followed by an immediate counter-attack against the Japanese in New Guinea and the Solomon Islands. American marines supported by Australians and New Zealanders began the long task of driving the Japanese back; a task made infinitely more unpleasant and dangerous by the other enemies they had to face — jungle, disease and the debilitating effect of the steamy tropical heat. Rather than attempt to drive the Japanese from every island in their path the Allies adopted an 'island-hopping' programme, which trapped the Japanese between two fronts, cut their supply lines and made it a much easier matter to clean out isolated pockets of resistance while the main advance continued.

The atomic bomb. By mid-1944 the American advance had reached the island of Saipan in the Mariana group and from this base huge B29s, better known as Super Fortresses, began to bomb Japan itself. In the early months of 1945 the islands of Iowa Jima and Okinawa were captured after desperate fighting and heavy casualties. Japan lay only 400 miles to the north and victory was only a matter of time. But it was unlikely that the Japanese would surrender easily and it was probable that many more lives would be lost before final victory was won.

But the events of a few seconds on August 6 and 9, 1945, not only ended the war but also altered the future of the entire world. The two atomic bombs that were dropped on the cities of Hiroshima and Nagasaki on these two days killed over 100,000 people and seriously injured as many more — and almost destroyed the two cities. On August 14 the Japanese agreed to an unconditional surrender.

OCCUPIED JAPAN

In 1945 Japan was not only defeated but also exhausted. Eight years of war had strained the country's resources to the limit. The bulk of the Japanese navy had been sunk, many important cities had been devastated by American bombing and thousands of ex-soldiers found themselves without either homes or jobs when they returned to Japan. For these reasons the occupying army of American, Australian and New Zealand troops under the command of General Douglas MacArthur was welcomed by many Japanese who were disillusioned about the future of their country.

Occupation policy. As in Germany, the Allied occupation aimed to punish Japan but also to restore the Japanese economy and to educate the people towards democracy. All military and patriotic societies were dissolved and cadet training in schools was abolished. A new constitution was introduced which was in marked contrast to the original constitution of 1889 (see page 124). The new document showed the extent of American influence in its preamble, which began, 'We, the Japanese people, acting through our duly elected representatives in the National Diet (or Parliament) . . . do proclaim that sovereign power resides with the people.' Women received equal rights with men, including the vote; trade unions were recognised; education became compulsory to the age of fifteen; the Emperor renounced his divine origin and became a constitutional monarch; and the Cabinet of Ministers,

headed by the Prime Minister, now became responsible to the
Diet. On the surface at least, Japan had been transformed into
a democracy.

Economic reconstruction. We have seen that the prewar industry, trade and finance of Japan had been dominated by the
zaibatsu (see page 126). All attempts by the Occupation to
destroy their power, because they had supported the militarists
in the 1930s, met with failure. Japanese industry showed no signs
of recovery and had to be heavily subsidised by Amercan dollars
to prevent wholesale starvation of city workers. Gradually large
businesses developed again and industry began to recover.

Japan, like nineteenth century Ireland, had long suffered from
the system of absentee landlords. Almost three-quarters of the
farmlands of Japan were occupied by farmers who paid rent for
their holdings to rich owners who often lived in the cities and
had no interest in their lands except for the rents they produced.
By forcing such landowners to sell and by redistributing these
lands to small, independent farmers, the Occupation carried out
an agricultural revolution in Japan which greatly improved the
position of farmers. Today no peasants in Asia are better off
than the Japanese.

The Peace Treaty, 1951. Because of disagreement between the
Soviet Union and the United States there was considerable delay
in the signing of a peace treaty with Japan. By 1951 the world
situation had changed. The communist revolution had succeeded
in China and the Korean War had already broken out (see page
207). Japan was no longer a menace to world peace but had
become an important base for American troops and a necessary
link in the western defence system along the Pacific coast of Asia.
By the treaty, Japan was once more reduced to the four main
islands which it had occupied almost a hundred years earlier
when Commodore Perry sailed into Tokyo Bay. The Japanese
Pacific islands became strategic trusteeships of the United Nations
to be controlled by the United States; Formosa, the Pescadores
and Manchuria were returned to China; southern Sakhalin was
returned to the Soviet Union and Korea was to be a trusteeship
of China, Russia and America for five years. Although the treaty
was rejected by the Soviet Union and India and disliked by many
other countries, it was signed by New Zealand and Australia in
return for the ANZUS Pact which provided for the joint defence
of the Pacific. As the treaty allowed Japan to rearm, this seemed
a wise and reasonable precaution.

THE NEW JAPAN

The revival of Japanese industry in the 1950s was remarkable. By the 1970s Japan ranked after the United States and the Soviet Union as the third most important economic power in the world. Japan has become the most important shipbuilding nation in the world, and for a country that has to import all its iron and most of its steel, this is no mean achievement. Japanese trade with the United States and the countries of South-East Asia and the South Pacific is greater than it has ever been. Transistor radios, television sets, computers, cameras, machine tools, cars and manufactured goods of every description flow off Japanese production lines in ever increasing numbers to supply the world's markets. Japan has become the second greatest investor in developing countries with a special interest in Australasia, South-East Asia and South America. In return she has become the biggest importer of raw materials in the world. Despite this her trade was very much balanced in her favour and she has had to invest so heavily overseas so that the developing countries can afford to buy her goods in return. The tremendous economic growth seemed uncheckable until the mid-1970s when it did suffer a series of shocks. First, the oil crisis showed just how dependent Japan was on the producers of key raw materials. At one time the Japanese Government had to make pro-Arab statements in order to guarantee oil supplies from the Middle East. Second, the country was hit hard by the general recession in world trade: there was heavy unemployment and an actual decline in production. Nevertheless the postwar industrial achievement of the country has been amazing.

In agriculture the results have been similar. 'Rice before flowers' is the Japanese way of saying that reforms that do not benefit the ordinary people are of little value. Although the average size of a farm is only two and a half acres, hard-working Japanese farmers, tilling the soil that they now own, have so greatly increased production that Japan is almost self-sufficient in rice, the staple food. Shortage of arable land still remains the chief agricultural problem (see page 127) and more and more peasant farmers and their families are moving to the large cities seeking work in the new shops, offices and factories.

Democracy on trial. Democracy is undoubtedly the most difficult system of government in the world. New nations in Africa and Asia have experienced its difficulties (see Chapter 10) and it could not be expected that six short years of Allied occupation of Japan would be sufficient to introduce a method of government which, in the western world, had developed gradually over many centuries. The result has been considerable confusion in Japan where the old ways have been discredited and often abandoned but where the new ways are often not understood. For the most part the country has been ruled by conservative-inclined governments under the highly respected constitutional head of state, Emperor Hirohito. The Socialists have formed the main opposition in the National Diet and the Communists have attracted less than two per cent of the votes at the general elections. On the other hand there has been a resurgence of extreme right-wing militarist movements outside Parliament and extremely militant left-wing groups, generally dominated by students. Both sides have remained relatively weak in terms of popular appeal, but there is always the fear that a major economic setback for the country could strengthen them immensely.

Japan in world affairs. Although there was a natural anti-American reaction in Japan following the occupation, this was short-lived and Japan has continued to work in close co-operation with the United States in world affairs. A security pact was signed between the two countries in 1952 and in 1955 Japan was admitted to the United Nations. Quite soon after the war the United States saw the advantage of rebuilding a strong Japan as part of her network around the Communist bloc. Japan was limited by the peace treaties to no more than self defence forces, but the Americans positively encouraged the growth of these and the development of mutual defence commitments between Japan, South Korea and Taiwan, all under the general umbrella of American nuclear power.

In the early 1970s Japanese governments sought a greater freedom of action from the United States especially dissociating themselves from American policy in Vietnam. At the same time the United States, alarmed by her imbalance in trade, sought to restrict Japanese imports. As a result the Japanese, while remaining basically in the American orbit, developed economic links with the Soviet Union, particularly in plans to develop Siberia, and subsequently with China, which was potentially the greatest of all markets for Japanese goods. The Chinese had for long regarded the new Japan of the 1950s and 1960s as just as great a danger as the Japan of the 1930s, but the Chinese also wanted economic co-operation. So, with the detente with America and Japan's increasing detachment from Taiwan, the way became open for improved relationships and trade.

The future for Japan remains obscure. The country is one of the economic leaders of the world, but has deliberately not yet developed her military and economic potential to the full. Japan could easily become a nuclear power, but remains very vulnerable to shifts in world trade; she has scored the greatest economic successes under a parliamentary democracy but the parliamentary system itself is still very unstable.

NOTEBOOK SUMMARY
Japan since 1870

END OF ISOLATION
1. The closed door — chief features
2. The Perry expedition
3. Change in government

MODERNISATION OF JAPAN
1. Government
   Collapse of feudalism
   Central government
   Constitution
   Influence of Ito
2. Economic development
   Trade restrictions
   Modernisation — note examples
   Position of Government
   Position of *zaibatsu*
3. Education — Methods adopted — Progress made
4. Position 1890

PROBLEMS AND AMBITIONS
1. Geographic problems and their importance
2. Population — possible solutions
3. Markets — Needs — Problems
4. Imperialism — Possible areas of expansion — Difficulties
5. Militarism — Western examples — Military tradition
6. Shinto — Definition — Influence
7. Position 1890

EXPANSION AND EQUALITY, 1894-1914
1. War with China, 1894
   Cause
   Japanese gains
   European opposition — effect
2. Manchuria
   Boxer Rebellion — importance for Japan
   Alliance with Britain — date and importance
   War with Russia — causes and results
3. Korea
4. Equality with West
   Extraterritorial rights
   Control of trade
   Significance of equality

EASTERN GIANT, 1914-41
1. World War I — immediate gains
2. Twenty-one Demands
   Main groups
   Japanese gains

3. Washington Conference
Reasons
Terms affecting Japan
4. Japan in the 1920s
Growth of nationalism — reasons
Limited democracy — reasons
Growth of militarism — reasons and results
5. Manchuria (refer also to Chapter 3, pages 56-7)
Reasons for intervention (summarised)
Acquisition
Results
6. War with China
Cause
Results by 1939
7. World War II
Japanese alliances
Japanese ambitions
Japanese expansion — results
Pearl Harbour — reason and results
8. Greater Japan — note greatest extent of Japanese Empire

DEFEAT OF JAPAN
1. Turning point — where, when and reasons
2. Island-hopping — significance
3. Atomic bombs — reason — significance
4. Effect of war on Japan

OCCUPIED JAPAN
1. Occupation policy
Aims
Changes made in Japan
2. Economic reconstruction
Industry
Agriculture
3. Peace Treaty, 1951·
Terms — Importance of Japan — Safeguards

THE NEW JAPAN
1. Industrial revival — chief features and results
2. Agriculture — results
3. Government — progress with democracy
4. World affairs: Relations with U.S.A. — other relationships

WORDS TO KNOW
The following words used in this chapter need to be understood. Most of them have been explained in the text but all of them should form part of a history student's vocabulary. Make a list in the back of your notebook, with meanings, of those words that are new to you. Learn these and use them in your essays:

Absentee landlord, balance of trade, Bushido, constitutional monarchy, Diet, extraterritorial rights, imperialism, island-hopping, Meiji, militarism, nationalism, samurai, Shinto, shogun, zaibatsu.

BOOKS TO READ OR CONSULT

Beasley, W. G. *The Modern History of Japan,* London, Weidenfeld & Nicolson, 1963.
Reischauer, E. O. *Japan, Past and Present,* London, Duckworth, 1964 (3rd ed.).
Storry, R. *A History of Modern Japan,* Harmondsworth, Penguin, 1963 (Rev. ed.).

QUESTIONS FOR ESSAYS OR DISCUSSION

1. (a) For what reasons did Japan enter World War II?
   (b) What long-term preparations had been made within Japan since 1870 to fit her for a role of world conquest?
2. (a) Why did Japan adopt an expansionist policy in the 1930s?
   (b) Trace the steps in Japan's expansion and defeat, 1931-45.
   (c) How has Japan fared since 1945?
3. (a) What circumstances caused Japan to be an imperialist nation and drove it along the path of overseas expansion between 1894 and 1937?
   (b) Trace the chief steps in Japan's territorial expansion in that period.
4. Give an account of the rise of modern Japan to the position it held in 1940.
5. (a) By what right could Japan claim equality with the nations of Europe by 1914?
   (b) In what ways, during the 1920s, did the Japanese consider this equality was not recognised?
   (c) What were the consequences of this Japanese feeling of inequality?

7

THE FOREIGN POLICY OF THE U.S.A. 1870-1945

In the first half of the nineteenth century the United States of America could be compared with a boy in his early teens. Childhood had been left behind and the young man was passing through a period of rapid physical growth and facing new problems within himself which he must solve before he was ready to take his place as an adult in society. The United States entered its period of adolescence at the start of the nineteenth century, by which time its initial problems had been solved, the Constitution was firmly established and its physical growth had begun. In the next fifty years exploration and settlement moved rapidly west of the Mississippi River, culminating in the acquisition of California on the Pacific coast in 1848. By mid-century the United States stretched from the Atlantic to the Pacific and from Mexico in the south to the Canadian boundary in the north; it included an area almost twice as large as the whole of Europe (excluding Russia).

This rapid physical growth was accompanied by serious internal problems which included the economic development of this vast territory, the absorption of immigrants from many different European countries and the settling of the increasingly difficult question of Negro slavery. In an age when the most common advice to new arrivals was, 'Go west young man, go west', the people of America became more and more absorbed with their own problems and less and less interested in matters beyond the American continent. Furthermore, with so many of its people coming from so many European countries, no American Government wished to involve itself in European wars or disputes. If these people were to be welded into a single nation it was important that they should not have their new loyalties disrupted by being involved in the disputes of the lands from which they and their ancestors had come.

The Monroe Doctrine. The determination of the United States to keep itself clear of involvement in European affairs was made clear early in the nineteenth century. In 1823, in his annual message to Congress, President Monroe said the United States was not interested in European affairs and it expected a similar attitude to American affairs by European nations. He warned the nations of Europe that any attempt to extend their influence or possessions in any part of the American continent would almost certainly involve them in war with the United States. The spirit of the Monroe Doctrine, as his speech became called, was later captured by two American poets who told the European nations that:

'With what you have, we have no quarrel.
We only draw one simple moral
From Labrador to Darien
And South to Horn and back again,
"These gates are shut. Respect these gates."
Yours truly,
The United States.'[1]

Although the Monroe Doctrine was primarily concerned with the defence of the. American continent from outside attack, it became accepted by many people in both America and Europe as an indication that the United States intended to take no further part in world affairs that did not directly affect it.

Isolationism. During the first half of the nineteenth century the majority of American eyes were turned inwards. National and personal energies were directed towards developing the rich natural resources of the continent. American life and thought were dominated by the moving frontier; the steadily advancing line of settlement which moved away from rather than towards Europe. It was not until 1869 that the first trans-continental railway was completed, and even then communications were so slow and un-reliable that the pioneers in the west were often unaware of happenings in the eastern cities of New York and Baltimore, let alone events in London and Paris. When the Monroe Doctrine is related to the political, social and economic problems that faced the American nation in this period, the development of an isola-tionist outlook becomes easier to understand.

AMERICAN IMPERIALISM

For twenty years following the Civil War, Americans not only persisted in their isolationist outlook but became almost com-pletely indifferent to events outside their own country. The reasons for this are easy to see. The bloodshed and devastation of the Civil War in the 1860s had left the nation with tremendous prob-lems of reconstruction. These problems absorbed most of the attention of the Government and the energies of the people. At

[1] Vincent Benét, Rosemary and Stephen, *A Book of Americans,* Rinehart & Co., 1933, p. 57.

the same time, with the more rapid opening up of the west following the development of the railways (four trans-continental railways were completed by 1884), the attention of eastern industrialists was drawn naturally to the new market provided for their goods. Internal development and reconstruction progressed rapidly, aided by the discovery and exploitation of valuable natural resources (especially coal and iron) and a policy of high customs duties which protected the new industries from overseas competition.

Foreign trade. By 1890 American overseas trade was 400 per cent greater than at the close of the Civil War in 1865. Much of this was the result of increased industrial production which enabled American manufacturers to supply the home market and to have an ever-growing surplus for export. Concurrent with this development was the increase in agricultural production, especially meat and wheat, made possible by the railways and the invention of barbed fencing wire. By 1890 the frontier had disappeared and the farmer joined the manufacturer in seeking overseas markets. Thus, although an isolationist outlook continued, Americans found that economic pressure drew them inevitably into competition for world markets. In the belief that 'trade follows the flag' many European nations were busily engaged in turning their markets into colonies (see pages 15-16). Would the United States be forced to follow suit?

The Far East. Americans had long been interested in the Far East. In the 1840s a trade agreement had been negotiated with China while in 1853 Commodore Perry had forced the reluctant Japanese to open their doors to American traders (see page 122). Perry reported that, 'It is self-evident that the course of coming events will ere long make it necessary for the United States to extend its jurisdiction (control) beyond the limits of the western continent.' However, the American Government was not prepared to join the European nations in their scramble to establish special trading posts and 'spheres of influence' in the Far East. Rather, it became the champion of the 'open door' policy, and advocated equal rights for all in the Far Eastern trade.

The Hay Note, 1898. The victory of Japan over China (see page 130) in 1895 and the American acquisition of the Philippine Islands from Spain in 1898 had an important bearing on American Far Eastern policy, for the one exposed the weakness of China while the other increased American interest in the China trade. To safeguard American trade, Secretary of State John Hay sought the agreement of other nations to a guarantee of equal trading rights for all. When the Boxer Rebellion broke out in

FIG. 21

China in 1900 (see page 170) and there was a real danger of China being divided among the European nations and Japan, American policy was extended to 'preserve Chinese territorial and administrative entity'. In other words, the United States became the champion of the continued existence of an independent China. But the fiction was more apparent than the fact and, although able to secure some modification of the Twenty-one Demands in 1915 (see page 132), the United States was finally forced to recognise the 'special interests' of Japan in China.

Pacific possessions. In 1867 the United States purchased Alaska from Russia and annexed Midway Island in the central North Pacific. However, thirty years were to pass before further possessions were gained in this area. The Spanish Pacific territories of the Philippine Islands and Guam were purchased from Spain for $20 million in 1898 following the Cuban War (see page 149). American motives were mixed: some saw the opportunity for evangelism and the chance to improve the living conditions of the natives while others hoped to develop the islands for American trade.

Missionaries and traders had long been active in the Hawaiian and Samoan Islands. With the acquisition of the Philippines and increasing trade with China, Hawaii became an important coaling station, and, with Wake Island, was annexed in 1898. The harbour of Pago Pago in eastern Samoa had been an important

Fig. 22 — Roosevelt and his 'Rough Riders' on a crest overlooking Santiago during the Spanish-American War, 1898.

port of call for American traders and whalers for over twenty years before Samoa was divided between American and Germany in 1899. Ten years earlier a storm had destroyed warships of these nations in the harbour at Apia when there was danger of a serious international incident. By the turn of the century the United States had become an important Pacific Power with a string of island possessions across the ocean.

Caribbean conquests. By 1898 the only remnants of the former Spanish empire in America were the islands of Cuba and Puerto Rico in the Caribbean Sea. Americans had always believed that, sooner or later, Cuba would become part of the United States, but earlier unrest caused by Spanish misgovernment had not persuaded them to intervene on behalf of the Cubans. By the end of the century the position had changed. Increasing American investments, especially in the sugar industry, and increasing American trade with the island provided an economic reason for greater interest. The possibility of a canal being cut to link the Atlantic and Pacific Oceans provided a strategic reason for American interest because Cuba lay directly across the Pacific approaches. Therefore, when another revolution broke out in

Cuba in 1895 American interest was greater than it had been on previous occasions.

For three years the United States Government wavered but matters came to an unexpected climax when the battleship *Maine* was blown up in Havana harbour in 1898. Two hundred and sixty American sailors died in the disaster and war fever swept the country, stimulated by such newspaper headlines as, 'Remember the Maine! To hell with Spain!' Whether the *Maine* explosion was accidental or deliberate was never proved but war resulted. In less than two months Spain was defeated and sued for peace. Puerto Rico became an American possession and, in keeping with earlier promises, Cuba gained its independence — but at a price. The Cubans were forced to sell two naval stations to the United States and to allow its intervention to restore order or to provide protection. In effect, if not in name, Cuba became an American protectorate (see map, page 147).

The Panama Canal. For over three hundred years men had talked of cutting a canal through the isthmus of Central America. An attempt by the French engineer de Lesseps in the 1880s had proved a costly failure, being defeated by malaria and yellow fever in the swamps of Panama. His permission to build the canal (known as a concession) was then purchased by an American company. Congress finally agreed to purchase this concession from the company for $40 million in 1902 when a supposedly extinct volcano erupted on the other possible route through Nicaragua. But the Colombian Government, which owned the territory through which it was intended to build the canal, did not agree to this proposal and challenged the right of the American company to sell the concession without its permission.

A revolt promptly broke out in Panama, with the secret support of both the American company and President Theodore Roosevelt, culminating in the creation of the Republic of Panama. The new republic quickly sold the permanent lease of a ten-mile strip (the Canal Zone) to the United States Government, which in its turn paid over the $40 million to the Canal Company. The land was now available for building the canal but the manner in which it had been acquired reflected no credit on President Roosevelt and made other Latin American States fear for their future dealings with their powerful northern neighbour. The opening of the Panama Canal in 1914 was an important step in the emergence of the United States as a world Power. By allowing the free movement of the American fleet from one ocean to the other the canal virtually doubled the size of the navy without another ship having been built.

FIG. 23 — Two German U-boats off the coast of America during World War I.

FIG. 24 — The United States enters the war, 1917 — an American tank landing in France.

AMERICA AND WORLD WAR I

In the years preceding World War I the United States Government played an active part in world politics on two important occasions. The first of these was the mediation of President Theodore Roosevelt in the Russo-Japanese War in 1905. In his typical swashbuckling manner, Roosevelt made threats and promises that no American Government would have been prepared to keep and his successful negotiation of the Treaty of Portsmouth gave the United States a position in world affairs that it did not seek. When war threatened between France and Germany in Morocco later in the same year (see page 24) Roosevelt again used his influence to bring the two parties to the conference table at Algeciras. However, Roosevelt's successor, President Taft, did not continue this policy and the United States took no part in either the Balkan or the later Moroccan crises.

Neutrality in 1914. When Europe erupted into war in 1914 (see page 25) the United States remained neutral. Many Americans believed that as the war was not of their making it was of no concern to them. For over a century the United States had been neutral in European affairs and had emerged as a champion of the rights of neutral nations. Of prime importance in this regard was the freedom of the seas which safeguarded the right of American ships to sail anywhere in the world without interference. Any attempt by the warring nations to interfere with this right would undoubtedly have serious consequences and an important effect on American public opinion.

Sympathy for the Allies. Although President Woodrow Wilson asked the nation to 'be neutral in fact as well as in name', this was not completely possible. The American nation was composed of people from many countries but the majority of these were English speaking while, to the north, lay the nation of Canada, a strong friend of the United States. The common republican and democratic ideals that America had long shared with France also helped to produce a public opinion that favoured the Allies rather than the Central Powers. Furthermore, since the Spanish War of 1898 the German Kaiser had been regarded with increasing suspicion in the United States. If America was forced into the war, there was little doubt as to which side it would support. Meanwhile the Allies were buying munitions from the United States in ever increasing quantities.[1]

While German submarine warfare was not the only reason for

[1] There was never an official refusal to sell munitions to Germany but the Allied naval blockade effectively prevented German purchases.

American entry into World War I, it provided the immediate cause. In May 1915 German U-boats sank a British passenger liner, the *Lusitania,* without warning, causing the loss of over a thousand lives including 128 Americans. Indignation swept the country and a declaration of war seemed imminent but President Wilson, determined on peace if at all possible, secured a guarantee from the Germans that they would sink no further passenger ships — without warning! For the next eighteen months an uneasy peace continued until, in January 1917, the German High Command announced that U-boats would sink on sight all merchant ships in the vicinity of the British Isles and in the Mediterranean Sea.

America at war. March 1917 was the fateful month. Anti-German opinion had been growing steadily as the sabotage of American industries by German agents increased. It became an outcry with the publication, at the beginning of March, of a proposed alliance between Mexico and Germany if the United States entered the war. In return for its support, Mexico was to regain territory stretching from Texas to Nevada which it had lost to the United States almost a hundred years earlier. Two weeks later Tsar Nicholas II abdicated (see page 98) and Russia became a republic and consequently a more acceptable ally to the American people. Before the end of the month five American ships had been torpedoed and American national honour could no longer be satisfied by anything less than a declaration of war on Germany. On April 2, 1917, President Wilson asked Congress to recognise 'the state of war which had been thrust upon it'. Four days later America was at war.

'It is a fearful thing', said Wilson, who had worked so hard for peace, 'to lead this great peaceful people into war . . . but the right is more precious than peace.'

When America joined the Allies the war in the west had reached a stalemate. For almost three years the opposing armies had faced each other from their trenches in northern France. Attacks and counter-attacks across the no man's land of Flanders and the Somme resulted in appalling loss of life but in little advance or retreat by either side. American troops began arriving in Europe in October 1917. Five months later the final collapse of Russia in the east freed the German armies to concentrate their full energies in a last desperate effort on the western front. But by this time the thin trickle of American 'doughboys' had become a flood as American troops landed in France at the rate of a quarter of a million a month. Meanwhile the American navy assisted the British blockade which was slowly strangling the

German economy. Faced with the combined strength of the Western Powers and exhausted by the failure of the spring campaign in 1918, Germany was forced to sue for peace and the armistice was signed in November, 1918.

Wilson and the peace. The part played by President Wilson at the peace conference at Versailles and in the formation of the League of Nations has already been discussed in previous chapters (see pages 32 and 70). We must now examine the reasons for the failure of the American Congress to support the President in his desire to produce a world organisation that would ensure a lasting peace with justice and freedom for all. At first sight this refusal to join the League of Nations may seem a simple restatement of American isolationism but there were also other issues.

Wilson had appealed to the nation for a vote of confidence in the mid-term election of 1918 but Republican majorities were returned in both houses of Congress. When he left for Versailles he no longer spoke for the American nation, and to make matters worse, he failed to include a single Republican in his peace delegation. Americans were concerned that the Treaty of Versailles largely ignored the honourable terms proposed in the Fourteen Points and that membership of the League of Nations would restrict their freedom to act independently. Even so, the Senate may have been prepared to ratify the Treaty if the President had agreed to some alterations intended to protect American interests. Rather than do this, Wilson set out on an exhausting speaking tour to appeal to the nation for its support. The strain was too much for his already frail and overworked body and before his tour was half completed he collapsed and suffered a stroke from which he never fully recovered. Meanwhile, diehard Republican senators increased their hostility and rejected the treaty, leaving the United States to make its own peace with Germany and free to continue its policy of isolation. A sweeping Republican victory in the elections of 1920 appeared to endorse this decision.

RETURN TO ISOLATION, 1919-39

Increasing involvement in world trade, however, prevented a complete return to isolation. America could no longer claim in 1923, as it had done in 1823, that it was not interested in European affairs. In spite of its vast natural resources the United States was no longer self-sufficient and needed to import increasing quantities of rubber and other raw materials for its expanding industries. At the same time this industrial expansion was producing an increasing surplus of manufactured goods for distribution on world markets. Financially, the United States emerged from World War I as the richest nation in the world. Former foreign loans had been repaid and replaced by overseas borrowing on the American money market. If American politicians could continue to remain aloof from the affairs of Europe, American financiers, farmers and manufacturers could not.

Debt repayments. The vast sum of $10,000 million had been lent to the Allies during World War I. Its repayment was complicated by the fact that many of the allied countries had also borrowed among themselves. Thus Britain, the largest American debtor, could not hope to repay her debts until she in turn had collected her loans to France and Italy. Suggestions that all wartime debts should be cancelled were rejected by the Americans, most of whom seemed to accept the attitude of the new President, Calvin Coolidge, who remarked, 'They hired the money, didn't they?' Attempts to repay the debts from trade profits also failed because the United States returned to a policy of high customs duties to protect its own industries from foreign competition. In fact, because the postwar expansion of American industry was so rapid, the United States found itself forced to increase its loans to other countries to enable them to buy American manufactured goods!

The issue was even further confused by the question of German reparations (see page 35). A farcical 'money-go-round' developed whereby American loans to Germany were being used to pay reparations to the Allies who in their turn used the same money to repay their war debts to the United States! With the collapse of world trade in the depression which began in 1929 (see page 52) the impossibility of continuing this pretence was finally recognised and, when Germany announced the abandonment of further reparation payments in 1931, debt repayments also ceased. America replied by refusing any further loans to countries which had defaulted on their war debts. Meanwhile, America had lost much good will in Europe by insisting on repayments and yet making it almost impossible for its debtors to pay.

Immigration by quota. By 1910 the population of the United States had passed ninety million, of which almost one person in three was an immigrant. Some remained in the eastern cities but the majority were quickly absorbed in the apparently limitless lands on the frontier. But by the end of World War I the frontier had disappeared and eastern cities were beginning to develop the same unfortunate social evils that many new settlers had left Europe to escape. In order to protect the 'American way of life' the Government decided that the time had come to close the floodgates of migration and reduce the flow to a well controlled stream.

The Immigration Act of 1921 introduced a quota system which so restricted the number of immigrants from different parts of the world that immigration from Asia, Africa and eastern and southern Europe almost ceased. In 1924 the restrictions were tightened to exclude any migrants from the greater part of Asia while numbers from other parts of the world were further reduced. With the settlement of the west and the increasing industrialisation of the east the United States no longer felt able to accept:

'Your huddled masses yearning to breathe free,
The wretched refuse of your teeming shore',

as the inscription on the Statue of Liberty proclaimed.[1]

World peace. Although the United States rejected membership of the League of Nations it did not ignore the League. From 1922 onwards American observers attended meetings of a number of the League's special commissions and in 1934 America joined the International Labour Organisation (see page 74). Throughout the period between the wars the United States co-operated with the League in its attempts to ensure world peace. The American concern for peace has already been seen by its initiative in calling the Washington Conference in 1922 and in its promotion of the Kellogg-Briand Pact in 1928 (see page 50). The various disarmament conferences of the early 1930s were also attended by American representatives. Nevertheless, in spite of America's obvious interest in the cause of world peace, its failure to join the League of Nations remained an important reason for the League's weakness.

Neutrality. As war again began to threaten Europe in the 1930s Americans withdrew further into their isolationist shell. The sinking of American shipping in the early stages of World War I had not been forgotten and fear that a new war in Europe would once again involve the loss of American lives resulted in the passing of Neutrality Acts in 1935 and 1937. These Acts made it illegal to sell military equipment or to make loans to countries which were at war. They provided, too, that other goods would only be supplied on a 'cash and carry' basis. In other words, warring countries wanting to buy American goods would have to provide their own ships and pay for the goods when they were collected. At the same time American spending on defence was increased. However, when the war between China and Japan broke out in 1937 (see page 134), the President did not declare

[1] Lazarus, E. I., *Poems,* Houghton Mifflin, 'The New Colossus', p. 202.

a 'state of war' to exist so that the United States was able to send both arms and supplies to China. It was apparent that the Neutrality Acts were designed to prevent American involvement in Europe rather than in Asia.

ABANDONMENT OF ISOLATION

While Churchill in England foretold the increasing danger from the Fascist dictators in the 1930s, his warnings were repeated in America by the new President, Franklin Delano Roosevelt (see pages 61-2). The first Democrat to hold the office since the resignation of Woodrow Wilson in 1920, Roosevelt soon found himself faced with the same problem that had faced Wilson. However, when war broke out in 1939, he did not repeat Wilson's message of 1914 (see page 151) but said to the nation, 'I cannot ask that every American remain neutral in thought. Even a neutral cannot be asked to close his mind or his conscience.'

America's attitude. Once again Americans were sympathetic towards the Allies but once again they were equally determined to preserve their neutrality. However, Roosevelt was able to secure an amendment to the neutrality laws which would enable Britain and France to buy arms and munitions as well as other supplies on a 'cash and carry' basis.

But the stalemate of World War I (see page 152) was not repeated in 1939. After a slow start (the 'phoney war') the German military machine crashed into action. By June 1940 Belgium had surrendered, France had collapsed and the British Expeditionary Force of more than a quarter of a million men had been miraculously snatched from the bombed beaches of Dunkirk. In August the Battle of Britain began as the might of the German Luftwaffe was concentrated on bombing and destroying the cities of south-eastern England. While the future of the world was being decided by the heroism of the pilots of the Royal Air Force — the famous 'Few' — Americans could not make up their minds. Was England's war their war or should America remain neutral?

Lend-Lease. One American at least had no doubts as to the course of action his nation should follow. As the German U-boat campaign began to increase its toll of Allied shipping President Roosevelt gave Britain fifty destroyers for the right to establish American bases in Newfoundland and on British islands in the West Indies. Immediately following his election for an unprecedented third term in November 1940, Roosevelt introduced legislation to allow the United States to supply arms, munitions and other goods to the Allies *without charge* on the understanding that they would be returned at the end of the war — if they were still useable. As one bitter isolationist opponent remarked, it was rather like lending chewing gum, 'You don't want it back.'

By 1945, America had provided, under lend-lease alone, supplies to more than twice the value of its total expenditure in World War I. In fact, if not in name, lend-lease was a declaration of war on Germany. While the Americans were still anxious to preserve their neutrality, they were at least prepared to supply the equipment to those who, by defeating Germany, would protect the United States. Realising the significance of lend-lease, Hitler began the sinking of American merchant vessels early in 1941. But still the United States did not enter the war.

Pearl Harbour. Throughout 1941 the United States became more deeply involved in the Allied cause, although there was no actual declaration of war. Following the German invasion of Russia in June, lend-lease was extended to that country; in August Roosevelt met Churchill in secret off the coast of Newfoundland to discuss both the war and the peace (see page 79); in September, after a U-boat attacked an American destroyer, the President ordered the navy to shoot any enemy submarines on sight and, in November, the Neutrality Acts were amended to allow American ships to deliver munitions to British ports. Any doubts as to the extent of American participation in the war were dramatically removed on the morning of Sunday, December 7, when Japanese dive bombers attacked the naval base at Pearl Harbour (see page 136) and the airfield at Manila. America was at war.

America and Britain. When Churchill met Roosevelt in Washington two weeks after the bombing of Pearl Harbour, two momentous decisions were made. By agreeing to pool their entire economic and military resources they reached, in the words of General Marshall, 'the most complete unification of military effort ever achieved by two nations.' Although the fury of the American people was directed against Japan rather than against Germany, and although their interests lay, as we have seen, in the Pacific and the Far East rather than in Europe, President Roosevelt agreed with Churchill that their common goal should be 'Hitler first'.

While general agreement had been reached on these two basic issues, many practical problems remained to be solved. General MacArthur and Admiral King could not see beyond the war with Japan which they were determined to win, and to win quickly. They were most reluctant to allow forces and equipment to be diverted from the Pacific theatre. In Europe the American Chiefs of Staff believed that a direct assault across the English

Channel should be attempted immediately. The tragic failure of the Dieppe raid, in which 3,500 of the 5,000 Canadian troops engaged were casualties, partly convinced them of the futility of such an attempt. Yet they had little sympathy with British proposals for a North African campaign or for an invasion of Italy, 'the underbelly of the Axis', as preliminaries to the establishment of a second front in France. Their reluctance to provide equipment was largely responsible for the German occupation of Italy after the fall of Mussolini in July 1943. They preferred to save their strength for a direct attack.

America and Russia. Since the German invasion of Russia in June 1941 Stalin had been demanding the establishment of a second front in France, regardless of the cost, in order to relieve German pressure on his own forces. The reluctance of Churchill to agree until the operation had at least some hope of success made Stalin extremely hostile towards Britain.[1] However, when Churchill, Roosevelt and Stalin met for the first time at Teheran, in November 1943, the situation on the Russian front was greatly changed. Anglo-American bombing of German munitions factories, the diversion of German troops to Italy, the provision of American lend-lease equipment and the heroic Russian resistance at Stalingrad had all contributed to this. In Churchill's eyes, it was no longer a question of saving Russia from Germany, but rather of saving Europe from Russia.

Churchill's fears were not shared by President Roosevelt, who apparently trusted Stalin and sincerely believed that his only concern was for Russia's security. On his return to Washington, Roosevelt felt well pleased with the friendship he had established with Stalin. 'I believe that we are going to get along very well with him and the Russian people — very well indeed', he told the American nation. But Stalin's insistence at Teheran that British and American troops should be used only in western Europe, 'not only determined the military strategy for 1944, but adjusted the political balance of postwar Europe in favour of the Soviet Union.'[2] Many of the problems that have defied solution in the postwar world can be attributed to Roosevelt's misjudgment of Stalin and his motives at Teheran in 1943.

The Fate of Europe. Roosevelt thought it inevitable that the Soviet Union would emerge from the war as the dominant Power in Europe but he believed it was of greater importance for world peace that Russia and America should 'develop and maintain the

[1]His own motives in World War II have already been discussed. See pages 109-10.
[2]Wilmot, Chester, *The Struggle For Europe*, London, Collins, 1952.

most friendly relations'. Furthermore, few Americans were concerned with the future of Europe and were reluctant to see their troops involved in the European war for any other reason than the defeat of Germany. Any thought of their being used to safeguard British postwar interests in Europe would have been unacceptable, especially in 1944 when Roosevelt was seeking a fourth term as President. Once the defeat of Germany was assured, American policy was dominated by the need to secure Russian assistance for the defeat of Japan and agreement to establish an international organisation to safeguard world peace. The fate of Europe seemed of secondary importance.

The Tragedy of Yalta. When the 'Big Three' met again at Yalta in February 1945, Roosevelt secured both of these aims in private talks with Stalin. Although Roosevelt had often showed himself to be suspicious of British imperialism, he accepted Russian demands for the return of their losses in the 1904-05 war with Japan (see page 130) as being 'a very reasonable suggestion from our ally.' Satisfied that the Soviet Union would emerge as the dominant Power in Asia, Stalin next turned his attention to Europe, where he secured agreements with Churchill and Roosevelt that were sufficiently vague to allow Russia to do almost whatever it wished in eastern Europe without actually breaking its Yalta promises. There can be little doubt that the Yalta Conference was a victory for Russian imperialism in Europe and in Asia. As the mediator between Churchill and Stalin, Roosevelt had a decisive role. His failure to understand the political situation in Europe and his misplaced trust in Stalin's future intentions cast a tragic shadow on the memory of a great statesman.

Winning the peace. Following the defeat of Germany and Japan, Americans were no longer able to ignore the rest of the world and to retire once more into their own corner. Although some isolationists remained, millions of Americans supported the sentiments expressed by President Roosevelt in December 1941 when, following the bombing of Pearl Harbour, he declared, 'We are going to win the war and we are going to win the peace that follows.' Although he did not live to see his prophecy fulfilled,[1] Roosevelt did more than any other man to break the tradition of American isolationism. His work was continued by the new President, Harry S. Truman. The United States became a foundation member of the United Nations when it was formed in 1945 (see Chapter 4), and has continued to play an major role in world affairs, as will be described in Chapter 9.

---

[1] Roosevelt died shortly after his election for a fourth term as President. The law has since been changed to prevent more than two terms.

U.S.A. AND LATIN AMERICA

The Monroe Doctrine. Spanish power in the Americas dated back to the sixteenth century but by the start of the nineteenth century Spain was a spent force. Inspired by the example of the revolt of the American colonies from Britain in 1776 and the humiliation of Spain by Napoleon Bonaparte, the Spanish American colonies declared their independence in the early years of the nineteenth century. After the defeat of Napoleon there seemed a strong possibility that Spain, supported by the great Powers of continental Europe, would try to regain its lost possessions. Britain, anxious to preserve its newly developed markets in these countries, offered to support the United States in preventing any intervention in Central or South America. However, President Monroe felt that, for the sake of national prestige, the United States should act alone. With the comforting knowledge of British sympathy, he rejected the offer and announced that the United States would not allow intervention by *any* European Power in this area (pages 144-5). Although the Monroe Doctrine depended on the support of the British navy for its enforcement, the future policy of the United States towards Latin America had been made clear.

'Big Brother'. After the American Civil War the interest of the United States in its southern neighbours quickened. Rather than allow European nations to interfere in these countries, it preferred to act itself. Sometimes this intervention was to assist them, as when Venezuela was supported in its dispute with Britain in 1895 concerning its boundary with British Guiana, or when the United States came to the aid of Cuba against Spain in 1898 (see page 149). On other occasions the United States collected debts owing to European nations rather than allow these Powers to collect them. This policy, developed principally by 'Teddy' Roosevelt, is known as the 'Roosevelt corollary' to the Monroe Doctrine. In effect, it meant that the United States would intervene in Latin America in order to prevent European intervention. While this policy was important for American protection it was not popular in the central and southern republics which resented American intrusion as much as European.

Dollar diplomacy. Another way in which the United States increased its influence in Latin America in the late nineteenth and early twentieth centuries was by large-scale investment. For instance, after Cuban independence, American money was used for the development of the Cuban sugar industry, mines and railways. The need to safeguard American financial interests became a ready excuse for using American troops to restore law and order in Cuba and other States where unstable government tended to be the rule rather than the exception. Venezuela, Haiti, Santo Domingo and Nicaragua were others to come strongly under the influence of dollar diplomacy. While such countries received the benefits of improving living standards, health and education programmes and public works schemes, they still regarded the intervention as foreign and resented it. Furthermore, most of the profits of these investments went to the American shareholders in much the same way as British investors had earlier benefited from the activities of the East India Company. (Study map on page 147.)

'Good Neighbour'. Theodore Roosevelt once said, 'Speak softly and carry a big stick and you will go far.' He used his 'big stick' to increase American influence in the Caribbean area and to secure the Canal Zone (see page 149) but the side effects were unfortunate because his policy developed a legacy of dislike for the United States among the republics of Latin America. Woodrow Wilson tried to improve relations but met with only limited success. However, the new policy was continued after World War I by the Republicans and in 1928 President Hoover undertook a good-will tour of South America. Meanwhile, American troops were withdrawn from Santo Domingo in 1924 and a dispute with Mexico over oil and mineral rights was settled peacefully. These beginnings provided the foundations on which the second Roosevelt was able to build much improved relations with Latin America in the 1930s. His 'good neighbour' policy did much to repair the damage done by his namesake at the turn of the century.

Pan-Americanism. As early as 1889 representatives of eighteen American States attended a conference in Washington to discuss closer co-operation. Although little came of it at the time, this conference provided a starting point in the movement towards Pan-Americanism. Periodic meetings continued but it was not until the seventh meeting, at Montevideo in 1933, that real progress was achieved. In that year all members agreed that no American republic should intervene in the affairs of another, even to collect debts. This recognition by the United States of the equal rights of all American States, great and small, was the most important single contribution it could make to the Pan-American ideal. As evidence of its good faith the remaining American troops were withdrawn from Haiti and Nicaragua.

At the same time it was agreed that any threat to any part of the American continent should be regarded as a common danger. By 1938 this agreement developed into a pledge from the States of Latin America that they would join together to defend any of their members from outside attack. As a party to this agreement, the United States retained its role as the natural protector of Latin America but the old antagonisms had gone. The bad neighbour of the days of Theodore Roosevelt had become the good neighbour during the presidency of his cousin, Franklin Roosevelt. In the postwar era these relations were further strengthened in the Rio Treaty of 1947 and by the formation of the Organisation of American States in 1948. The OAS has since become an important force in the United Nations.

A WORLD POWER

In the century from 1870 the United States moved from isolation to a position of world leadership. In particular, in the decades after World War II the United States was the predominant power throughout the world outside the Communist bloc and the dominant influence in the United Nations. In the 1970s her power has been checked. This is the result not only of the greater military capability of the Communist powers but of setbacks in areas which were particularly important to the United States such as Cuba (see page 217) and South-East Asia (see page 209) and of the increasing influence in the United Nations and elsewhere of the independent, Third World nations. These developments have, in their turn, brought a reaction towards isolationism amongst some sections of the American people. These developments in America's world role are studied in Chapter 9.

NOTEBOOK SUMMARY
The Foreign Policy of the U.S.A. 1870-1945

TRADITION OF ISOLATION
1. Main features of early 19th century
   Physical growth
   Internal problems — economic, social and racial
2. Monroe Doctrine
   Terms and date
   Significance (see also pages 144-5)
3. Isolationism — justification

AMERICAN IMPERIALISM
1. Economic background
   Internal development
   Foreign trade

2. The Far East
   Early interest
   Policy
   Hay Note — reasons and effect
3. The Pacific
   Early possessions — before 1870
   Gains from Spanish War — reasons
   Other acquisitions
   Position in 1900
4. The Caribbean
   Attitude towards Cuba — note economic and strategic interests
   Reason for Spanish War
   Results
5. Panama Canal
   Early attempt
   American intervention — note effect on Latin America
   Importance of canal

WORLD WAR I
1. Work for peace
   Russo-Japanese War
   Morocco
2. Neutrality
   Reasons
   Concerns
3. Attitude to War
   Reasons for sympathy to Allies
   Reasons for opposition to Germany
   Reasons for entry to war
   Effect of entry to war
4. Wilson and the peace
   Wilson's ideals (see Chapter 2, page 32)
   Wilson's achievements (see Chapter 4, page 70)
   Wilson's failure — note reasons for American rejection of proposals

RETURN TO ISOLATION, 1919-39
1. Economic involvement — examine the following factors that pre-
   vented a return to complete isolation from European affairs.
   Markets and raw materials
   Overseas loans — note American attitude and its effect
   German reparations — their effect
2. Immigration
   Restrictions imposed
   Reasons and results
3. World peace — note American participation
4. Neutrality
   Reason for Neutrality Acts
   Terms
   Aid for China

ABANDONMENT OF ISOLATION
1. American Attitude to World War II
   President Roosevelt
   American people
2. Aid to the Allies
   Ways in which aid was given
   Increasing American involvement
3. Pearl Harbour — effect
4. America and Britain
   Terms of co-operation
   Problems of co-operation
   Different points of view
5. America and Russia
   Roosevelt's attitude to Stalin
   Importance of Teheran
6. American policy
   Three main aims
   Gains from Yalta
   Failure at Yalta — note significance
7. Postwar attitude

U.S.A. AND LATIN AMERICA
1. The Monroe Doctrine
   Reason for it
   Importance for Latin America
2. Extension of American influence
   Intervention — reasons and examples
   Investment — examples and results
   Attitude of Latin American States
3. Improved relations
   Changed policy — men responsible and actions taken
   Results
4. Pan-Americanism
   Early developments
   Position of U.S.A.
   Progress after World War II

WORDS TO KNOW

The following words used in this chapter need to be understood. Most of them have been explained in the text but all of them should form part of a history student's vocabulary. Make a list in the back of your notebook, with meanings, of those words that are new to you. Learn these and use them in your essays:

'Cash and carry', concession, dollar diplomacy, evangelism, freedom of the seas, frontier, immigration quota, imperialism, isolationism, Kaiser, lend-lease, Monroe Doctrine, neutrality, 'open door', Pan-American, protectorate, reparations, republican, 'sphere of influence', strategic.

BOOKS TO READ OR CONSULT

Bailey, T. A. *Woodrow Wilson and the Great Betrayal*, New York, Macmillan, 1945.

Brock, W. R. *The Character of American History*, New York, Macmillan, 1960.

Buchan, A. *The U.S.A.* (The Modern World Series), London, O.U.P., 1963.

Catchpole, B. *A Map History of the United States*, Heinemann Educational Books, 1974.

Dulles, F. R. *America's Rise to World Power*, London, Hamilton, 1955.

Hill, C. P. *The USA since the First World War*, London, Allen and Unwin, 1967.

Morison, S. E. and Commager, H. S. *The Growth of the American Republic*, New York, O.U.P., 1942 (3rd Ed.).

Wilmot, C. *The Struggle for Europe*, London, Collins, 1952.

QUESTIONS FOR ESSAYS OR DISCUSSION

1. (a) For what reasons has isolationism appealed to a large section of the American people?

   (b) State two occasions between 1914 and 1924 when U.S. isolationist policy has been of considerable significance for the rest of the world.

   (c) What steps did the U.S. Government take to protect herself from the need to participate when it seemed that World War II was likely?

2. Write an account of each of the following:

   (a) The attitude of the United States of America to the League of Nations.

   (b) The proposals made by the United States in 1899 for the control of trade by outside nations with China, and the reasons for the proposed policy.

   (c) The position of the United States as a Pacific Power before World War II.

3. Compare and contrast the attitude of the United States to the world wars between 1914 and 1917 and between 1939 and 1941. Account for the differences.

4. Describe and explain American policy in Central and Latin America to 1945.

5. 'The foreign policy of President F. D. Roosevelt was a disastrous failure.' Discuss.

8

CHINA SINCE 1900

When our forefathers, the Ancient Britons, were still savages, living in simple huts and decorating their bodies with woad, the Chinese had already developed a society that was centuries old. During the two thousand years before the birth of Christ, the way of life that was to be typical of almost another two thousand years was gradually developing. Chinese legends tell us that this civilisation is even more ancient and although, as yet, we have no proof, this could very likely be true. Discoveries show that at this early period a system of character writing related to modern Chinese had already been developed, bronze was being used with great skill, and animals such as dogs, pigs, fowls and elephants were domesticated.

Development in isolation. For centuries the East, and especially China, has been shrouded in mystery and little known to westerners. If we consider the physical boundaries of distance and desert, of mountain ranges and malarial tropical jungles that isolate China from the rest of the world, the reason for this becomes easier to understand. Unlike the progress of our own civilisation which can be compared with a chain reaction moving ever westward, the culture of China developed in almost complete isolation except for its contact with the crude and uncivilised nomads of central Asia.

Superiority complex. Because of this isolation, there arose quite naturally in China a belief that theirs was the only truly civilised way of life. This belief in the superiority of all things Chinese was accompanied by a contempt for anything that was not of Chinese origin, as was demonstrated by the reply of the Chinese Emperor to an ambassador of King George III in 1793. The Emperor, asked to allow British trade with China, replied, 'You, O King, live in a distant region, but desiring humbly to share the blessings of our civilisation, you have sent an ambassador respectfully bearing your letter . . . We possess all things: we are not interested in strange or costly objects, and we have no use for your country's products. I have accepted your tribute offerings only because of the devotion that made you send them so far . . .'

The outstanding thinker, teacher and scholar of ancient China was undoubtedly Confucius. His code of behaviour, which he taught almost five hundred years before the birth of Christ, dominated the life of China for centuries. With his disciple Mencius he became a legendary figure, and statements beginning, 'According to the teaching of Mencius and Confucius . . .' were treated with the same reverence that we reserve for passages from the Holy Bible. The chief concern of Confucius, as of all ancient Chinese scholars, was to find a system of government that would produce an ideal society. Unfortunately, by seeking his answers in the methods of the past, he turned Chinese eyes backwards and this made them less able to resist the forward looking westerners who were to invade their land in the nineteenth century.

CHINA IN 1900

In ancient China there were between five and six thousand separate States, each controlled by a prince who thought of himself as independent. In distant Peking, in a magnificent palace, lived an unseen and unknown Emperor. Periodically there were strong emperors who were able to control much of the country. Periodically also, there were foreign invasions by the tribes of central Asia — the Huns, Mongols and Manchus in particular, none of whom were kept out by the 1500-mile Great Wall built along the northern border about 200 B.C. In the periods between these extremes there was sometimes peace and sometimes civil war, depending on the strength and ambitions of local princes and warlords. These local rulers, whose position we could compare with that of the feudal barons of medieval France and England, used armies of hired soldiers to fight their wars, while, in the countryside, the mass of the people toiled on unceasingly and unconscious of events around them.

When another civil war broke out in the mid-nineteenth century no one would have forecast that this was the beginning of the end of ancient China. But the Taiping Rebellion, which raged through the greater part of China from 1850 to 1864, so greatly weakened the Manchu dynasty (or imperial ruling house) that it never recovered. Once again the Chinese warlords seized the chance to revolt against the Emperor but this time they were supported by the foreign Powers who wished to weaken China for their own advantage.

Western barbarians. Since Marco Polo travelled overland to Cathay (China) from Italy seven hundred years ago, Cathay has

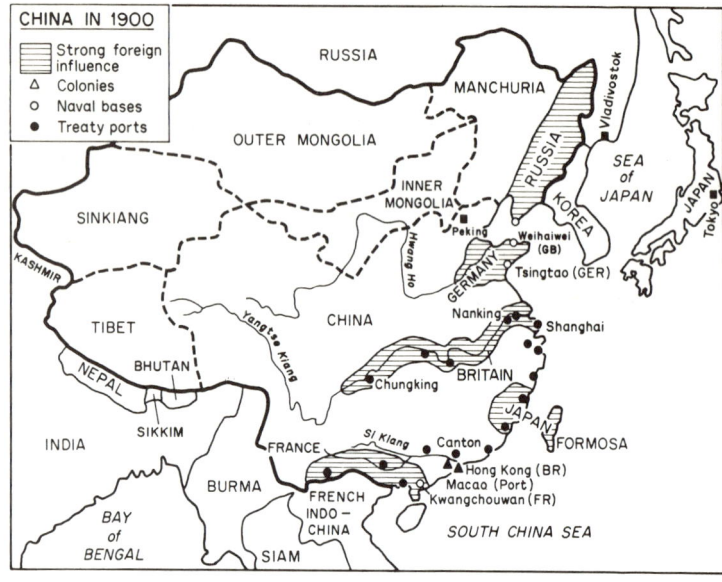

CHINA IN 1900

- ▨ Strong foreign influence
- △ Colonies
- ○ Naval bases
- ● Treaty ports

RUSSIA

MANCHURIA

OUTER MONGOLIA

Vladivostok

SEA of JAPAN

INNER MONGOLIA

SINKIANG

KASHMIR

Peking

Weihaiwei (GB)

Tsingtao (GER)

KOREA

RUSSIA

GERMANY

Hwang Ho

JAPAN

Tokyo

TIBET

CHINA

Nanking

Shanghai

Yangtse Kiang

BHUTAN

Chungking

BRITAIN

NEPAL

SIKKIM

INDIA

FRANCE

Si Klang

Canton

JAPAN

FORMOSA

BURMA

FRENCH INDO-CHINA

Hong Kong (BR)

Macao (Port)

Kwangchouwan (FR)

BAY of BENGAL

SIAM

SOUTH CHINA SEA

Fɪɢ. 25

held an increasing fascination for the people of Europe. But even after the first Portuguese ships reached China two hundred and fifty years later they were only able to trade with the coastal city of Canton and even there they were unwelcome visitors. It was not until the nineteenth century that European influence was extended in China.

The lead in this movement for commercial expansion came, understandably, from Britain, whose trading activities had been growing steadily for two hundred years. Following the Opium War (1839-42) China was forced to cede Hong Kong to Britain and to open five further ports to foreign trade. The other Western Powers were quick to take advantage of the gains that Britain had made and further concessions were forced from China in such quick succession that, by the end of the century, some of the Powers were talking freely of dividing China among themselves, as they had done with Africa (see map).

Population jumps. For centuries frequent civil wars and regular famines kept the population of China small enough to allow the peasants to win a reasonable living from the land they cultivated. Because of this slow growth of population and an almost complete isolation from the western world the Chinese way of life was able to continue unchanged for centuries. However, by 1900 the population had increased from about 100 million in 1650 to almost 400 million. Widespread peace, new heavy yielding crops (such as kaoliang and corn) and increasing settlement of the fertile Yangtse plain no doubt contributed to this rapid growth of population. If all the reasons are not certain the results are unmistakable — China had become a land of teeming millions.

Unfortunately the area of land under cultivation did not grow nearly as rapidly. In 1700 there was an acre of cultivated land for every person in the country, but by 1900 this had shrunk to less than half an acre. This increasing shortage of land led to rising rents and the income of many peasants was reduced to starvation level. Matters were made even worse by the Chinese custom of sharing a father's land among his sons. This frequent subdivision of farms forced many to sell their small uneconomic share and drift to the cities to look for work while others became hired labourers on the land their families had farmed for centuries.

Peasant discontent. By the end of the nineteenth century cheap, western factory made goods, which were now being distributed on a large scale, had undermined and often destroyed native village industries, the only source of income of millions of peasant families. Furthermore, the Chinese merchants who distributed these goods became increasingly rich and used their new wealth to buy vast areas of land. As they had no interest in their properties apart from the rents they would yield, the sufferings of the peasants grew further. As the nineteenth century progressed, peasant discontent and uprisings increased. They still failed because they lacked leaders and organisation but they became more and more difficult to control.

The events of the nineteenth and preceding centuries provide the key to the understanding of the events of the twentieth century. The rapidly increasing population and the increasing pressure on the cultivated land meant that it would not be possible to continue the centuries-old Chinese way of life indefinitely. At the same time China was exposed to the shattering impact of the western imperial countries whose merchants and traders steadily increased the influence and extended the commercial power of the countries they represented. Defeat by Japan in 1895 (see page 130) and the crushing of the anti-western Boxer Rebellion in 1901 increased the belief that, after centuries of resistance to foreigners, China was in danger of breaking up and was at the mercy of the West. It was against this background that the revolution of 1911 was launched. This revolution, which reached its climax with the success of the Communists in 1949, and the destruction of a way of life over two thousand years old, was thus not an isolated event in Chinese history but the culmination of a movement whose roots can be traced back into the past.

A LAND OF REVOLUTION

China faced the start of the present century in a desperate state. Before modern China could emerge in mid-century, the foreign Manchu dynasty had to be overthrown, the influence of Europe and America reduced, and the Japanese expelled. This was completed in fifty years — fifty years torn by civil strife and foreign war.

The Boxer Rebellion. The Boxers were members of a semi-religious secret society who believed that their faith would protect them from the bullets of their enemies. In 1900 they killed a number of foreign missionaries and diplomats as a protest against the increasing foreign influence in China. Western retaliation was rapid and effective. The forces of eight countries combined to attack and occupy Peking and, in 1901, China had to accept a treaty which further strengthened foreign influence. As well as being compelled to pay a heavy indemnity, China had to agree to the stationing of troops in strategic areas to protect foreign interests. The failure of the Boxer Rebellion appeared to drive another nail into the Chinese coffin.

The Kuomintang. The revolution which was to establish the republic suffered ten failures before it succeeded. In 1895 the first attempt to seize Canton failed and Dr Sun Yat-sen, China's first modern doctor and one of the leaders of the revolt, escaped to London with a price on his head. Undeterred, he spent the next fifteen years travelling in the United States, Europe and Japan organising the forces of revolution and collecting huge sums of money for the cause. In 1905 the *Kuomintang,* or National People's Party, was established with Dr Sun as its president. Newspapers and pamphlets quickly spread its revolutionary ideas throughout China and thousands joined its ranks. Members took an oath to work for 'the termination of foreign domination, the restoration of sovereign power to the Chinese people, the establishment of a democratic government and the equalisation of land rights'. It is these aims that have been summarised as the 'Three Principles of the People' — nationalism, democracy and livelihood.

Revolution, 1911. That the Manchu dynasty had lost the 'mandate of Heaven' and was nearing its end was obvious to all. What would succeed it was less obvious, but when a small local rebellion broke out in the south in October 1911, those who wished to overthrow the Manchus quickly took advantage of it. Within a few days they had captured the great cities of Wuchang, Hankow and Hanyang, the most important urban area in central China. Before two months had passed fifteen of the eighteen provinces had joined the revolution and Sun Yat-sen, who was on a lecture tour in the United States, hastened home to be elected the first president of Asia's first republic. But, to prevent a civil war, he resigned in favour of Yuan Shih-kai who controlled the three northern provinces and the strongest military force in the country.

The republic now seemed assured. To celebrate their newly won independence the Chinese cut off their pigtails and replaced the Imperial yellow dragon with a new five-coloured flag signifying the five racial groups included in the Chinese nation: the Hans (the true Chinese), Manchus, Mongols, Moslems and Tibetans.

Civil war. It was easier to destroy the empire than to build the republic. Yuan attempted, with brief success, to re-establish the empire but died in 1916 and, for the next ten years, chaos reigned as China was once more in the grip of civil war. The outlying provinces of Mongolia, Turkestan and Tibet declared their independence, as they had always done whenever the imperial government was weak, and the Government in Peking was powerless to resist. Japan, taking advantage of China's weakness, issued the Twenty-one Demands in 1915, which if accepted in full, would have virtually made China a Japanese colony. Only the fact that the Western Powers were not prepared to lose their interests in China to the Japanese saved its independence (see page 132).

Meanwhile Dr Sun, regretting his trust in Yuan, was active in the south where a rival Republican Government was established with its capital at Canton. He had hoped to see the creation in China of a democracy on British and American lines, but despairing of receiving help from the Western Powers who continued to recognise the Government in Peking, he turned to Russia and, in 1923, sent Chiang Kai-shek to Moscow to study the Soviet system. Chiang returned in 1924 with Russian advisers, led by Borodin. who reorganised the Kuomintang on communist lines. Under his guidance it was quickly transformed into a party of obedient followers who would act without question on instructions from their leaders. At the same time preparations began for the conquest of China and the now famous Whampoa Military Academy was established, under the leadership of Chiang

Kai-shek, to train the future officers for the revolutionary army.

Dr Sun—national hero. However, Dr Sun was not to taste the fruits of victory. His death in 1925 provided China with a national hero — a Chinese Lenin — whose authority and wisdom could no longer be challenged. It has been said that in death Dr Sun was more powerful than he had ever been in life. His 'last will and testament', signed on his deathbed, became the symbol of the Kuomintang and all school children were required to learn it by heart. It states: 'For forty years I have devoted myself to the cause of the National Revolution, the object of which is to raise China to a position of independence and equality among the nations of the world. The experience of these forty years has convinced me that, to attain this goal, the people must be aroused, and that we must associate ourselves in a common struggle with all the peoples of the world who treat us as equals.' No further justification needed to be sought for the assistance from Communist Russia which, alone of the great Powers, seemed prepared to treat the Chinese as equals.

A United China. The death of Dr Sun also allowed the party's strong man, Chiang Kai-shek, to take control. In 1926, in alliance with the Chinese Communist Party and supported by Russian

Fig. 26 — Chiang Kai-shek (1887–1975).

military equipment, the Kuomintang army began its northward march. Meeting with little organised resistance it had, by mid-1928, captured Peking and once again restored unity to China. The new blue-sky-and-white-sun flag soon fluttered over Nanking, which was now restored as the capital, and Dr Sun was ceremoniously reburied there at the foot of the Purple Mountains. The outside world thought that China's troubles were over but the new unity was short-lived.

ENTER THE COMMUNISTS

Before the Russian Revolution there was little interest in communism in China. The failure of Western countries to support Dr Sun and the success of the Russians in dealing with a problem similar to that which had faced the Chinese provided a natural opportunity for closer relations between the two countries. An agent of the Comintern (see page 104) visited China in 1920 and in the following year the first congress of the Chinese Communist Party met in Shanghai. In these early days the newly formed party attracted little interest or popular support and drew its members entirely from the intellectual classes — students, university professors and writers. Its greatest hope of success appeared to lie in joining forces with an established and powerful party. The Kuomintang was the obvious choice.

Break with the Kuomintang. Chiang had always been uneasy about the alliance with Moscow and, in December 1927, diplomatic relations with the Soviet Union were broken off. Borodin fled and the communists were expelled from the Kuomintang. However, communist influence continued in the south. Although the official leadership of the party remained in Shanghai the most important events were taking place in the hills of Kiangsi, where Mao Tse-tung and Chuh Teh were building a peasant Red Army, massacring the rural gentry and redistributing their lands among the tenant farmers. Industrial workers had made up the bulk of the armies that had carried through the Russian Revolution. In China it was to be achieved by peasant armies.

The Long March. But Mao was not left in peace to develop his ideas: Chiang maintained a rigid blockade and embarked on a number of campaigns to destroy the communists. Through sheer weight of numbers and equipment it appeared as if he was going to succeed. In 1934 the communists decided to break out of Kiangsi. Thus began the famous Long March which was to last for a year and to involve a journey of 6000 miles on foot over some of the most rugged country in the world. The route crossed

FIG. 27 — A speaker addressing a meeting of the Communists after the Long March.

twenty-four large rivers and eighteen mountains, many of them snow covered. Fifteen major battles were fought while smaller encounters were almost a daily occurrence. More than 100,000 set out from Kiangsi but, in spite of recruitment along the route, fewer than 20,000 reached Shensi province where the new headquarters were established at Yenan in 1935. Here, in the remote northwest, living in caves scooped out of the hillsides, the communists were able to try out their ideas although, periodically, they had to withstand further attacks because Chiang was determined to destroy them or drive them out of China.

Meanwhile, in China Proper, and especially in the Yangtse Valley, a great programme of modernisation was in progress.[1] Roads and railways, hospitals and factories, irrigation and education were all receiving attention. Led by Madame Chiang Kaishek, the emancipation of women began. Above all, with German assistance, a modern regular army was being established. But the most serious problem — the land — remained untouched. In the provinces the leaders of the party were the rural gentry, the traditional scholar-landlord class which had for so long governed

[1]China Proper is a historical name used to distinguish the provinces of China from the Outlying Territories of Inner and Outer Mongolia, Manchuria, Tibet and Sinkiang (see map, page 168).

China. Any large-scale land reform would have been to their disadvantage and, as the Central Government was afraid to challenge them, nothing was done. The position of the peasants continued to decline and, with over sixty per cent of the main crop taken for rent, their lot was worse than at the beginning of the century.

BLACK DRAGON OR RED FLAG?

The state of affairs within China was not generally known to the outside world and once again it appeared as if China's troubles were almost over. However, this was not to be the case. Across the Yellow Sea the Japanese watched with growing concern the revival and modernisation of China. They feared that there would not be room in Asia for a strong Japan and a strong China. To ensure their position a war would be necessary before China's recovery was complete. This threat was serious enough in itself but there was a much more deadly enemy within. Communism had been defeated but not destroyed and already preparations were under way for the conquest of the whole country. It was under the shadow of these two threats that China entered the 1930s.

The threat from Japan. In 1910, following her defeat of China in 1895 (see page 129) and Russia in 1905 (see page 130), Japan had taken possession of the valuable grain-growing lands of Korea and had also gained a foothold in Manchuria. This desirable area, rich in raw materials and food, was to the Japanese a natural region for expansion and, during the next twenty years, their influence steadily increased. But the reunification of China under Chiang Kai-shek threatened to destroy Japan's ambitions and in 1931, following an incident, she seized the province and renamed it Manchukuo — an independent State under Japanese protection! Protests from China and the League of Nations proved ineffective and, from this new and valuable base, the Japanese began to extend their influence south of the Great Wall (see page 133).

Despite the growing danger from Japan, Chiang continued in his determination to destroy the communists first. But they, seeing the chance to win popular support, pressed for an end to the civil war and a united front against Japan. Their propaganda was effective in the north where, in 1936, troops engaged against them refused to continue the fight. Chiang hastened to Sian to enforce his orders and was there kidnapped by his mutinous troops. For

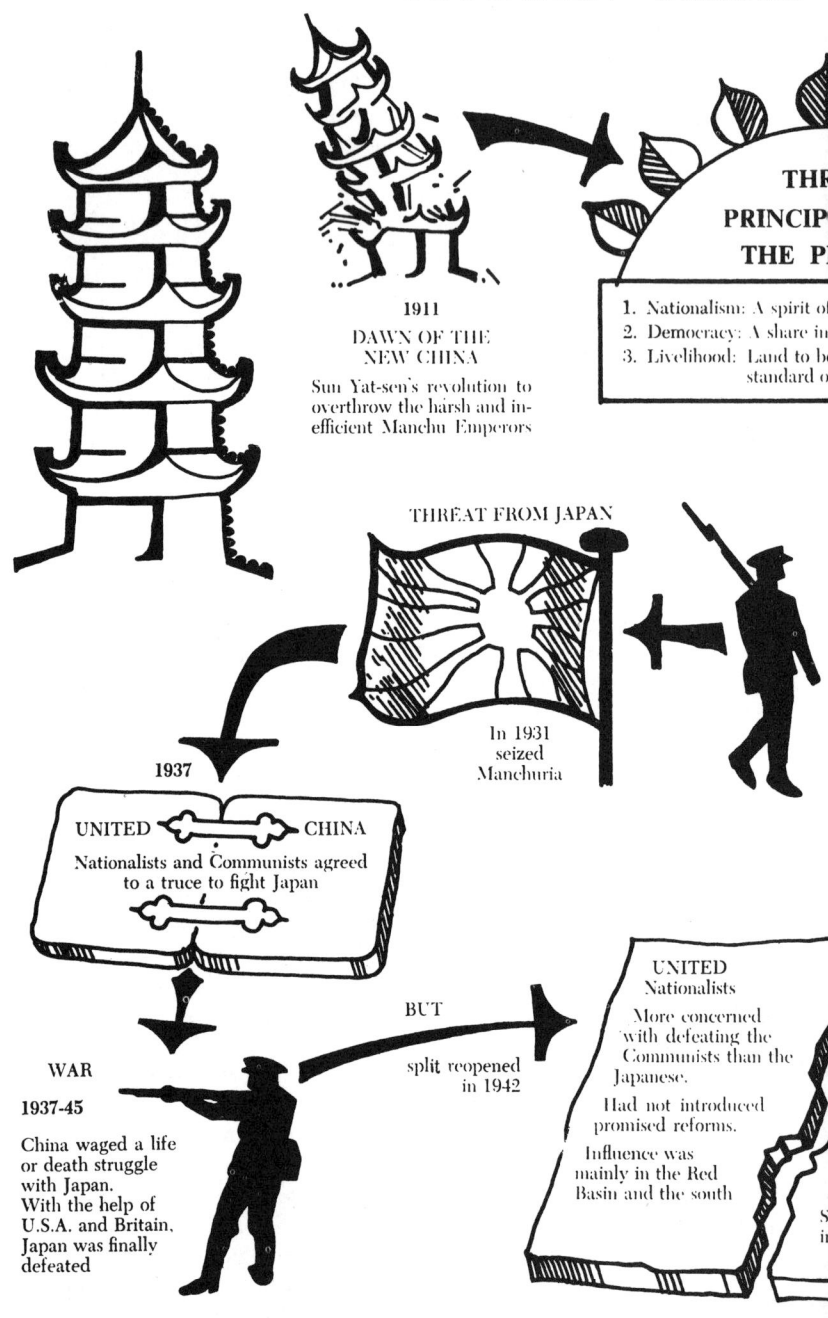

1911
DAWN OF THE
NEW CHINA

Sun Yat-sen's revolution to
overthrow the harsh and in-
efficient Manchu Emperors

**THE
PRINCIP
THE PI**

1. Nationalism: A spirit o
2. Democracy: A share in
3. Livelihood: Land to be
standard o

THREAT FROM JAPAN

In 1931
seized
Manchuria

1937

UNITED ⟷ CHINA

Nationalists and Communists agreed
to a truce to fight Japan

WAR

1937-45

China waged a life
or death struggle
with Japan.
With the help of
U.S.A. and Britain,
Japan was finally
defeated

BUT

split reopened
in 1942

UNITED
Nationalists

More concerned
with defeating the
Communists than the
Japanese.

Had not introduced
promised reforms.

Influence was
mainly in the Red
Basin and the south

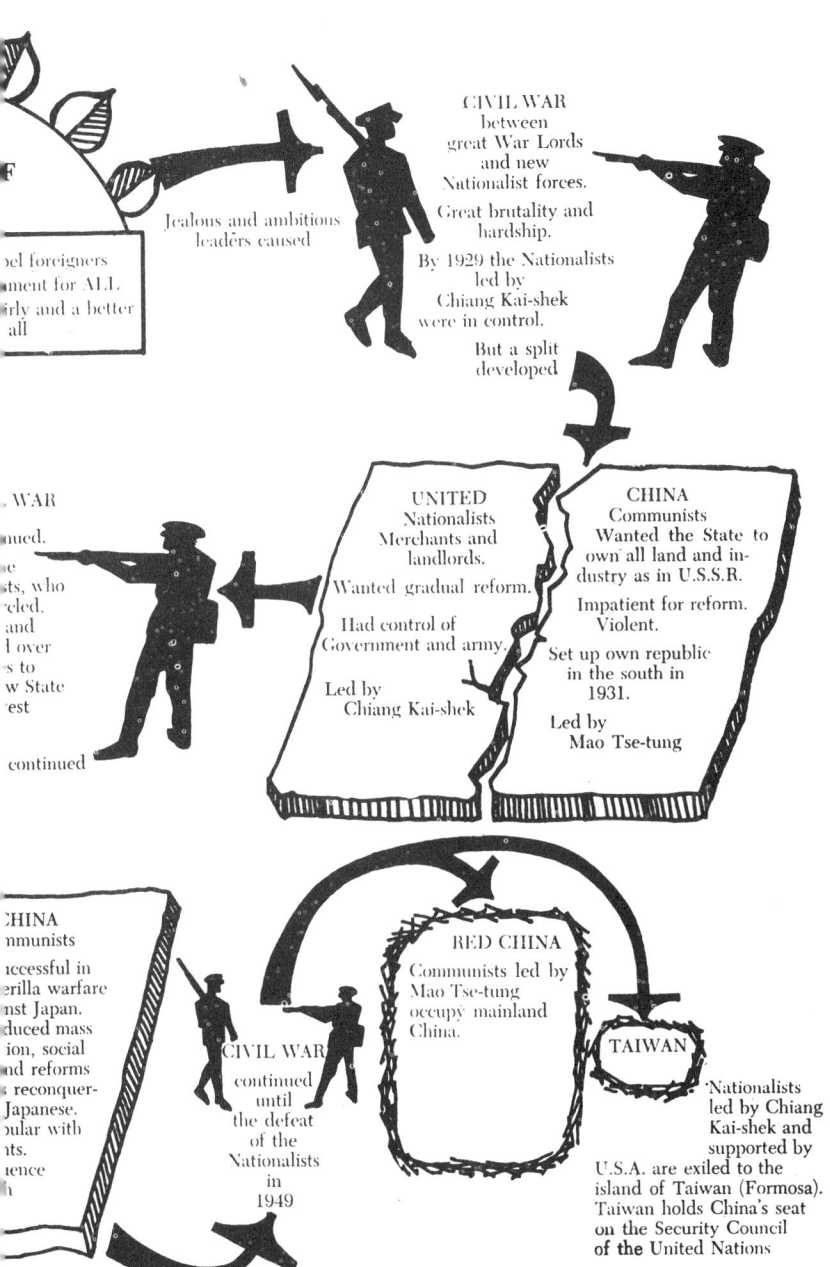

CIVIL WAR
between
great War Lords
and new
Nationalist forces.

Great brutality and
hardship.

By 1929 the Nationalists
led by
Chiang Kai-shek
were in control.

But a split
developed

Jealous and ambitious
leaders caused

...el foreigners
...ment for ALL
...irly and a better
all

...WAR
...nued.

...e
...ts, who
...cled,
...and
...l over
...s to
...w State
...est

continued

UNITED
Nationalists
Merchants and
landlords.

Wanted gradual reform.

Had control of
Government and army.

Led by
Chiang Kai-shek

CHINA
Communists
Wanted the State to
own all land and in-
dustry as in U.S.S.R.

Impatient for reform.
Violent.

Set up own republic
in the south in
1931.

Led by
Mao Tse-tung

...HINA
...mmunists

...ccessful in
...erilla warfare
...nst Japan.
...duced mass
...ion, social
...nd reforms
...; reconquer-
...Japanese.
...ular with
...ts.
...ience
...h

CIVIL WAR
continued
until
the defeat
of the
Nationalists
in
1949

RED CHINA
Communists led by
Mao Tse-tung
occupy mainland
China.

TAIWAN

Nationalists
led by Chiang
Kai-shek and
supported by
U.S.A. are exiled to the
island of Taiwan (Formosa).
Taiwan holds China's seat
on the Security Council
of the United Nations

days his fate hung in the balance, but such was the force of his personality that he was released and returned in triumph to Nanking taking his former captor with him as a hostage. However, presumably as the price of his freedom, he had agreed to end the civil war and to form a united front with the communists.

Undeclared war with Japan. This was the very step that the Japanese most feared and, before the arrangements were completed, they began an undeclared war with an attack at the Marco Polo Bridge near Peking in mid-1937 (see pages 134-5). The detailed story of the eight years of war that followed does not concern us here. By slowly retreating to the hills the Chinese hoped to force their opponents to lengthen their communication and supply lines and so expose them to guerilla attacks. But the rapid Japanese advance and the fall of Shanghai and Nanking forced the Kuomintang Government to retreat to the Szechwan Basin where they established their wartime capital at Chungking. Little further territory fell into Japanese hands but, as they controlled the coastal areas and almost all the routes into the interior, they began slowly but surely to strangle China.

United Front collapses. Within the territory that remained under Chinese control a tense drama was being staged. As the war continued and the Japanese economic stranglehold tightened, the Kuomintang Government grew weaker. After the Japanese occupation of Rangoon in 1941 the Burma Road was closed and China's last link with the west was destroyed. Lacking in food, money, leaders, and equipment and cut off from all contact with the outside world except by the hazardous air route over the Himalayas, China steadily lost its strength and morale. At the same time the communists in the north were growing stronger. Here they waged a successful guerilla war behind the Japanese lines and, by introducing land reforms in the country areas, greatly extended their influence in north and central China. There could be no doubt that the communists were using the war for their own advantage and this ended the United Front in 1941. For the remainder of the war the two Chinese sides, while still nominally at war with Japan, were more concerned with watching each other, and with preparing for what was obviously going to be a further struggle for leadership of the Chinese nation.

When the Japanese were defeated in 1945 (see page 137) these two opposing groups raced to occupy the areas given up by the retreating Japanese forces. As the recognised Government of China, the Kuomintang had the advantage and secured control of all the principal coastal cities. But in the north the Japanese surrendered to the Russians who gave their weapons to the communists, thus providing the Chinese Red Army with up-to-date equipment.

Two years of discussions followed, during which American General George C. Marshall tried, without success, to persuade the two sides to reach an agreement. Once again the control of Manchuria was to be the issue which started a war. If China's economy was to recover, its valuable lands had to be used to the full. As the approach to them was in communist hands a full-scale civil war developed again in 1947 when, rejecting the advice of General Marshall, the Kuomintang Government attempted to reoccupy Manchuria.

Communist success. The result of this last stage in the struggle to establish the Chinese Republic was not long in doubt. The Kuomintang armies lacked the will to fight and, following the communist offer to pay cash for the weapons of all deserters, whole battalions soon laid down their arms. With the siege and eventual surrender of the best of Chiang's armies the whole of north China quickly fell into communist hands. Their efficient and well organised armies rapidly swept southwards. By the end of 1949 resistance on the mainland had collapsed and Chiang, with the remnant of his troops, retired to the island of Formosa (or Taiwan) where, under American protection, he was safe for the moment from further attacks. The civil war was over and the new red flag of the People's Republic of China flew over the Government buildings in Peking, now restored as the national capital.

The Chinese Revolution, which began in 1911 and was completed in 1949, took place in stages. It began with the attempt to overthrow the Manchu emperors by the Nationalists represented by the Kuomintang Party. Largely because of the failure of the western nations to support this new Nationalist government in China, the Kuomintang joined forces with the newly developed Chinese Communist Party in the early 1920s. However, this alliance did not long survive the death of Dr Sun, and Chiang Kai-shek set out in the early 1930s to destroy the Communist Party. His failure to do so and the threat from Japan produced a second United Front in the mid-thirties but this proved to be as impermanent as the first. The defeat of Japan in 1945 allowed the final phase of the revolution to proceed and this ended with the exile of the Nationalist Government to the island of Formosa. The Chinese Revolution had ended and the stage was set for the Communist Revolution to begin. (Study chart on pages 176-7.)

COMMUNIST CHINA

A country worn out after fifty years of foreign and civil war and still smarting from a century or more of insults and attacks by the West welcomed any strong government that could restore order and self-respect. Opposition to the Nationalists rather than support for the communists was responsible for the collapse of Chiang Kai-shek's Government. But as the new Government also rapidly reunited the country, dismissed dishonest officials, destroyed the landlords, and distributed their land among the peasants, it quickly gained popularity with the mass of the people. Chinese scholars returned from overseas, eager to play their part in building the new China. For the first time in modern history the future for China looked bright.

The Communist Party. China has never known democracy as it is understood in Western countries and has always been governed by a ruling class. Like the Kuomintang before it, the Communist Party became the only political party in China. In the past the able and the ambitious had sought positions in the Government by passing the civil service examinations which were based on a knowledge of the Confucian classics. Now the Communist Party offered the only way to positions of power in the country and membership was eagerly sought after. Party membership was also popular because of the additional privileges it carried, such as additional food in periods of scarcity. To build a strong China the party itself needed to be strong and, as in Russia, careful selection has remained the basis of membership. Only two per cent of the population — or fewer than fourteen million of more than 700 million Chinese people — are members of the Communist Party.

As in the Soviet Union, the party is a highly centralised body. The top leaders of the party form the Politburo, which could be compared in its purpose with our Cabinet — the real Government of the country. But whereas our Cabinet has to be able to justify its actions in Parliament, which meets in regular sessions, the Politburo has only to report twice a year to the body which elects it — the Central Committee — and this is purely a matter of routine because its decisions are not questioned. The Central Committee in its turn is elected every three years by the National Party Congress but, in practice, this simply involves approving a list submitted by the Central Committee itself. This great pyramid is dominated by the Presidium, a small committee elected by the Politburo, and the Presidium in its turn is controlled by its chairman, the most powerful man in China. His work in the years from 1925 to 1949 made Mao Tse-tung the obvious choice as the first chairman of the Presidium.

Chairman Mao. There are many similarities in the life stories of Sun Yat-sen and Mao Tse-tung (pronounced Mau Zuh-doong). Both were the sons of prosperous farmers in south China and both were able to go to school instead of having to spend their entire youth working in the fields as was the lot of most Chinese boys. University studies followed for both, but whereas Sun's studies took him overseas to western countries, it was the writings of Lenin and Karl Marx that attracted Mao. As we have seen, Sun Yat-sen devoted his life to the overthrow of the Manchu emperors and the establishment of a Chinese republic. Mao devoted his life to improving the lot of the peasants and became the leader of the peasant opposition to the land policy of the Kuomintang Government of Chiang Kai-shek. His success in this direction singled him out as the logical leader of the Communist Party, a position that he has held ever since, even although he resigned his chairmanship of the Presidium in 1958.

The central organisation of the party in Peking is repeated in twenty-eight different local areas where the decisions of the Central Government are carried out. The main responsibility for this belongs to the *kan-pu*. These are the local officials who control the smallest units of the communist system, the cells. The *kan-pu* provide the link between the ordinary members and the party leaders. The fourteen million *cadres,* or active party workers, are employed in every kind of activity — in the largest cities and in the remotest villages. They are the party's eyes and ears and their loyalty and efficiency has enabled the development of a stronger and more dictatorial Government than China has ever before known.

CHANGING CHINA

One of the most immediate problems facing the new Government was the one its predecessor had failed to solve — the land. As in the French and Russian revolutions, the support of the peasants was won by giving them the ownership of the land they tilled. This had been completed and the former landlords liquidated, or destroyed, by 1952. As the peasants would now be opposed to any further change, and as the money for China's industrial expansion had to come mainly from the sale of farm crops, the land reform programme could not be allowed to stop there. It has been developed further in three main stages — co-operatives, collectives and communes.

First, local party members organised groups of peasant families into co-operatives where the members still owned their land but cultivated it and marketed the produce as a group. By the end of 1956 the party claimed that virtually the whole of the rural population had been organised in this way and considered that the time was ripe for the introduction of the next stage.

Collectives. Before the new landowners had time to establish any real spirit of independence, collective farming was introduced. Here individual farmers were paid only for their labour and, although members received small private plots and owned their houses and a few animals, their first duty was to work for 250 days a year on the collective farm. There was considerable opposition to this move but, as the poor peasants with nothing to lose were in favour and in a large majority, the programme advanced without the violence that was associated with the eviction of the *kulaks* in Russia (see page 108). By the end of 1957 when China's first Five-Year Plan was completed most of the co-operative farms had been changed into collectives. When the plan had been launched in 1953 one of its aims had been to increase agricultural production. Although there were failures, especially in the south where collective methods were not suited to the production of paddy rice, there were also great successes. Under large-scale methods made possible by the collectives, the production of wheat and other cereals in the north showed a marked increase.

Industrial development. China's position as a world Power will be judged by her industrial strength and the first Five-Year Plan aimed to make 'the Soviet Union of today the China of tomorrow'. Success in achieving this aim demanded State planning and control of industry — a feature we have come to associate with all communist governments. The emphasis was on heavy industry and on quantity rather than on quality. China needed steel mills, coal mines, power stations and chemical works, and it needed them in a hurry. This determination to break production records required long hours and strained the resources of both men and machines resulting in the manufacture of many shoddy and inadequate articles.

Nevertheless, progress was remarkable. By the end of the first plan, China had become the greatest coal producing nation in Asia and its output of steel had increased so considerably that it was able to manufacture almost three-quarters of the machinery it needed. At the same time railways were being extended and the huge task of controlling the Yellow River had begun. In the northwest a start had been made to develop enormous but previously unknown oil and mineral deposits.

Russian assistance again. The Soviet Union had looked to the West, and especially to the United States, for technical assistance during its first Five-Year Plan. China also looked west for help — west to Russia. During the operation of the first Five-Year Plan, Russian technical aid and money poured into China at a fantastic rate. Tens of thousands of skilled Russian workers installed and operated machinery in hundreds of factories, mines and mills built with Russian money. But this was not a gift. In return China had to repay the Soviet Union in kind. For many years to come China was pledged to export raw materials, manufactured goods and food to Russia. Even while its own people went hungry in bad seasons, the Russian debt had to be paid.

THE GREAT LEAP FORWARD

An ambitious second Five-Year Plan was introduced in 1958 which aimed to double the production of steel and electric power by 1962 and to increase the supply of grain by fifty per cent. Before this new programme had really started it was replaced by an even more ambitious one — the Great Leap Forward. This was based on the belief that, if everyone worked harder, production would be further increased. To achieve this goal, greater State control was necessary and accordingly the party began the revolutionary step of establishing communes.

Communes. While some attempt was made to develop communes which included both farm and factory workers, the new movement was largely concerned with agriculture. Each commune consisted of a number of collective farms merged into a single unit including as many as 5,000 or 10,000 families, compared with 150 families typical of the collectives. Private plots were abolished and, on the more advanced communes, farm buildings were torn down and barracks built to house the entire population. These, with their associated mess halls, kindergartens, and creches, had the 'advantages' of releasing mothers from domestic work to labour in the fields. On the collectives the peasants had been paid according to the amount they produced, but now they became wage earners who, like the factory workers in the cities, were paid a fixed wage irrespective of the work they did. By the end of 1958 the Government claimed that almost all peasant families were organised into communes. The final stage in the land reform programme had been completed.

In an attempt to step up industrial production, and especially the production of steel, encouragement was given for the establishment of small local plants. Thousands of workers built furnaces,

FIG. 28 — With plentiful manpower in place of machinery, Chinese
workers build a canal near Peking.

FIG. 29 — Leading members of the Chinese Government. Mao Tse-tung
sits in the bottom row, centre. Third from the left is Liu Shao-chi,
Mao's successor as Chairman after the Great Leap Forward, but
discredited during the Cultural Revolution. Second from the right is
Chou en-Lai, Premier until his death in 1976.

even in the yards attached to their houses. For a short time national control was relaxed as local enthusiasts were encouraged to play their part in helping to swell production. In this they were successful, but the iron and steel that was smelted in these backyard furnaces was of such inferior quality that it was useless for industry and the scheme was quickly abandoned.

Too much haste. 'Deep ploughing and close planting' was one of the slogans adopted for increasing production on the communes during the Great Leap Forward. But, in many areas, deep ploughing only served to bury the fertile topsoil while close planting resulted in many seeds rotting in the ground and young plants being choked. The formation of the communes allowed the Government to conscript millions of peasants for the public works. Dams, canals and irrigation schemes were built at a great rate with this forced labour, but many of the dams burst and in other areas insufficient planning of schemes destroyed the natural drainage and reduced yields from formerly fertile farmlands.

Failure. Early reports suggested that the Great Leap Forward had been an unqualified success but this was not so. Local officials, anxious to please their superiors, had exaggerated returns. As this process was repeated all the way along the line to Peking, the final figures received in the capital bore little relation to the actual amounts produced. On top of the practical difficulties of this reorganisation of social and economic life came natural disasters which had produced very bad harvests and forced China to import grain from Canada and Australia. China had tried to do too much too quickly. In August 1959 Prime Minister Chou en-Lai announced that quotas had been set too high. On the communes private plots were restored and many of the extreme features of commune life were abandoned.

It had been a great setback for the leadership and particularly for Mao Tse-tung himself who resigned the chairmanship of the Presidium although he remained head of the party and ideological leader of the country. The running of the business of the country passed to the new Chairman Liu Shao-chi and the prime minister Chou en-Lai. Both were veteran Communists, but they did modify the policies of the Great Leap Forward to some extent and the early 1960s saw a steady increase in economic achievement despite the diversion of a formidable amount of the national effort into the armed forces and into the attainment of nuclear weapons in 1964. Inevitably the mass methods of the Great Leap Forward were dropped and the old experts and managers brought back to positions of influence.

However this by no means meant the end of the process of social transformation. Nor was Mao displaced as the ultimate helmsman, steering the course of the Chinese Revolution in the long term. Within a few years the radicals were on the move again, this time in the amazing process known as the Great Cultural Revolution.

THE CHINESE PEOPLE UNDER COMMUNISM

The Communist Party had been engaged on the process of transforming Chinese society even before it came to power. After 1949 this process intensified. The Government had initiated first the Three Antis campaign — against corruption, waste and inefficiency, all weaknesses of the old regime; then the Five Antis campaign against tax evasion, bribery, fraud, and theft of government property and secrets. However a cleaning up of malpractices was not enough especially in a country as dominated by tradition as China. One of the main targets for transformation was the family.

The unity of the family has always been of first importance in Chinese life and in the Chinese language the same symbols are used to represent 'family', 'house', and 'home'. The strength of family ties was demonstrated strongly when the Government held the first census in 1953. Sons and daughters who had been away from home for more than twenty years were still regarded by their families as being only temporarily absent and were therefore included, in a special column provided for the purpose, as being permanent residents in the family home! In China it was said that 'parents are like Heaven', and it was important to honour them when alive and to revere them when dead.

In the Great Leap Forward the process of setting up communes certainly weakened the family. Wages were paid to individuals rather than the head of the family; in some cases children were looked after in nurseries whilst both parents worked, family graveyards were sometimes dug up and ancestor worship was discouraged. However, in the end a family pattern of life returned even though automatic respect for the older generation disappeared and both parents were still expected to work. On the positive side the Communists did a tremendous amount to improve the position of women, who had frequently been no better than possessions in traditional China. Now they were expected to have equal education and opportunities and to do the same range of jobs as men.

In the early days of the Revolution the new regime was concerned to involve all groups who were not actually opposed to the Communists outright to participate in public life. So professionals and businessmen were encouraged to carry on with their work and to draw at least some of the old rewards from their work and the Communists tried to win the support of the intellectuals who had always enjoyed great respect in Chinese society.

The Hundred Flowers. 'Let a hundred flowers bloom; let a hundred schools of thought contend' is an old Chinese quotation which we might interpret to mean freedom of speech. This was the title of a campaign introduced in 1956 to encourage university professors and other intellectuals to express their views on the new China. Throughout its long history China had depended on its scholars to provide the leaders of the nation. Before 1949 many of these scholars had been sympathetic towards the aims of the Communist Party but by 1956 they realised that their freedom of thought would be lost if they became members. Also, as many of them had been educated in the United States and other western countries, they were not prepared to accept the 'party line' which required them to 'Hate America' and 'Love the Soviet Union'. While they remained silent the party did not feel safe. It was necessary either to win their support or to disgrace them — no compromise was possible.

Rethinking. Because of suspicion of the party's motives the scholars were slow to accept the opportunity to speak freely but, encouraged by Chairman Mao, they gradually began to voice their criticisms. The trickle, once started, rapidly became a flood and the party quickly mounted its counter-attack. Loyal peasants and workers, 'encouraged' by the *kan-pu,* attended mass meetings at which the critics were attacked as Rightists, or wrong thinkers. Faced with the alternative of imprisonment or death, many scholars made public confessions of their wrong thinking in the past and promised in future to accept the 'real truth'. The 'Hundred Flowers' movement had succeeded. It had exposed and destroyed an important group of opponents and so had strengthened the control of the Communist Party in China.

Mass education. To make the future safe for communism, the real emphasis of education is on the training of the young. This is achieved through the new schools and also through the work of mass organisations that reach every person in the country. Among the most important are the Youth League and the Young Pioneers which have over twenty million members and which will provide the future members of the party.

Chinese women have also been given a much more important place in society under the new regime, and the All China Democratic Women's Federation, with over eighty million members, is an important political body. Similar national organisations cover factory workers, soldiers, agricultural and professional workers who, through regular meetings and conferences, are kept fully informed of the latest party line on every matter that affects their daily lives. These mass organisations, backed by the constant threat of force, have assisted the party to dominate the whole of Chinese society.

The threat of force, the removal of opponents, and the education of the masses are not enough in themselves to explain the success of the Communist Party. Much emphasis is placed on 'campaigns' which encourage people to work harder and to exceed the ever present production quotas. Those who do not co-operate are in danger of being condemned as 'Rightists' which may entail loss of both social and political rights. In the picturesque Chinese way they may become 'non-people' to distinguish them from the 'people' who support and accept the party. Then again, there is much praise and often there are special privileges for the workers who set good examples. They may become 'heroes of labour' and receive higher wages or more or better food. Finally the outstanding advances that have been made in China cannot be ignored. Many believe that present hardships are a necessary forerunner to the better society that is being built in China. This belief is a powerful weapon which the Communist Party would be foolish to ignore.

The Hundred Flowers turned into the dynamic commitment of the Great Leap Forward and even when that failed, the experiment of freedom of speech was not repeated. However this could not hide the fact that there were disagreements within the party itself and these were to break out finally in one of the most extraordinary incidents in modern China, the Great Cultural Revolution.

The Great Cultural Revolution. In 1966 newspapers and propaganda posters began to attack as 'reactionary élitists' first some professors at Peking University, then the powerful mayor of Peking and then a whole range of leading figures in the Government, the party and the armed forces including the head of state Liu Shao-chi. Young people, known as the Red Guards, spearheaded this movement and forced officials and managers to hand over power to local people's groups and criticise themselves for their past misdeeds. 'Decadent' foreign influences were denounced and everywhere Mao was glorified. Work in many schools, colleges and factories was disrupted by endless political debate.

Liu and many of his followers were pushed from power and some were killed. For a while extreme confusion and open violence spread through the country until eventually order was restored with the help of the army under its leader Lin Piao. Mao was now clearly back in control of the ideology of the country and Lin Piao was nominated as his successor. However Chou en-Lai had survived the Cultural Revolution and was the man left with the job of getting the economy back into action again.

In 1971 Lin Piao was killed, apparently fleeing from China by plane after trying to overthrow Mao himself. Thereafter a number of the old leaders who had been overthrown in the Cultural Revolution returned to office. The country was once more controlled by the alliance of Mao and Chou, but both were now old and in bad health and the future line to be followed by the country after their deaths was impossible to predict.

TAIWAN

In 1945, Formosa[1] was returned to China after fifty years of Japanese occupation (see page 130). Two years later, as the communist threat on the mainland increased, thousands of Chinese settled on the island and in 1949 Chiang Kai-shek transferred the capital of the Republic of China from Nanking to Taipei. Today Taiwan, a hundred miles from the coast, provides an interesting contrast with developments on the Chinese mainland.

One China or two? The fate of the Nationalist Government would not have been left long in doubt if it had not been for the Korean War in 1950 (see page 207). Preparations were in hand for American recognition of the Government in Peking when the war began but Communist Chinese support for North Korea altered the situation and Taiwan assumed a new strategic importance. This position was recognised by an American agreement in 1954 to protect Taiwan against attack from the mainland. Thus there are two Chinas. Because of its association with the West in World War II, Nationalist China became a foundation member of the United Nations. In 1971 the Americans abstained in the vote which replaced Taiwan by Communist China in the United Nations and this, together with President Nixon's visit to Peking in 1972, was a blow to Taiwan's prestige.

American aid has played a vital part in the development of Taiwan since 1950. Military aid has been most important and by the mid-sixties Taiwan had one of the best equipped and most efficient armies in Asia. Of the island's total population of 11,500,000, over half a million men (or one man in five) were in the armed forces! Taiwan has become a vital link in the United States 'defence perimeter', which extends from South Korea through Japan to the Philippines, Australia and New Zealand.

[1]Since 1949 the Chinese name Taiwan has replaced the Portuguese name Formosa.

Apart from its strategic importance, Taiwan has a social and economic importance. In industry, agriculture, education, and social welfare American aid has helped development. Next to Japan, Taiwan has become the most prosperous nation in Asia. The Kuomintang, having learned from its previous failure (see page 175), developed a sound agricultural programme based on peasant ownership of the land, which steadily increased food production both for home use and for export.

The Government in Taiwan has sought to develop close links with other states in Asia and Africa but in the end the Peking regime won world recognition at the expense of Taipeh. In 1975 Taiwan suffered further setbacks with the collapse of the anti-Communist regime in South Vietnam and with the death of Chiang Kai-shek. Chiang was succeeded by his son, but the Nationalist Government now lacked the prestige at home and abroad which the old Generalissimo had enjoyed. Taiwan might have achieved wider support if it had settled for being a separate state, but the Nationalist Government had always stood on the claim that there was only one China and that theirs was the rightful government. Now that this claim has become totally untenable the long-term future for Taiwan seems to be inevitable reunification with the mainland.

CHINA IN WORLD AFFAIRS

The overthrow of the Nationalist Government in 1949 caused an immediate reversal of Chinese foreign policy. Whereas Chiang Kai-shek had looked to the United States and Britain for support, Mao Tse-tung looked to the Soviet Union and, in 1950, the two nations signed a thirty-year treaty of friendship. The obvious and unquestioned leadership of the Soviet Union in the communist world remained unchallenged until the death of Stalin in 1953. When Stalin's unceasing hostility to the West was replaced by Krushchev's policy of peaceful coexistence (see page 113), Mao immediately attacked the new policy as a departure from the correct party line laid down by Marx, Lenin and Stalin.

Chinese-Russian tension. Mao's challenge was seen by many observers as an attempt to gain the leadership of the communist world. At the same time every encouragement was given to other communist countries to improve their diplomatic relations and increase their trade with China. The continued refusal of the Soviet Union to support China's aggressive policy in Asia, especially against India, and the support provided by China for Albania when it revolted against Russian control have increased the tension between the two nations and, in 1960, Russian economic and military aid to China ceased.

Thereafter the two countries have carried on an intense propaganda war against each other and have competed strongly for support both amongst the other Communist parties and in the neutral, Third World states. In this process the Russians had the advantage of greater resources available for military and economic aid whilst China was able to claim to have more in common with the developing countries. Even when they were supporting the same cause—for instance the North Vietnamese in the war against the Americans—there was little or no co-operation. On several occasions there were actual clashes between their troops, notably on the Ussuri River in the disputed area of Russia's far eastern provinces (see also page 118).

China, a nuclear power since 1964, and possessor of the world's largest land forces is not a match for Russia in an offensive war but the Russians remain acutely aware of the threat posed by this vast population to the south of her own empty lands in Asia.

China and the West. A small number of Western powers including Britain recognised the Communist regime almost as soon as it came to power, but for a long time China made little effort to win further diplomatic support in the West. The Chinese leaders concentrated first on their enormous internal problems, and externally were mainly interested in their position within the Communist bloc and with the Third World countries. Through the Korean, Taiwanese and Vietnamese crises a never-ending stream of propaganda was directed against America and her allies. In the late 1960s, however, China changed her position seeking closer relationships with capitalist countries such as Japan and France. This was partly for commercial reasons and partly in an attempt to encourage such countries, and in particular the EEC group, to adopt an independent attitude towards both Russia and the United States.

The 'third force'. At Bandung (see page 210) Chou en-Lai tried to form a common front with the other Third World leaders such as Nehru, and Nasser but it was not long before her rivalry with the other Asian giant, India, came into the open and soured the 'Bandung spirit'.

The Chinese leadership has been consistently concerned to extend their control directly or indirectly into all the areas once dominated by the Chinese empire. In 1951 the Red Army reasserted Chinese power in Tibet and, especially after the flight of the traditional ruler, the Dalai Lama, in 1959, the Government moved large numbers of Chinese settlers into the country. During the same period they pushed forward their ill-defined and much disputed border with India and heavily defeated the Indians in a short border war in 1962 (see page 294).

In other areas the Chinese were less completely successful. The

Chinese 'volunteer' army played a critical role in preventing the defeat of the North Koreans by United Nations forces in 1951 but the Koreans were fearful for their own independence from China and maintained close links with Russia to counterbalance Peking's influence. Mongolia has been a loyal ally of the Soviet Union since the time of the Russian Revolution and Taiwan remained, as we have seen (page 189) beyond China's grasp for the time being.

To the south, China had traditionally been the overlord of Indo-China and the Chinese gave considerable aid to the North Vietnamese in the long war with the Americans. However, here too the Russians rivalled them in influence and outbid them in material aid. Nor is it certain that a strong and united Vietnam, even under a Communist government, would want to take orders from Peking.

The greatest setback for Chinese influence came with the crushing of the Indonesian Communist Party which was largely made up of overseas Chinese (see pages 259–60). Nevertheless, China has a wide range of friendly contacts with neutralists of left-wing regimes in Asia — with Burma, Afghanistan, Cambodia and Pakistan, for instance — and gives aid and encouragement to Communist resistance movements in such countries as Thailand, Malaysia and the Philippines.

In Africa a number of countries have received Chinese economic aid and guidance from Chinese technical experts. Tanzania is the prime example and such aid is often welcomed because, although it may be less valuable in cash terms, it has seemed to the country concerned to have fewer strings attached than help from the West or from Russia. So, while China is still no match militarily for the super powers nor a rival in economic terms for them or for Japan or the EEC, the country has become one of the most potent forces in international relations.

The entry of Communist China to the United Nations in 1971 and the visit of President Nixon to Peking in 1972 seemed to herald a new role for China in world affairs. But the points of tension between China and America remain and there is no sign of an improvement in Sino-Russian relations. After a generation of isolation China is only slowly defining her new role and relationships in world affairs and these depend on an internal balance of power about which little is known in the West.

NOTEBOOK SUMMARY
China Since 1900

CHINA IN 1900

1. The background — Ancient origins — Isolation — Confucius
2. Government — 19th century developments — position in 1900
3. Foreign influence — reasons for it and its effects
4. Economic problems — note the problem and its effects
   Population — Land — Trade and industry
5. Background to revolution — summarise the chief events and problems of the 19th century that led to the revolution of 1911 — what steps were necessary before China could become a modern nation?

THE FIRST REVOLUTION, 1911

1. Boxer Rebellion — reasons and results
2. Kuomintang: Early development — Importance of Dr Sun — Aims
3. Revolution: Immediate cause — Progress — Establishment of republic
4. Civil War — reasons and effects
5. Foreign aid: From whom — reason — Effect
6. Dr Sun — his place in China
7. United China — how and when achieved

RISE OF COMMUNISM

1. Early development — Reasons — Sources of support
2. Break with Kuomintang — Reasons — Importance — Attitude of Chiang Kai-shek — Long March
3. Reforms in China
   Main improvements
   Chief failure and its significance for Government and peasants

CHINA'S PROBLEMS IN THE 1930s

1. Two main problems — reasons
2. Threat from Japan
   Japanese action and result
   Attitude of Chiang Kai-shek
   Attitude of communists
   United Front — reasons and result
   Japanese gains
3. Threat from communists
   Effect of war on Kuomintang
   Effect of war on communists
   Collapse of united front — result
   Defeat of Japan — consequences within China

THE SECOND REVOLUTION, 1947-49

1. Reasons
2. Immediate cause
3. Result
4. Reasons for Kuomintang failure and communist success

COMMUNIST CHINA
1. Government: Immediate policy — Attitude of the people
2. Communist Party
   Its position
   Attitude of the people
   Membership
   Organisation — chief features
   Chairman Mao — career and importance
   Party workers — their importance
3. Land policy
   Peasant ownership
   Co-operatives — how organised — reasons
   Collectives — how organised — reasons — progress
4. Industrial development: Goals — Methods — Achievements
5. Russian assistance: Extent of assistance — Cost to China

THE GREAT LEAP FORWARD
1. Purpose and method
2. Communes — how organised — progress
3. Steel — how produced — results
4. Results: Economic results — Political results — New policy

COMMUNISM AND THE PEOPLE
1. Family life — traditional importance — communist policy — effects
2. Effect on the people — reasons and results
3. Crushing of opposition — methods and results
4. Education — purpose and methods
5. Support for party — methods by which achieved

GREAT CULTURAL REVOLUTION
1. Overthrow of old Leaders
2. Effects in China
3. Problems for the future

TAIWAN
1. Position in world affairs — reasons
2. Relations with U.S.A.

CHINA IN WORLD AFFAIRS
1. Relations with Russia
   Effect of 1949 revolution
   Changed relations after 1956 — reasons and results
2. Relations with the West
   Attitude to U.S.A.
   Reasons
3. Relations with neutral nations
   Bandung Conference
   Success and failure in Asia and Africa
4. Future outlook

WORDS TO KNOW

The following words used in this chapter need to be understood. Most of them have been explained in the text but all of them should form part of a history student's vocabulary. Make a list in the back of your notebook, with meanings, of those words that are new to you. Learn these and use them in your essays:

Barbarian, Cadres, collective, commune, communism, co-operative, 'defence perimeter', democracy, diplomatic relations, dynasty, élitist, emancipation, feudal, gentry, guerilla, ideology, indemnity, kan-pu, kulak, Kuomintang, mandate, medieval, peaceful coexistence, Politburo, Presidium, Red Guards, sovereign, strategic, tenant.

BOOKS TO READ OR CONSULT

Bown, C. and Edwards, A. D. *Revolution in China*, Heinemann Educational Books, 1974.

Bown, C. *The Peoples Republic of China*, Heinemann Educational Books, 1975.

Catchpole, B. *A Map History of Modern China*, Heinemann Educational Books, 1976.

Robottom, J. *Modern China,* London, Longman, 1969.

QUESTIONS FOR ESSAYS OR DISCUSSION

1. (a) Why was there a rising in China in 1911 to overthrow the Manchu dynasty?
   (b) What form of government was established?
   (c) Why was the Kuomintang unable to retain power in China after 1945?
2. (a) Why did the Kuomintang fail to govern China effectively in the 1930s?
   (b) Why did the Chinese communists seize control in 1949?
   (c) What have been the main aims of the Chinese in their internal policies since 1950?
   (d) Why have the Chinese communists been so hostile to the U.S.A. since 1950?
3. Give an account of the chief changes in the way that China was controlled and governed between 1911 and 1950.
4. (a) Suggest why the Kuomintang, which was dominant in China in the 1930s, failed to maintain its hold on the Chinese people.
   (b) Why were the communists successful in taking over China?
   (c) What effect did the communist victory have on the economic life of China?
   (d) What has been China's role in international affairs since 1950?
5. (a) What were the chief problems that faced China at the start of the twentieth century?
   (b) In what ways did Dr Sun Yat-sen attempt to overcome these problems?
   (c) To what extent did the Kuomintang Government succeed and fail in its objectives up to 1928?

9

INTERNATIONAL RELATIONS SINCE 1945

When President Roosevelt and Prime Minister Churchill met at their secret rendezvous in August 1941 to sign the Atlantic Charter (see page 78), they laid the foundations on which they hoped to see the peace built. The sixth clause of the Charter stated that, 'After the final destruction of Nazi tyranny, they hope to see established a peace which will afford to all nations the means of dwelling in safety within their own boundaries, and which will afford assurance that all the men in all the lands may live out their lives in freedom from fear and want.' These high ideals were accompanied by a determination to ensure that all nations, 'great or small, victor or vanquished', would be able to gain a sufficient share of the world's wealth to guarantee their people a steadily improving standard of living, and that all peoples should be free 'to choose the form of government under which they will live.' The intention of the United States to share in the rebuilding of the world was made clear by President Roosevelt one year later when he declared that, 'When victory comes we shall stand shoulder to shoulder in seeking to nourish the great ideals for which we fight.'

United Nations. The establishment of the United Nations[1] was the first practical expression of the peace hopes of the Atlantic Charter. From the outset its chances of success seemed to be much greater than those of the League of Nations. First, it was much more representative than the League had ever been, including as it did all the important nations of the world as well as the great majority of the smaller States. Then again the extravagant ideals of 1919 had been replaced by much more down to earth proposals which recognised the possible dangers to future peace and were designed to provide practical safeguards. Finally, the spirit of international co-operation and good will seemed stronger and more widespread than at any other time in modern history. With the destruction of fascism it appeared to many people that peace was assured and that their energies could

[1]The United Nations is treated fully in Chapter 4.

now be concentrated on waging war on the problems of poverty, hunger, illiteracy and disease.

Danger signs. For almost two years following the collapse and surrender of Germany in May 1945, the Foreign Ministers of the four victorious allies argued over the terms of the peace treaties. At these meetings, which took place in London, Paris, and New York, differences quickly began to appear between Byrnes and Bevin, representing the United States and Britain, and Molotov, representing the Soviet Union. The French Foreign Minister, Bidault, tried, with a certain amount of success, to steer a middle course and thus allow the opposing groups to agree to a compromise solution in a number of cases. When the Peace Conference finally met in Paris in July 1946, this same disagreement was apparent and the Soviet Union and its satellite States were invariably opposed by the non-communist States. Peace treaties were eventually signed with Bulgaria, Finland, Hungary, Italy and Rumania in February 1947, but differences between the former allies had by this time become most marked. These differences delayed the signing of a peace treaty with Japan until 1951 and with Austria until 1955, while there has not yet been a treaty with Germany.

THE PROBLEM OF GERMANY

No area illustrates more vividly than Germany the differences that emerged between the former wartime allies. Agreement was reached in conferences at Yalta and Potsdam in 1945 that there should be a temporary division of Germany, for purposes of occupation, between Britain, France, the United States and the Soviet Union, but that Germany should continue to be regarded and treated as a united nation. An Allied Control Council was established in Berlin to ensure that a unified policy was followed.

Differences emerge. Unfortunately, from the outset, the Russians immediately treated their sector (East Germany) as a satellite State and trade between it and the rest of the country almost stopped. As Eastern Germany was the chief food producing area, this action caused serious food shortages in the west and forced the other three occupying Powers to take action to prevent wholesale starvation. The repeated refusal of the Russians to co-operate in the work of reconstruction forced the Western Allies to develop their own policy in the two-thirds of the country that was under their control. By 1948, Britain, France and the United States had agreed to combine their zones of occupation into a single economic unit and to introduce a new currency in order to prevent further inflation and to speed economic recovery.[1] Their decision was greatly resented by the Russians who regarded it as a threat to their own position in Germany.

Berlin blockade. Russian retaliation was swift. In May 1948 all road and rail routes into West Berlin were sealed off by Russian troops. When Germany had been divided into four occupation zones the capital city had been similarly divided, but its location in the Russian zone of Germany made the position of the western Powers extremely difficult when Russian co-operation was withdrawn. However, the challenge could not be ignored and, for over a year, the two million people of West Berlin were supplied with food, coal, medical supplies, and other necessities by a vast airlift. Day and night, at two-minute intervals, British and American transport planes landed at the two aerodromes in the western section of the city while Sunderland flying boats, landing on Lake Waann, added their contribution to the daily quota of over 4000 tons of supplies that poured into the besieged city. When the blockade was withdrawn in May 1949 over two million tons of supplies had been flown into Berlin from the west.

The Cold War. Not only had the airlift saved the people of West Berlin from starvation or Russian domination, but it had also proved to the world that the nations of the West had the determination and the strength to resist aggression. While these achievements may be regarded as triumphs, the tragedy of the Berlin blockade cannot be ignored. Within three short years the spirit of wartime co-operation and peacetime optimism had been abandoned to be replaced by suspicion and hostility.

Since 1948 'Power politics' have become more dangerous than ever before as rival statesmen, anxious to increase their prestige, have used every possible opportunity to discredit their opponents. This policy of 'brinkmanship', first apparent in the Berlin crisis, has repeatedly brought the world within sight of a nuclear war. Like the game of 'chicken', this Cold War, or war of nerves, depends on one side giving way before a collision occurs. If a situation develops in which neither side is prepared to retreat the consequences are too fearful to contemplate.

Two Germanies. Immediately after the Soviet abandonment of the Berlin blockade the Western Allies announced a new federal constitution for West Germany. For the next three years the new German Government in Bonn was supervised by the Allies but, in 1952, the military occupation was virtually ended and by 1955

[1]For an example of the effects of inflation refer to the situation in Germany after World War I (see page 36).

the German Federal Republic had become a fully independent nation. In the same year it joined the North Atlantic Treaty Organisation (see page 203) to become 'a free and equal partner of the West'. Political independence has been accompanied by rapid economic recovery so that today West Germany is probably the most prosperous State in western Europe — a marked contrast to the situation following World War I. This recovery was assisted by the return of the Saar in 1957. Although this important industrial area had been separated from Germany in 1945 the majority of its inhabitants are German and, when given the opportunity to decide their future, chose reunion with Germany.

Meanwhile, in the east, the Soviet Union established the German Democratic Republic in October 1949. In reply to NATO the Soviet Union announced the Warsaw Pact with its European satellites, including East Germany. One-third of Germany and one-quarter of its people were now behind the 'Iron Curtain'. East German reaction can best be judged by reports of strikes and demands for greater political freedom, and by the steady westward flow of refugees. Before the Berlin Wall was erected in 1961 over three million East German people had escaped to the west. This represented one person in seven of the entire population of East Germany and they had been moving to the west, through Berlin, at the rate of over five hundred a day for more than fifteen years! The building of the wall hardly needs any further explanation.

From the early 1960s East Germany began to enjoy the sort of economic expansion which West Germany had already seen in the previous decade. By 1975 it had the most advanced economy in eastern Europe. Such expansion had been dependent upon closing the escape route, and in its turn it meant that fewer people were inclined to take the risk. In this new situation it was easier to normalise relations between East and West Germany and for both to accept that they would remain divided in the foreseeable future.

In 1973 Chancellor Brandt of West Germany signed the Basic Treaty which recognised the regime in the East and improved relations with Russia. Both parts of Germany were now able to take their seats at the United Nations and both continued to lead their parts of Europe. On the other hand the basic differences in political ideology, symbolised by the Berlin Wall, remained and Berlin itself was still a vulnerable pressure point in East–West relations.

EUROPE DIVIDED — THE EAST

In 1946, Sir Winston Churchill said, 'an Iron Curtain' has descended across the continent. The map on page 111 makes his meaning clear. Following World War II almost one-third of the total land area of Europe passed into Russian hands or came directly under Russian control. Of the countries of eastern and southern Europe, only Finland, Austria, Greece and Czechoslovakia remained outside the communist bloc (group of States). Of all the new democracies created by the Treaty of Versailles, Czechoslovakia had been the most successful and, alone of these States, was able to stand out against communist pressure after World War II. However, as it was almost surrounded by Russian satellite States its chances of survival were slim and, in 1948, a communist *coup* overthrew the Government and carried the country behind the Iron Curtain.

Hungary crushed. Elections in Hungary at the end of the war produced a Government mainly representative of the small farmers who made up the bulk of the population. But Russian troops were still in the country and there was an active Communist Party. By 1952 Hungary had become securely attached to the Soviet bloc and private farms had been almost entirely replaced by collectives (see page 108). Following the death of Stalin in 1953 and the apparent relaxation of Russian control in the satellite States, there was a widespread demand for greater freedom and national recognition. Revolts in Budapest in October 1956 led to the establishment of a new Government led by Imre Nagy, the release of Cardinal Mindszenty (the head of the Hungarian Roman Catholic Church) whose earlier arrest and imprisonment had shocked the world, and an attempt to win freedom for Hungary. But Hungarian hopes were shortlived. Without hesitation, the Russians used force to destroy Hungarian freedom, and by early November Russian troops were again in control, Nagy had been 'tried' and shot as a traitor, and a new Government loyal to the Soviet Union had been installed in Budapest.

The United Nations General Assembly 'united for peace' (see page 83) and demanded the withdrawal of Russian troops from Hungary. It appointed a special investigating commission, led by New Zealander Sir Leslie Munro, and even discussed the possibility of imposing sanctions against the Soviet Union. But Russian troops remained and the United Nations Commission was denied entry. Preoccupied with the Suez crisis (see page 212), the United Nations took no further action except to condemn Russian brutality and to request the Secretary-General to take any further steps he could to solve the problem. Short of armed intervention there was little else the United Nations could have done in the circumstances. The Soviet Union had shown that a determined Great Power could still defy world opinion. In 1968–9 world opinion was even more shocked when the Russians crushed an attempt by the Czech Communists to assert their national autonomy whilst remaining within the eastern bloc. But once again there was little or nothing that the outside powers could do.

Successful resistance. Finland had fought against the Soviet Union in World War II and the victorious Russians extracted a harsh peace treaty from the Finns and annexed almost one-sixth of the country. But Finland was determined to maintain its independence and, by 1952, had paid the last of its wartime debts to Russia. As one modern historian has said, 'All in all, Finland post-1945 makes a rare story of a great national struggle, a story all too rare in the world of the Cold War'.[1]

Austria, like Germany, was occupied by the four Great Powers in 1945. Similar Russian tactics to those employed in East Germany hindered the rehabilitation of Austria until suddenly, and for no apparent reason, the Soviet Union announced its willingness to sign a peace treaty in 1955. As a result Austria regained its independence but was forced to sign a guarantee that it would never reunite with Germany and would always remain neutral. Perhaps the Soviet Union hoped to secure a similar agreement over Germany or perhaps the Austrian treaty was part of the new policy of peaceful co-existence (see page 113).

Greece and Turkey. In a special address to Congress in 1947, President Harry S. Truman, speaking of communist pressure on Greece and Turkey, said, 'I believe that it must be the policy of the United States to support free peoples who are resisting attempted subjugation by armed minorities or by outside pressures . . . The free peoples of the world look to us for support in maintaining their freedoms. If we falter in our leadership, we may endanger the peace of the world.' Two months later Congress voted $400 million to assist the recovery of Greece and Turkey.

To the western nations these two countries occupied a position of special importance as they guard the approaches to the Black Sea, Russia's southern outlet to the Mediterranean. Since 1944 a civil war had been raging in Greece. Communist guerilla bands, sheltering in the hills of neighbouring Albania, Yugoslavia and Bulgaria, conducted widespread raids across the Greek frontier but a Security Council resolution to prevent them was vetoed by the Soviet Union. However, in 1949, following its defection from the Soviet bloc, Yugoslavia closed its frontier to the guerillas, the raids stopped, and the British occupation force was withdrawn.

[1]Chambers, F. P., *This Age of Conflict,* Harcourt, Brace & World, New York, 1962, p. 671.

Bolstered by the American financial aid, Greece was able to settle its internal problems and, in 1952, both Greece and Turkey became members of the North Atlantic Treaty Organisation. However both countries suffered from political instability and in 1967, after a military *coup* in Greece, a highly repressive regime was established which made the country an outcast amongst the Western democracies. In 1974 the Greek Government instigated a *coup* in Cyprus—for long a crisis point with a Greek majority and a Turkish minority continually at odds with each other. The Turks invaded the island and effectively partitioned it; the Greek military regime collapsed; and Greece left NATO. The southern flank of the organisation had thus been severely weakened while Cyprus was left divided and potentially explosive.

Yugoslavia independent. Marshal Josef Tito provides an interesting study in the history of postwar Europe. The Government which he established in Belgrade in 1945 was modelled on the Russian constitution of 1936, but did not need the support of Russian troops to survive. At no stage has Marshal Tito been prepared to accept Russian domination and increasing tension between the two countries culminated in the expulsion of Yugoslavia from the Soviet bloc in 1948. Since then Tito has followed an independent policy, leaning towards China rather than Russia, accepting economic and military aid from the West, and joining in conferences of the neutral nations. In 1953 Yugoslavia, Greece and Turkey signed the Balkan Pact for their mutual defence.

EUROPE DIVIDED — THE WEST

The United States, which had resolutely turned its back on Europe in 1919, adopted an entirely different policy in 1945. Realising that the rapid recovery of European agriculture and industry was essential for the restoration of world trade and, therefore, for American prosperity, the United States introduced a large-scale programme of financial assistance for countries devastated by the war. Although this offer was rejected by the Soviet Union and its satellites as an attempt to extend American control into Europe, it was taken up by seventeen nations, mainly in western Europe (including West Germany, at this stage not independent), who joined together in the Organisation for European Economic Co-operation (OEEC) in 1948. In the next four years these countries received assistance to the value of $12,000 million which was equivalent to the expenditure of over £10 per head. By 1952, the determined efforts of the members of OEEC and the aid they had received under the Marshall Plan had restored much of the prosperity of western Europe. As food became more plentiful and factory production increased, people became more satisfied and the influence of Communist Parties in these countries declined rapidly.

Towards a united Europe. The idea of a united Europe is not new. Over a thousand years ago the Emperor Charlemagne had brought a brief unity to much of the continent but, after World War II, the idea again became popular. There were now two large and powerful nations which seemed to dominate the world and beside them the once proud nations of Europe appeared to be of little significance. Also French politicians saw in European unification a solution to their longstanding fear of Germany. A start had been made with the formation of the Benelux Union in 1944 (Belgium, the Netherlands and Luxembourg) and the offer of Marshall Aid in 1947 provided the incentive for further development in the form of OEEC.

It is doubtful whether anything more than economic co-operation would have resulted if it had not been for the sudden intensification of the Cold War early in 1948. The Soviet seizure of Czechoslovakia and the blockade of Berlin forced the nations of western Europe to realise the weakness of their position, and in May 1948 a 'Congress of Europe' met at The Hague in the Netherlands. Although the Council of Europe, which was established in that year and which has met regularly since then, has not accomplished a great deal, it has at least helped to prepare for closer co-operation in matters of trade and defence. Its supporters hope that it may yet lead to closer political co-operation and even envisage a United States of Europe.

North Atlantic Treaty Organisation. By the Treaty of Dunkirk with Britain in 1947, France gained security against a possible revival of German military ambitions. When this treaty was extended in 1948 by the Treaty of Brussels to include the Benelux countries, it had become obvious that the threat of Russian rather than German aggression would dominate the postwar era. Persistent Russian use of the veto in the United Nations Security Council and the maintenance of a large Russian army in eastern Europe emphasised the dangers of western disunity. These dangers were felt most keenly in the United States of America where an almost hysterical fear of Russia gripped the country. Prompted by the events of 1948 mentioned above the United States Government suggested a military alliance between the U.S.A., Canada, and the Brussels nations. These countries, together with Denmark, Iceland, Italy, Norway, and Portugal, signed the North Atlantic Pact in Washington in 1949. They have since been joined by both Greece and Turkey, in 1952, and by West Germany in 1955.

America in Europe. The North Atlantic Pact was the first military alliance signed with foreign countries in the history of the United States. As one statesman remarked, 'It placed the American frontier on the Rhine'. On the surface it suggests a complete abandonment of the traditional American isolationist policy (see page 145) but it must not be forgotten that the creation of NATO was very much in America's own interests. If the threat from Russia was as real as Americans believed, then it was essential for the United States to have strong allies in Europe. The establishment of a NATO army in Europe and the maintenance of large American forces and missile bases there are particularly resented by the Russians, who regard them as proof of Western aggressive intentions. The Western Allies, on the other hand, consider their presence essential to prevent any further extension of Russian power in Europe.

European Defence Community. From the outset the United States made it clear that its continued participation in NATO would depend on the European members co-operating for their own defence and agreeing to the rearming of Germany. This need became urgent with the explosion of a Russian atomic bomb in 1949 and the outbreak of the Korean War in 1950 (see page 207). The first proposal, put forward in the Council of Europe in 1951 by the French Foreign Minister, M. Robert Schuman, was for a European Defence Community with an international European army for the defence of western Europe. Schuman hoped that this would allow the rearming of Germany without any threat to France and that it would also be a further step towards European federation. But other Frenchmen feared the loss of French identity, while Britain, because of its heavy overseas commitments and its traditional reluctance to become involved in European affairs, refused to join. In August 1954, following its rejection by both nations, EDC was abandoned.

Western European Union. That the major nations of western Europe were not yet ready for the close co-operation envisaged in EDC was now obvious, but it was equally obvious that some form of military co-operation was essential. On the initiative of the British Foreign Secretary, Anthony Eden, a further conference assembled in London in September and within a month agreement had been reached on the establishment of a Western European Union. The Brussels nations, plus Italy and West Germany, agreed to the formation of a WEU army under a unified command but completely separate from the Council of Europe. Adequate safeguards were provided to prevent a dangerous revival of German military strength and there was also provision for the withdrawal of forces to meet overseas emergencies. The WEU army is under the command of the Supreme Allied Commander in Europe (SACEUR) who is appointed by NATO, so that, for all practical purposes, NATO and WEU are closely linked to provide for the defence of the countries of western Europe and Anglo-America. However by the mid-1970s NATO had been considerably weakened. De Gaulle had withdrawn French military co-operation; Greece had left the organisation altogether; and Portugal was governed by an unstable left-wing regime.

European Economic Community. The first attempt at economic co-operation was the establishment of the European Coal and Steel Community in 1951 by France, Italy, West Germany and the Benelux countries. These nations, now known as the 'Six', pooled their resources and abolished tariffs on coal, iron and steel in an endeavour to increase the efficiency and strength of their heavy industries. The success achieved by ECSC was so encouraging that the Six agreed to work towards the establishment of a European common market. By the Treaty of Rome, signed in 1957, the Six created an atomic energy commission (Euratom) to pool their nuclear resources, and a European Economic Community, generally known as the Common Market or EEC. An immediate reduction of tariffs began and the ultimate aim of the Common Market was to abolish all Customs duties and trade restrictions within the area. It was also hoped by many that this practical co-operation would lead to closer political union than had yet been achieved by the Council of Europe (see page 203).

European Free Trade Association. The creation of the Common Market placed Great Britain in a more difficult position than had any previous move towards a united Europe. Traditional British distrust of close political and military ties with the Continent had already reduced the effectiveness of the Council of Europe and contributed to the failure of EDC. Commonwealth commitments, fears for the future of its heavily subsidised agriculture and for its national independence, prevented Britain joining the Common Market. But it could not ignore such an important development in an area with which it had one-sixth of its trade. During 1959, Britain, Norway, Sweden, Denmark, Austria, Switzerland, and Portugal — usually known as the 'Seven' — formed the European Free Trade Association (EFTA), a much looser agreement than EEC. In 1961 they were joined by Finland.

Because of their scattered location, the Seven were in a much weaker trading position than were the Six. The danger of trade rivalry was quickly appreciated and throughout 1961 and 1962 Britain negotiated with the Six for entry to the Common Market. If adequate safeguards for Commonwealth trade had been provided it seems likely that Britain and the other members of EFTA would have joined EEC. Unfortunately, when there appeared some possibility of success, President de Gaulle refused to continue the talks. His chief reason was assumed to have been concern that the inclusion of Britain would weaken the position of France in western Europe where, under his leadership, much former French prestige had been regained.

Britain tried again to negotiate membership in 1967 and again she was rejected. It was only after the resignation of De Gaulle that a treaty was successfully negotiated by the British Prime Minister, Edward Heath, and Britain, Ireland and Denmark became full members of the EEC in January 1973. The Norwegian Government had also signed the treaty, but this agreement was subsequently rejected in a referendum of the Norwegian people. In 1975 the British themselves held a referendum on renegotiated terms which Harold Wilson's Labour Government had agreed and the British people voted by a majority of two to one to remain members.

The EEC now forms a formidable economic bloc with a productive capacity to rival that of Russia or America. However, progress towards unification has been slower and more difficult than the founders had hoped. National conflict of interest has arisen on many points. For instance countries have been deeply divided over the Common Agricultural Policy which appeared to operate in the interests of the peasant farmers in France at the expense of the more industrialised areas such as Britain. Countries with deep economic problems such as Britain and Italy had hoped for more regional aid than the more successful states such as Germany were prepared to pay for and all nine countries tended to go their own way in the economic and energy crises of the 1970s. On the key issue of energy there was inevitably a divergence of interest between Britain with her North Sea reserves and the rest.

So far the European Parliament has been allowed little or no power by the Commission or the individual states and the future role which the Community can play as a political entity is uncertain. Yet for all that it is a remarkable development from the shattered wreck of Europe in 1945.

EXPLOSION IN THE FAR EAST

Worsening international relations in Europe in the late 1940s were matched by an equally serious turn of events in Asia. With the final breakdown of negotiations between the Chinese communists and the Kuomintang Government in 1947 (see page 179), the uneasy peace which had continued since 1945 dissolved into further civil war. This ended in 1949 with the complete triumph of the communist armies and the establishment of the People's Republic of China. The communist bloc now stretched from central Europe right across the Asian continent and included almost one-quarter of the land surface and over one-third of the people of the entire world. The Berlin airlift (see page 198) and the formation of NATO (see page 203) were a clear indication that the western nations were not prepared to allow any further expansion of communist influence in Europe. Asia, with its serious economic problems and its hatred of western imperialism, provided another opportunity for expansion which could not be ignored.

Stalemate in Korea. With the defeat of Japan in 1945, Korea was occupied from the south by American forces and from the north by the Russians. They met at the 38th parallel in central Korea and it was agreed that the country should be placed under joint control until such time as it was ready for independence. As in Germany, the two halves of Korea, the industrial north and the rice growing south, made a natural economic whole but political reunification soon proved impossible. The failure of the occupying Powers to agree brought a United Nations commission of investigation to the country in 1947 but it was refused admission to the Russian zone. In 1948 the United States announced the formation of the independent Democratic Republic of Korea in the south, matched immediately by the Russian sponsorship of the People's Republic of Korea in the north. Although the withdrawal of Soviet and American forces in 1949 reduced tension in the area there seemed little likelihood of agreement on reunification.

The Korean War. The Korean situation changed with startling suddenness on June 25, 1950 when North Korean forces poured across the 38th parallel and began the invasion of South Korea in an attempt to reunite the country by force. Temporary Russian absence from the Security Council, because of the council's refusal to admit Red China to the United Nations, allowed international condemnation of this North Korean aggression and a United Nations force under the command of the American General McArthur was hastily assembled. Initially the North Korean army enjoyed great success. Within three months it had overrun all but the southeast corner of the peninsula but the rapid build-up of United Nations forces quickly reversed the position and by October the 38th parallel had been regained.

Because of the refusal of North Korea to surrender, the UN General Assembly decided that its armies should cross the frontier in order to establish a 'unified, independent and democratic government' in Korea.[1] Within a month of this decision American troops, the bulk of the United Nations force, had almost reached the Yalu River, the northern boundary of Korea with China. The invasion of North Korea was promptly denounced by China as imperialist aggression, and the entire character of the war was changed by the entry of almost a quarter of a million Chinese troops on the side of North Korea. Regardless of tremendous losses, the Chinese advanced relentlessly through the difficult mountainous country of North Korea until by June 1951, a year after the war had started, the opposing forces again faced each other across the 38th parallel.

Peace in Korea. A Soviet appeal for a cease-fire in Korea allowed the world to step back from the brink of a possible third world war. The Cold War in Europe had become a hot war in Asia which threatened to engulf the whole world. Only the dismissal of General McArthur by President Truman had stopped the bombing of Chinese cities and the possible invasion of mainland China by Chiang Kai-shek's forces. Either of these actions would have had disastrous consequences for world peace. Two years of protracted discussions followed before an armistice was finally signed in July 1953.

Thousands of lives had been lost, the poverty and misery of the Korean people had greatly increased, and no progress had been made towards reunification. Had the war been fought in vain? If nothing else was achieved at least the Korean War demonstrated that, in Asia as in Europe, the nations of the free world were sufficiently determined and sufficiently strong to resist aggression.[2] This in itself was an important achievement.

Exit Indo-China. While United Nations forces were fighting in the mountains and mud of Korea, French troops were engaged in a losing battle in the steamy jungles of Indo-China. Japanese occupation from 1940 to 1945 had hastened the development of a strong nationalist movement in Indo-China and French attempts to regain control of the area were met with determined resistance, especially from the Viet Minh led by Ho Chi-minh. Intermittent fighting continued from 1946 to 1953 when, following the Korean armistice, Chinese support for the Viet Minh was greatly increased.

[1]The return of the Soviet representative to the Security Council prevented any further effective action and the responsibility for maintaining peace passed to the General Assembly (see page 83).

[2]Compare with Germany (page 198).

In 1954 a large French force surrendered after a heroic resistance at Dien Bien Phu and two months later a cease-fire agreement was signed at Geneva.

Enter Vietnam. For France the war in Indo-China was a disaster. Not only was it costly in men and in money but also in international prestige. By the Geneva agreement both sides withdrew their forces from Laos and Cambodia while Vietnam became the third nation to suffer from growing conflict between East and West, being divided at the 17th parallel (see map, page 227). This left the main rice-growing area in the South under an American-backed government and the main industrial area in the North under the Communist regime of Ho Chi-minh. However many Communist supporters remained in the South and the President, an ardent Catholic, incurred not only their enmity but also the hostility of many Buddhists and intellectuals by his corrupt and autocratic methods. In 1955–6 there were guerilla risings in the South which marked the beginning of a new twenty-year war.

American military advisers were sent in by President Kennedy in 1962, but the Communist guerillas, the Vietcong, advanced to control half the country and in 1963 Diem was assassinated by his own troops. Successive regimes in South Vietnam thereafter failed to win the hearts of their own people or to inflict decisive defeats on the Vietcong who received much support from the North.

In 1964, after a clash with North Vietnamese forces in the Gulf of Tonking, the Americans began a full-scale campaign of bombardment against the North and committed a growing number of combat troops in the South. Other countries such as Australia, New Zealand and South Korea also sent token forces to help in the South but the war with its massive costs and appalling devastation provoked growing protest both in the United States itself and around the world.

Yet the Vietcong could not be defeated and American intervention in Cambodia to cut off Communist supplies threw that hitherto peaceful country into a bitter civil war. There was also intermittent fighting between left- and right-wing forces in Laos.

There were long drawn out attempts to negotiate a settlement and after 1968 President Nixon and his Secretary of State, Kissinger, made an all out effort to secure an agreement which would allow the withdrawal of American troops in good order. The last American troops left in January 1973 and the defence of the South was left to the South Vietnam army strengthened with massive amounts of American equipment and arms.

However the peace settlement was a sham. Vietcong and North Vietnamese pressure continued until in the spring of 1975, after the dramatic collapse of the Government in Saigon, Communist forces overran the whole of South Vietnam. At about the same time Cambodia also fell to the Communists and Laos came virtually under their control.

South-East Asia Treaty Organisation. A direct result of the wars in Korea and Indo-China was the formation of the South-East Asia Treaty Organisation (SEATO) in 1954 at a conference at Manila. This version of NATO in Asia was signed by Australia, Britain, France, New Zealand, Pakistan, the Philippines, Thailand and the United States, who pledged themselves to work together to protect their interests and to prevent the advance of communism in South-East Asia. Although the terms of the Geneva agreement prevented Laos, Cambodia or South Vietnam from joining SEATO, the members agreed to come to their assistance if requested. Because SEATO had no permanent forces such as NATO it depended entirely on the willingness of its members to supply troops in the event of trouble. In September 1975, having failed in its task of creating an effective anti-Communist organisation in the area, SEATO was formally dissolved.

Bandung Conference, 1955. Many Asian nations were uneasy about the establishment of SEATO and regarded it as an attempt by the nations of the West to maintain their influence under cover of the threat of communist expansion. When the first Afro-Asian conference assembled at Bandung in Indonesia it was attended by almost all the independent nations of both continents. The favourable impression made by the Chinese Prime Minister, Chou-en-Lai, did much to undermine SEATO and to convince those present of China's peaceful intentions in South-East Asia. Apart from this, the Bandung Conference was also an important milestone in the development of the Afro-Asian bloc of uncommitted nations (see page 218).

TROUBLE IN THE MIDDLE EAST

The Middle East is the focal point of the Arab world, which stretches for some 4,000 miles from Morocco to the Persian Gulf across the Sahara and Arabian deserts. Apart from the fortunate inhabitants of the oil States clustered around the Persian Gulf, the remainder of its eighty-five million people live in extreme poverty as nomadic herdsmen or as subsistence farmers in scattered desert oases. Yet despite its poverty the Arab world, and the Middle East in particular, is of immense importance in international affairs. From east to west it offers a natural route from Asia into Africa, while from north to south the Suez Canal and the Red Sea provide a vital link in the sea communications of the world. Most important of all, beneath its barren surface, it contains over two-fifths of the world's known oil reserves.[1] It is little wonder that trouble in the Middle East attracts the attention of the entire world.

The Arab League. Until 1945 most of the States of the Arab world were under the control of European nations — Britain, France and Italy. The rapid growth of Arab nationalism since World War II, the traditional disunity among the Arab peoples and the instability of Governments in most States have made co-operation between them very difficult. Although the Arab League was formed in 1945 (see map, page 226), it was based on common hatreds rather than on a spirit of co-operation. Apart from the Moslem religion and a common Arabic language, the chief unifying forces were opposition to the Europeans (anti-colonialism) and, above all, hatred of the Jews. The creation of Israel as a Jewish national State was the most important single factor in the development of Arab unity.

The Problem of Palestine. When Palestine became a British mandate (see page 75) after World War I Britain announced that it would become a 'national home for the Jews' who, for more than a thousand years, had been a people without a country. At the same time the British promised to protect the interests of the Arabs in Palestine. For the next thirty years Britain endeavoured to keep its promises to both groups but the position was complicated by the return of thousands of Jews to their 'Promised Land' following Hitler's *pogroms* (or massacres) in the 1930s. Meanwhile, as the number of Jews increased, Arab opinion hardened and became determined to destroy Jewish Palestine. Finally, despairing of a solution, Britain made the problem a United Nations responsibility in 1947.

Matters came to a head in 1948 when the United Nations decided to partition Palestine between the Jews and the Arabs. The proclamation of the Jewish State of Israel resulted in an Arab invasion (see page 87) and, although United Nations mediators quickly restored peace, it was apparent that no final solution had been found. Continued Arab refusal to recognise Israel and the determination of almost a million Arab refugees to return to their former homes in Palestine made a permanent settlement impossible. With the western nations committed to the preservation of Israel and the Arab States equally determined on its destruction, the situation became increasingly explosive. It was aggravated by the remarkable economic progress made by the

---

[1]Most of the oilfields have been developed by European and American companies. A Soviet attempt to force oil concessions from Persia in 1946 was rejected by the United Nations Security Council.

Jews which was in marked contrast to the continued poverty of the surrounding Arab States. The extension of the Cold War to the Middle East could only be a matter of time.

Britain leaves Suez. A main cause of disagreement between Britain and Egypt was the continued presence of British troops in the Suez Canal Zone and the refusal of Britain to evacuate the Sudan. Although the twenty-year treaty governing occupation of the zone was due to expire in 1956, Egyptian demands for withdrawal from both areas increased after the overthrow of King Farouk by a military *coup* in 1952 (see page 270). On the understanding that Britain could continue to service the base and reoccupy it if either Turkey or any Arab State was attacked, British troops were withdrawn in 1954. At the same time the Sudan was given the right to decide its own future, and it chose independence rather than the unification Egypt had hoped for. Unfortunately the British withdrawal did not result in an improvement in Anglo-Egyptian relations, and the Egyptian leader, Nasser, who was already receiving arms from the Soviet Union, continued to pursue an anti-Western policy.

Western support for Israel and Britain's presence in the Canal Zone and the Sudan had led to the Arab League rejecting a British offer of a Middle East Defence Organisation in 1952. A similar American offer had been rejected in 1953. Concern for the safety of Middle East communications and the vital supplies of oil from the area led the Western Powers to negotiate a defence agreement with the northern States of the area in 1955. This Baghdad Pact was signed by Turkey (already a member of NATO), Pakistan already a member of SEATO, Iran (Persia) and Iraq, the chief opponent of Egypt for the leadership of the Arab world. Britain also signed the pact and the United States promised to work in close co-operation. Following the overthrow of Iraq's pro-Western Government in 1958, it withdrew from the pact which was renamed the Central Treaty Organisation.

Suez Again, 1956. Resentment at Iraq's alliance with the West led Nasser, now President of Egypt, to seek new ways of proving Egyptian leadership of the Arab world. In 1956, following a large purchase of arms from Czechoslovakia in defiance of Western restrictions,[1] he formed a counter-alliance against Iraq, with Syria and Saudi-Arabia. The Western reply was the withdrawal of offers of financial assistance for the construction of the Aswan Dam, a key project in the economic development of Egypt.

[1] In an attempt to prevent a renewal of Israeli-Arab hostilities, Britain, France and the U.S.A. had carefully controlled the supply of arms and munitions to both sides since 1951.

Nasser immediately nationalised the Suez Canal and announced that the profits from its operation would be used to construct the dam. In his attempts to establish the superiority of Egypt in the Middle East, Nasser was obviously prepared to play off East against West.

Fearful of growing Egyptian military strength and resentful that its ships were denied passage through the Suez Canal, Israel attacked Egypt on October 29, 1956. Within days Israeli forces had over-run the weak Egyptian opposition and were within reach of the Suez Canal. Britain and France, anxious for the safety of the canal, called on both sides for a cease-fire. Egyptian refusal to comply with this demand resulted in an Anglo-French invasion. The United States protested strongly against this action; Russia immediately threatened rocket attacks on Paris and London; and the United Nations General Assembly 'united for peace', following British and French vetoes in the Security Council, and demanded that the forces be withdrawn (see page 87). Britain and France withdrew in favour of a United Nations force and peace was restored, but the chief significance of the crisis was to bring the United States and the Soviet Union into direct conflict in yet another part of the globe.

The Eisenhower Doctrine. The Suez crisis served to introduce both the United States and the Soviet Union to the Middle East as rival champions of local nations in what many Afro-Asian States regarded as a continuation of the struggle against European imperialism. In 1957 President Eisenhower guaranteed American assistance to any Middle Eastern nation that felt itself threatened from communism. Jordan and Lebanon took advantage of this offer in 1958.

The Six Days War. In 1966–7 tension mounted again between Israel and her Arab neighbours. The former had received considerable military aid from the United States and France, whilst the Arabs were being armed by the Soviet Union. In 1967 President Nasser successfully demanded the removal of the United Nations peace-keeping force from Egypt's frontier with Israel and both sides began to mobilise their troops. Then, in June, in a lightning six-day campaign, the Israelis crushed the forces of Egypt, Jordan and Syria and extended their frontiers to the Suez Canal, the river Jordan and the Syrian Heights. This dramatic victory did nothing to solve the long-term problems of the area and indeed inflamed Arab nationalism still further. Both the Arabs and Israel continued to re-arm with increasingly sophisticated weapons. There was continuous sporadic fighting along the new frontiers between the Israelis and both regular Arab armies and the guerilla forces of the Palestinian refugee groups. The Suez Canal remained closed. The result was insecurity for Israel, political instability in the Arab states and the constant threat of another major conflict in which the big powers could easily be involved directly or indirectly in a confrontation.

Israel found herself under pressure at two levels. On the one hand the Arab states kept up a diplomatic offensive against her with the threat of full scale war always in the background. After Nasser's death in 1971 Gaddafi, the extreme Arab nationalist leader of Libya, set the pace in these activities. But even more immediate pressure came from the Palestinian guerillas operating in and around Israel's borders and committing terrorist attacks on Israel — hi-jacking planes, destroying property — around the world. Each attack provoked an Israeli counter-attack, usually against the guerilla bases in Lebanon.

In October 1973 Egypt and Syria launched a surprise offensive against Israel on two fronts. The Israelis were initially taken off-guard and their defence perimeter was broken. Although after several weeks of very tough fighting the Israelis regained the upper hand militarily, the process had shaken and weakened the country and she had to give way to American pressure to agree to an armistice under the mediation of the American Secretary of State, Henry Kissinger.

In the course of the war the Arabs had achieved greater unity and greater military success than ever before. What was significant was not so much the small contingents from a number of Arab states that went to fight on the Syrian front, but the joint action by the oil-producing states to put economic pressure on the industrial countries of the West. This produced both an immediate world energy crisis and a recognition of an important power shift (see page 218).

In the meantime the relative success of the Arabs in the war made it a little easier for the Arab leaders to reach a limited settlement with Israel. By 1975 Kissinger had negotiated an Israeli–Egyptian agreement which meant that in return for a limited withdrawal in Sinai on the Israelis' part, the Egyptians renounced war for a limited period and in effect recognised Israel's right to exist within her pre-1967 boundaries. Apart from anything else this allowed the Suez Canal to be reopened. An agreement with Syria was more difficult to reach but Kissinger had made some progress on this front too. The problem that showed no sign of resolution was that of the Palestinian refugees whose position was generally ignored by the Israelis and exploited for their own ends by the Arab states. The guerillas therefore showed no sign of relenting in their terror campaign and the presence of their bases in the Lebanon brought that country into virtual civil war in 1975.

Meanwhile Israel remained almost completely dependent upon America for military aid and on contributions from the Jewish communities around the world for economic survival. She came under threat of expulsion from the United Nations and its agencies because of the majority which the Arabs with their Communist and Third World allies could now mobilise.

'PEACEFUL COEXISTENCE'

The year 1953 was a turning point in postwar international relations. Since 1946 the Cold War had been steadily increasing in intensity. Civil war in Greece (page 201), oil disputes in Iran (page 210), the blockade of Berlin (page 198), and communist successes in Czechoslovakia (page 200) and China (page 207) had culminated in the outbreak of a shooting war in Korea in 1950 (pages 207-8).

In November 1952 General Dwight Eisenhower, the Republican candidate, won the election for the American Presidency and in March 1953 Stalin died. Within a few months an armistice was signed in Korea and, under the leadership first of Malenkov and later of Bulganin and Krushchev, the Soviet Union appeared to relax its earlier hostility towards the West.

The Bomb. When the United States dropped the first atomic bomb on Hiroshima in 1945, American scientists forecast that other countries would be able to follow the American lead 'within two to five years'. The explosion of the first Russian atomic bomb in 1949 confirmed this forecast and, at one stroke, altered the strategic balance of power. By 1953 both the United States and the Soviet Union had developed the even more deadly hydrogen bombs and Sir Winston Churchill spoke of the 'balance of terror' which had been created. By 1975 Britain, France, China and India had all exploded nuclear devices and a large number of other countries such as Japan, Israel, South Africa and Germany had the potential to do so.

In 1963 America, Britain and Russia had signed a limited agreement on the testing of nuclear weapons and this had been endorsed by most other nations — but not by France and China. A hot line was also set up between Moscow and Washington to help reduce the chance of nuclear war by accident. However both Russia and America continued to develop increasingly destructive and sophisticated missile systems and there was still no control over underground nuclear tests. Both sides were keenly aware both of the dangers and the enormous costs of these systems and a series of talks were held in Vienna and Helsinki on strategic arms limitation. Nixon and Brezhnev signed treaties on the control of missiles and the avoidance of nuclear war in 1972 and 1973 and the major powers had already agreed on treaties for the peaceful development of the Antarctic and of Outer Space. Yet in practice pitifully little had been achieved to reduce the danger of nuclear holocaust.

The space race. In their bid to overtake the West the Russians have always recognised the importance of scientific research. Since 1945 vast sums of money — which could ill be spared from the development of agriculture and consumer industries — have been appropriated for the space programme. The success of 'Sputnik I', the first earth satellite launched on October 4, 1957 was a tremendous psychological victory to the Russians. By their success, three months before the Americans shot 'Explorer I' into orbit, the Russians were acclaimed as the leading scientific nation in the world. Their prestige was further enhanced by the first space flight by Major Yuri Gagarin in April 1963, one month before the flight by the American, Commander Alan Shepard. In July 1969 the Americans scored the greatest popular success of the 'space-race' by landing two men on the moon and bringing them back safely loaded with lunar samples and photographs for scientific analysis. Each new 'first' in this costly field of international rivalry has important propaganda value, but whether the governments of underdeveloped and hungry countries are impressed is an open question.

The policy of peaceful co-existence did not mark the end of international conflict by other means — for instance economic and propaganda wars — for areas of influence throughout the world and in particular amongst the neutralist countries. Nevertheless the policy did keep the super powers out of direct armed conflict. After the first thaw in the Cold War under Krushchev relations between Russia and America deteriorated again with the crises in the Middle East and American intervention in South-East Asia. After 1968, Nixon made a determined effort, with the help of his foreign affairs expert Henry Kissinger to reach a major detente with both Russia and China. However his efforts were partly undermined by the progressive collapse of the President's prestige at home with his involvement in a series of political scandals known as the Watergate affair. This finally brought about his resignation from office in 1974. However his successor President Ford continued with a detente policy and with Kissinger in charge of his foreign affairs team.

CRISIS IN THE CARIBBEAN

Despite the apparent unity of the Organisation of American States (see page 161) many problems remain in Latin America. While the strength of Roman Catholicism has checked the spread of communism, the continent has by no means escaped the effects of the Cold War. Nor has the American 'good neighbour' policy been a complete success. In 1958 Vice-President Nixon barely escaped with his life while on a good-will tour of Latin American States. At the same time a Soviet ambassador offering aid and trade was well received in many countries. Brazil and other republics were quick to see that they, too, could benefit from rivalry between East and West and, under a new 'good partner' policy, American economic aid was increased.

Castro in Cuba. The overthrow of the twenty-five-year-old dictatorship of Fulgencio Batista by Fidel Castro in 1958 was welcomed in many countries and the new Government was quickly recognised by the United States, the Soviet Union, Britain and most of the other States of Latin America. However, by 1960 relations between the United States and Cuba had deteriorated as Castro began the nationalisation of American oil and sugar refineries on the island. In reply the United States placed an embargo (or trade boycott) on Cuban sugar and broke off diplomatic relations. Cuban refugees, sponsored and equipped by the United States, attempted an unsuccessful invasion of Cuba in 1961 and, in January 1962, Cuba was expelled from the Organisation of American States.

The missile scare. Throughout 1962 there was a steady flow of Soviet arms into Cuba — paid for, ironically, by Cuban sugar. In October, in a dramatic announcement, President Kennedy declared that he had positive proof of the existence of Soviet missile bases in Cuba. He demanded their immediate withdrawal and stated that the United States navy would blockade Cuba in order to search all vessels bound for Cuban ports. (During the Napoleonic Wars, British insistence on the right to search American merchant vessels bound for European ports had led to war between the two countries in 1812. When faced with a similar threat to *its* safety in 1962, the American Government adopted the same policy — but in peacetime.) Fortunately the Russian ships turned back before reaching the American blockade, the bases were dismantled and the most serious crisis of the Cold War was ended.

THE FUTURE

The United Nations. In the crises of the post-war world high hopes have been pinned on the United Nations, but the United Nations could only be truly effective when the big powers with the veto on the Security Council chose to let it be so.

However there have been several important shifts in the Organisation since the height of the Cold War. The first is that the power blocs no longer act with the same unity of purpose. On the Western side NATO has been considerably weakened by internal divisions and, for instance, America's European allies showed no enthusiasm for her Vietnamese policies. SEATO and CENTO, the Western organised security pacts covering the Far East and the Middle East have ceased to function altogether.

In Europe the Warsaw pact shows greater superficial unity and mobilises much more powerful conventional forces. Yet here too the old united front against the West has been considerably weakened as the East European states show less and less enthusiasm for blind obedience to Russia. And beyond this the fundamental split in the Communist world between the Russians and Chinese remains as deep as it has ever been.

The other great change which has had considerable effects on international politics as a whole and on the United Nations in particular has been the increasing influence of the Third World. The neutralist states of Africa, Asia and Latin America can dominate the United Nations and its agencies when they can unite on an issue. Although far behind the big powers militarily and technologically they do have considerable moral power with which to pressurise the big powers and they can play one off against another. Moreover in certain areas, of which by far the most important is oil, they have certain economic sanctions in their control as well.

Oil and the Power of the Producers. One of the most significant aspects of the post-war world has been a growing awareness of the deep divide in terms of nutrition, medical treatment, education and almost all measures of material well-being between the industrialised nations and the poorer, developing countries of the Third World. Although the latter came gradually to control the majority of the seats at the United Nations and although they make up some two-thirds of mankind, they remain deeply dependent on the rich countries for economic and technical aid, for supplies of all but the simplest consumer goods, and for markets for their own exports — mostly foodstuffs and other raw materials.

However by the 1970s a world shortage of a number of primary materials emphasised the complementary dependence of the industrialised states on the basic producers. The most important of all these primary products and the most critical in political and economic terms was oil.

In 1972–3 America felt the bite of an oil-shortage and it became apparent for the first time that the country was no longer self-sufficient in this key product. Russia was able to supply her own needs and new areas of supply such as Nigeria were opening up, but the major source of supply for the industrialised world was the Middle

East. In 1973 the Saudi Arabians made it plain that they would use their control of the largest reserves in the world to pressurise the Western world to take a more favourable view of Arab policies. Meanwhile the other Arab and non-Arab (for instance Iran) members of the Oil Producers and Exporters Conference were taking a greater share of the oil companies profits, or in some cases nationalising the companies outright. They were also forcing a general increase in the price of oil.

These policies were intensified as a result of the 1973 Arab–Israeli war. The Arab states immediately reduced output and demanded dramatically higher prices for their oil products. For a while America was boycotted altogether and other states, such as Japan, were forced to make pro-Arab statements in order to secure their vital supplies of oil.

The results of this crisis were far-reaching. The Arab states not only flexed their muscles politically, but the vast incomes they derived from oil exports made them a potent force in the world investment market. The rise in oil prices produced a world-wide inflation which ironically hit the other Third World countries hardest of all. Meanwhile it also meant huge balance of payments deficits for major importers such as Britain. OPEC's action also served as a stimulus to countries such as Britain to develop their own energy resources more vigorously. However it was clear that for several decades to come at the very least the oil producers would wield considerable power in world affairs.

International co-operation. Despite the apparent failure of collective security and the development of a Cold War between East and West, there are a number of important fields where international co-operation has been most marked and most successful. In the Antarctic, where international agreement bans the establishment of military bases, there has been much co-operation in scientific research. This sharing of information reached its peak during the International Geophysical Year in 1958, not only in the Antarctic but in many other scientific projects in other parts of the world. The success achieved by the many specialised agencies of the United Nations is another important example of the great progress that can be made for the betterment of mankind when the nations of the world choose to co-operate rather than to compete.

In the belief that the cause of world peace would be assisted by informing people of these successes, the General Assembly of the United Nations instituted 1965 as International Co-operation Year and used it to publicise throughout the world the work of the countless organisations that are already striving for world peace through international co-operation. These include such bodies as the International Red Cross, the World Council of Churches, many volunteer service schemes, the Colombo Plan and the host of UN Specialised Agencies such as UNICEF, WHO, FAO, and UNESCO. One hope for world peace may be provided by the emergence of a 'third force' to balance the opponents in the Cold War but the prospects of permanent world peace are more likely to be strengthened if the nations and peoples of the world can show their determination to work together in these ways so that all may eventually enjoy freedom from want and freedom from fear.

FIG. 30 — Brezhnev, Secretary-General of the Soviet Communist Party talking to Nixon, then President of the United States of America, with the aid of an interpreter.

NOTEBOOK SUMMARY

POSTWAR WORLD

1. The Atlantic Charter — its aims
2. The United Nations — its chances of success
3. The peace treaties — note the danger signs

THE PROBLEM OF GERMANY

1. Allied policy
   Agreement at Yalta
   Russian attitude — result
   Western attitude — result
2. Berlin Blockade
   Russian action — reason
   Western action — result
   Significance for international relations
3. Two Germanies
   Emergence of West Germany
   Emergence of East Germany
   International significance — note Germany and Berlin

EUROPE DIVIDED

A. *Eastern Europe*

1. Iron Curtain
   Meaning
   States included
2. Hungary — Revolt in 1956 — attempt and failure
   Czechoslovakia 1948 and 1968
   International importance
3. Successful resistance
   Finland
   Austria
   Greece and Turkey — note western attitude and aid
   Yugoslavia — reason for success — result

B. *Western Europe*

1. Marshall Aid
   What was it and who accepted it?
   Formation and importance of OEEC
2. Political co-operation
   Reasons for it
   First steps — Benelux, OEEC
   Council of Europe — importance
3. Military co-operation
   Reasons for it
   NATO — formation — membership
   American attitude and participation
   EDC — reasons for the proposal and for its failure
   WEU — terms and importance

4. Economic co-operation
   EEC — stages of establishment
   members
   terms and aims
   British attitude — rejection — membership
   Divisions in EEC
   EFTA — formation and membership
   compare its position with EEC
   International significance of economic co-operation

THE FAR EAST
1. China — significance of communist success
2. Korea
   Postwar situation and problems
   Korean War — reason
   United Nations attitude and action
   significance of Chinese intervention
   Peace
   Importance of war
3. Indo-China
   Postwar situation and problems
   Withdrawal of France
   Problems of independence
   American Intervention
   Communist victory
   Effect in Asia
4. Bandung Conference
   Reasons for it
   Importance

THE MIDDLE EAST
1. The Arabs
   Features of Arab world
   Importance of Arab world
   Arab League — reasons for formation
   weaknesses
2. The Jews
   Palestine — British problems
   reasons and results
   United Nations decision
   Palestine war — international significance
3. Egypt, Israel and the Suez Canal
   British withdrawal from Canal Zone — reasons and results
   Middle East defence — Western attitude
   Arab attitude
   Formation of Baghdad Pact — note
   change to CENTO
   Egypt and the West
   Israeli-Egyptian war — reasons
   Anglo-French attitude and action

United Nations action — international significance
4. Eisenhower Doctrine — its terms and significance
5. Six Days War and its aftermath.
6. War of 1973 and aftermath
   Position of Israel

PEACEFUL COEXISTENCE
1. Changed international relations after 1953 — reasons
2. Nuclear weapons — importance in international relations
3. Disarmament — problems and progress
4. Space race — its importance
5. Coexistence — reasons for change of Russian policy
   meaning of Russian policy

LATIN AMERICA
1. Involvement in Cold War
2. Cuba
   Emergence of Castro
   Relations with U.S.A.
   Relations with U.S.S.R.
   Missile scare — chief features
   international significance

PROSPECTS FOR THE FUTURE
1. Failure of collective security — reasons and results
2. East against West — reasons for hostility and results
3. The 'Third World'
   what is it?
   what are its aims?
   what power does it have?
4. International co-operation
   Examples of success
   Significance

WORDS TO KNOW
The following words used in this chapter need to be understood. Most of them have been explained in the text but all of them should form part of a history student's vocabulary. Make a list in the back of your notebook, with meanings, of those words which are new to you. Learn these and use them in your essays:

Brinkmanship, coup, Cold War, defence perimeter, detente, Fascism, humanitarian, isolationist, mediation, peaceful coexistence, rehabilitation, referendum, sanctions, satellite States, stalemate, strategic, subjugation, subsistence farming.

BOOKS TO READ OR CONSULT
Boyd, A. *An Atlas of World Affairs*, London, Methuen, 1962.
Catchpole, B. *A Map History of the Modern World*, London, Heinemann, 1974.

Crowley, D. *The Background to Current Affairs,* London, Macmillan, 1973.

Higgins, H. *The Cold War,* London, Heinemann Educational Books, 1974.

Higgins, H. *Vietnam,* London, Heinemann Educational Books, 1975.

QUESTIONS FOR ESSAYS OR DISCUSSION

1. (a) How has the U.S.A. pursued an 'internationalist' policy since 1945?

   (b) Discuss any *one* tension spot where the U.S.A. is involved, outlining the reasons for U.S. involvement.

2. Suggest reasons for the 'Cold War' between the U.S.S.R. and the Western Allies since 1945. Then explain the issue in *three* main international clashes that have occurred between these two power blocs since 1945.

3. (a) Explain the different attitudes of Russia and the West to Germany after World War II.

   (b) Show the importance of Berlin in international relations since 1945.

   (c) Describe the emergence of two Germanies since 1945 and explain the international importance of this development.

4. Describe steps taken towards closer political, economic and military co-operation in western Europe since 1945. What has prompted these developments and what success have they achieved?

5. By an examination of the main events in *either* the Far East *or* the Middle East since 1945:

   (a) Indicate, with reasons, the two chief areas that have been involved in international disputes.

   (b) Choose *one* of these areas and carefully describe the events that have occurred there.

   (c) Examine the importance for international relations of the events in the area you have described.

10

NEW NATIONS IN AFRICA AND ASIA

COLLAPSE OF COLONIALISM

The maps on pages 226 and 227 indicate the extent of the colonial revolution that has swept the world in the years following World War II. Over two-thirds of the world's people in more than fifty different countries have taken their places among the free and independent nations of the world. By 1965 there were thirty-seven independent States in Africa where in 1945 there had been only four, while in Asia the number had grown from fourteen to thirty-two. The emergence of Afro-Asian nationalism and the corresponding retreat of European colonialism is one of the most important developments in modern history (see page 218).

Colonialism under fire. The reasons for European imperialism have already been fully examined in Chapter One (see pages 15 to 20). There can be no doubt that, in many cases, the native people in these colonies were exploited and unjustly treated by their European masters. In many areas raw materials and cheap native labour were used to benefit distant shareholders in European cities while local living conditions remained primitive in the extreme. The justice of these criticisms of colonialism cannot be denied but those who condemn it as 'the rule of injustice, oppression and exploitation' ignore, or conveniently forget, the other side of the picture.

It is a well established truth that 'nothing is wholly good or wholly evil', and European imperialism has brought advantages as well as disadvantages to colonial peoples. Well-known names such as Livingstone and Schweitzer have their counterparts in the lives of thousands of unknown missionaries, civil servants and settlers who have devoted their lives to the advancement of native welfare far from the comfort and security of their European homelands. The building of roads and railways, the establishment of mines, factories and commercial agriculture, the development of education and health services and the introduction of a money

F<small>IG</small>. 31

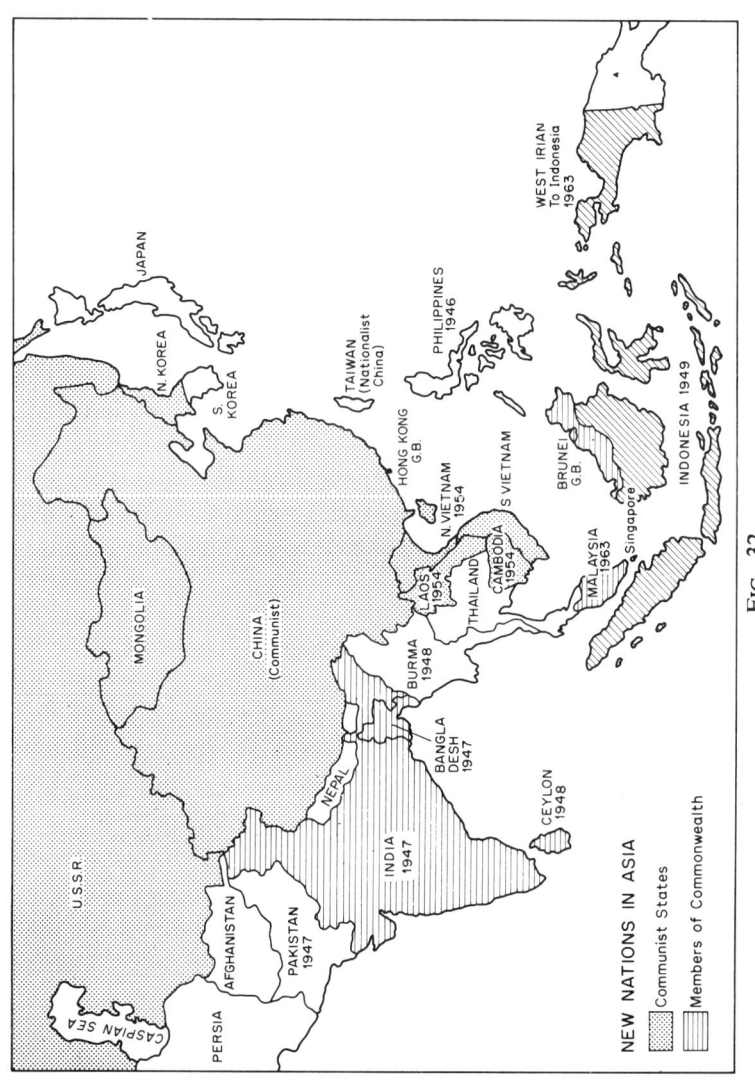

FIG. 32

economy have brought benefits to the ruled as well as to the rulers. Even President Nkrumah of Ghana, a bitter critic of colonialism, recognised that Ghana achieved independence, 'with all the machinery of a modern State'. Many other newly independent nations have received equal, if unrecognised, benefits from their former European masters.

An inevitable process. The loyalty of colonial troops in World War II provides ample evidence that colonialism was not regarded as 'wholly evil'. But colonialism contained within it the seeds of its own destruction and its decline in the postwar world should not be regarded as the eclipse of the nations of Europe but rather as the inevitable emergence of the nations of Africa and Asia. In our society a dependent baby is transformed into an independent adult in eighteen years. If the period of training is open to argument, there can be no disputing the end result. When the process of growth is regarded as a partnership between parents and children the transition from adolescence to adulthood is generally smooth, but in other circumstances the passage may well be a stormy one. If the emergence of new nations can be viewed in the same light, much of the bitterness and recrimination associated with it can surely be avoided.

EMERGENT NATIONALISM

Between the wars most of the colonial Powers paid more attention to keeping law and order in their territories than to the needs of the people under their control. However, in some areas, notably in British Africa and India and the American controlled Philippines, considerable political progress was made. In India and many of the British African colonies local government was increasingly placed in the hands of the native people, while in the Philippines the date for independence had been announced. Much less progress towards local participation had been made in Dutch, French, Belgian, Portuguese or Spanish colonies which were, in general, governed directly from The Hague, Paris, Brussels, Lisbon and Madrid.

Higher living standards. In the villages of Africa and Asia the coming of the white man had little impact. Illiteracy, poverty, and disease remained virtually unchecked and life continued very much as it had done for centuries. The new European towns and plantations, established to promote trade or to develop industry, presented a different story. Here the local people made direct contact with the benefits of European civilisation. The white *sahib* or *bwana,* who never worked with his hands, whose house was light and airy and kept by native servants, whose food and clothing was plentiful and rich, made a tremendous impression on the simple folk among whom he lived. Although local living standards improved they seldom approached those of the foreign rulers. It is little wonder that resentment increased as colonial people sought a greater share of the wealth which they helped to create.

The favoured few. Even today almost ninety per cent of the people of Africa are illiterate and the percentage is little lower in Asia. Apart from the work of Christian missionaries little attempt was made by many colonial governments to educate the native inhabitants before 1945. Schools were provided for the children of civil servants and European settlers but few places were available for any others. The small number of boys who received higher education, often at English or American universities, were the sons of the rich and members of a privileged class. As they studied the origins of the American Revolution or the struggle between the English Parliament and the Stuart kings at Oxford or Harvard they could not fail to consider the position of their own people. It was these young men who, in the years after 1945, were to become the leaders of the independence movements.

Declining white prestige. The western victory in Europe in 1945 was a defeat in Asia and Africa. In Asia Japanese armies had shattered the myth of the invincible white man, while in Europe the fall of France, the defeat of Italy, and the German occupation of Belgium and the Netherlands freed their colonies from foreign control. After peace was restored, returning soldiers brought with them a host of new ideas, new experiences, and above all, a new confidence in themselves and in the future. Africa and Asia had come of age. There could be no return to former days. It was time to move forward and not to look backward. The goal — independence.

BACKGROUND TO INDEPENDENCE

British Colonies. Policies of colonial Powers, like attitudes of parents, vary considerably. When the British Government accepted Lord Durham's report on Canada in 1839 it recognised that, sooner or later, the colonies of white settlement would have to be granted self-government and independence.[1] In the present century, following the lead given by Lord Lugard in Nigeria, a similar policy has been adopted towards British colonies in Africa

[1]Following his investigation of rebellions in Canada in 1837, Lord Durham recommended that, with some reservations, Canada should be given responsible government or, in other words, the right to elect its own parliament and to control its own affairs.

and Asia. By the operation of a 'dual mandate' or 'double trust', Britain has accepted the responsibility of developing societies, 'able to participate in the life of the modern world as communities in their own right'.[1] With eventual independence assured, differences have centred on its timing and have seldom been long-standing. Accordingly, the majority of British colonies have had relatively smooth passages from dependence to independence, and have elected to retain membership of the Commonwealth of Nations.

French colonies. The French endeavoured, by a policy of assimilation, to make Frenchmen out of Africans. From 1946 French colonies elected their own representatives to the National Assembly (or Parliament) in Paris and every effort was made to make France and her colonies so interdependent that they would never wish to separate. This policy was not altogether successful. The French had lost control of Indo-China after a bloody and ruinous war and repeated the experience in Algeria. Most of the rest of the African colonies attained independence peacefully but only a minority wished to maintain membership of the French Community, the equivalent of the British Commonwealth.

Other countries. Different policies have been adopted by other countries, generally with less success. Belgium placed the chief emphasis on economic progress and native welfare. But the high standards achieved in these fields did not compensate for the complete lack of political training which contributed to the chaos in the Congo in 1960. Dutch, Spanish and Portuguese policies have shown least concern for the welfare and advancement of their colonial peoples. Limited social reform, widespread poverty, and the absence of any training in government contributed to the Indonesian hatred of their Dutch masters and to the collapse into civil war of such territories as Angola and Portuguese Timor when the colonial government withdrew in 1975.

PROBLEMS OF INDEPENDENCE

Government. The most immediate problem facing newly independent nations is the problem of government. Even the most elementary study of history shows that there is no easy solution to this age-old problem. The pharaohs of Ancient Egypt, the city States of Ancient Greece, and the emperors of Rome all faced problems similar to those which exist in Africa and Asia today. But these ancient governments had the advantage of good communications and loyal and experienced civil servants. The expulsion of European officials, the isolation of thousands of primitive

[1]Mair, L. P., *Native Policies in Africa*, London, 1936, page 12.

villages, and the lack of schools and facilities for higher education have made the task of government immeasurably more difficult in many new nations. Tribal rather than national loyalties, religious feuds, language differences and racial strife have helped to make the picture even more complex and the task of government correspondingly more difficult. Yet, without ordered government, progress of any sort is impossible.

Many emergent nations have attempted to introduce Western democratic methods of government, often with the same consequences as occurred in the new nations of eastern Europe after World War I when they were faced with serious economic and political problems which they could not solve (see page 56). The system of government known as Western democracy has evolve ' slowly through the centuries before reaching its present form. Attempts to apply the system to newly independent nations are fraught with difficulties because it must develop from within and cannot be imposed from without. Such attempts frequently result in apparent failure as a single man, or a single party, or the army emerges to provide the strong government essential for rapid development.

Strong government of the sort we have just described carries with it its own dangers, the most serious of which is the loss of individual rights and liberties. But these results should not be regarded as final, for unless government is acceptable to the governed, sooner or later trouble occurs. With increasing maturity, the new nations of the world will adapt their political institutions to meet their changing needs and to serve their changing purposes.

Economic problems. Closely related to, and largely dependent on, the problem of government is that of economic development. Like the young man who leaves school too soon, many new nations find great difficulty in surviving in a highly competitive world. Many are small, both in size and in population, lacking in raw materials and technical skill, and largely dependent on the continuation of foreign aid. Without money it is impossible to build dams, power stations, railways, harbours, mines, and factories, but without these things it is difficult to earn the money needed to provide them! Foreign aid can break this vicious circle although, while such assistance can rightly be regarded as a responsibility of the more developed countries, it will not and should not provide the complete answer to economic problems.

The economic problems of these countries are complicated by the unequal distribution of the world's wealth. No nation in Asia or Africa enjoys a standard of living comparable with that of New Zealand, Australia, the United States, Canada, or the nations of Western Europe, where almost two-thirds of the world's wealth is shared by only fifteen per cent of the world's people. Meanwhile, the conquest of tropical diseases through the advances in medical science, and the prevention of floods and droughts through the advances in civil engineering, are contributing to a rapid increase in world population, especially in the underdeveloped areas of Africa and Asia where the death rate was formerly so high.[1] To prevent the aggravation of existing social problems rapid economic development is essential to provide employment for this increasing population.

Social problems. Improved health services and better facilities for education are the most pressing social needs in most newly independent countries. That the high standard of living in western countries has been a gradual development is of little interest to hungry, unhealthy and illiterate people in the mid-twentieth century. They want results and they want them quickly. Unfortunately, the generally low per capita income (i.e. earnings per head of population) resulting from the low level of employment and economic development allows governments much smaller returns from taxation than are available in western countries. Again, foreign aid, partly through the specialised agencies of the United Nations (see pages 85-6), is making an important contribution to raising living standards, although here also the ultimate solution must depend on increased production and increased national wealth.

International problems. The close relationship of problems facing new nations should now be apparent, as should the need for foreign aid. This latter need creates problems in itself. Although the futility of expecting military support in return for economic aid has been proved, few foreign nations, Eastern or Western, are willing to spend large amounts on foreign aid without the prospect of some return for their investment. Western aid is open to the charge of neo-colonialism (or a new attempt at imperialism) from some, while communist aid is regarded by others as part of a policy of infiltration (or peaceful extension of communist influence). Faced with the problem of securing both international recognition and foreign aid, it is hardly surprising that most of the emergent nations prefer to follow a policy of *neutralism,* refusing to become committed to either side in the Cold War struggle. In these circumstances the appearance of Pan-African, Pan-Asian and Afro-Asian movements is only to be expected. They will allow strength through unity in the

[1] World population is increasing at a *net rate* (i.e., surplus of births over deaths) of approximately 130 per minute. 'Every time the clock ticks there is another mouth to feed.'

international sphere without involving commitment to East or West.

Case studies. The following short studies provide examples of the ways in which different nations have approached independence and have attempted to deal with the problems associated with its achievement. Although backgrounds and methods differ the basic problems remain the same.

GHANA

Early history. Portuguese explorers, feeling their way along the west coast of Africa in the late fifteenth century, were the first Europeans to make a landfall on the Gold Coast. The quantity and purity of the precious metal which they found there not only gave the area its name but also quickly encouraged trade rivalry. In the sixteenth century, and especially during the reign of Queen Elizabeth, English sailors became keen competitors for west African gold and for the equally valuable cargoes of Negro slaves for the growing market in North and Central America. Until the British abolition of the slave trade in 1807 and the final abolition of slavery on the American continent in 1888 (in Brazil) there was little change in the pattern of economic activity. Apart from Christian missionaries there was also little European settlement in this area, labelled 'the white man's grave' because of its steamy jungles, malarial swamps and tropical fevers.

A British possession. Increasing European trading and colonising activity in the surrounding areas and the withdrawal of Dutch and Danish competitors in the mid-nineteenth century prompted the British Government to annex the coastal strip, known as the Gold Coast Colony, in 1874. Although this strip contained the established forts and trading posts, its successful development depended on the peaceful co-operation of the powerful Ashanti tribes of the interior. When this was not forthcoming, British troops were used to suppress civil war and rebellion and, in 1902, the area was annexed. At the same time a protectorate was established over the Northern Territories which lay between Ashanti and French North Africa. In the meantime, treaties with France and Germany had settled the eastern and western boundaries with the Ivory Coast and Togoland. When Germany was defeated in World War I, Togoland was divided between Britain and France as a mandate of the League of Nations (see page 75) and, from 1922, British Togoland was administered as part of the Gold Coast Dependency.

Economic and social development. The introduction of cacao (cocoa) in 1870, by a Negro labourer returning to the Gold

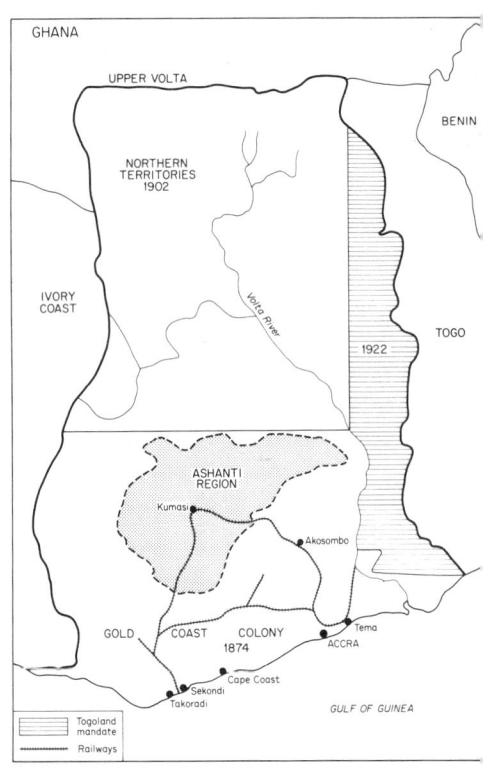

FIG. 33 — Kwame Nkrumah, first Prime Minister of Ghana.

FIG. 34

FIG. 35 — African tribal chiefs gather on the lawn of Parliament Building in Accra as the first Ghana Parliament assembles on the day the state of Ghana was born, 6 March 1957.

Coast from working in a Spanish cocoa plantation on nearby Fernando Po (see map, page 226), had a remarkable effect on the economy. By 1920 local farmers, with almost no European assistance, were exporting more than 100,000 tons of cocoa beans a year. Gold mining also continued to flourish as new areas were opened up and, next to cocoa, gold was the most important export. By 1919 the building of railways had begun, more than 1,000 miles of roads had been laid, twenty government and over four hundred mission schools had been established and a Government technical school and training college had been opened in Accra, the capital city. But much remained to be done. With the return of world peace, Sir Gordon Guggisberg was appointed as Governor of the Gold Coast and, under his able and inspired leadership in the next decade, the foundations were laid on which future independence could be built.

BACKGROUND TO INDEPENDENCE, 1919-1939

At the end of World War I, the Gold Coast was a Crown Colony still in the early stages of political development. The following chart shows that, at the upper end of the administration, the Governor remained in direct control of affairs while, at the local level, the role of the African chiefs was paramount. It is important to study the composition and selection of the Legislative Council, because it is here that the gradual development of self-government took place as the unofficial members became elected representatives and finally held the majority of the seats in a Parliament which had the right to make laws and levy taxes. This pattern of political development is well proved and has been applied to the great majority of British colonies.

Indirect rule. In keeping with established colonial policy a determined attempt was made to preserve the authority of the chiefs in local affairs. While this policy achieved considerable success in the primitive tribal areas of the Northern Territories, it was much less acceptable in the coastal areas where the increasing wealth and education of many Africans greatly reduced the authority and prestige of the chiefs. Educated city dwellers — largely away from tribal customs — saw indirect rule as an attempt to keep 'illiterate, pro-British chiefs in office',[1] and sought the rapid replacement of tribal institutions by parliamentary government. This clash between education and tradition would have been difficult to avoid, but the increasing education of the

[1]Bourret, F. M., *Ghana, The Road to Independence, 1919-57*, London, O.U.P., 1960, page 47.

chiefs during the 1930s and 1940s saw the more general willingness of the two groups to work together to win for Africans a greater share in the government of the colony.

Political progress. Restrictions made necessary by the war produced a growing awareness among many Africans of the importance of politics, and during the 1920s there developed a strong demand for increased African representation in the Legislative Council. In 1925 a new constitution established a system of provincial councils made up of the head chiefs in each area. These councils not only provided valuable training in government, but also elected six chiefs to the Legislative Council. A further three African members were elected to represent the coastal towns of Accra, Cape Coast, and Sekondi. Although the official majority in the council remained, the introduction of elected members was an important step on the road to self-government. Unfortunately this progress was not matched in the Civil Service, where forty posts were held by educated Africans in 1939, only thirteen more than in 1925. Plans to remedy this situation were disrupted by the outbreak of war.

One crop economy. Cocoa, the foundation of Gold Coast prosperity in the 1920s, almost brought ruin to the dependency in the 1930s. The cocoa crop was produced on more than a quarter of a million small farms (averaging less than five acres) by African farmers who had paid little attention to drainage, pruning, and disease — especially the growing threat from 'swollen shoot' which endangered millions of trees in the 1930s. The position was made more serious by the heavy indebtedness of the cocoa farmers, who frequently borrowed on their next season's crop at exorbitant rates of interest (native moneylenders seldom charged less than 50 per cent interest!), and by the confusion over landownership as increasing land values encouraged the sale of unsurveyed tribal holdings.

When the world cocoa price dropped from £50 to £20 a ton in 1931, Gold Coast revenue dropped sharply from £4 million to £2 million because cocoa beans accounted for more than three-quarters of the country's export earnings. The dangers of a one-crop economy were brought home to both the farmers and the Government and, during the thirties, the Department of Agriculture encouraged diversified farming by the introduction of bananas, citrus fruits and coconuts and the increased production of rubber and palm oil.

Government policy. There is considerable truth in the charge that the Gold Coast Government gave too little help to agriculture and marketing during this period, but to suggest that this was the

Gold Coast Government, 1920

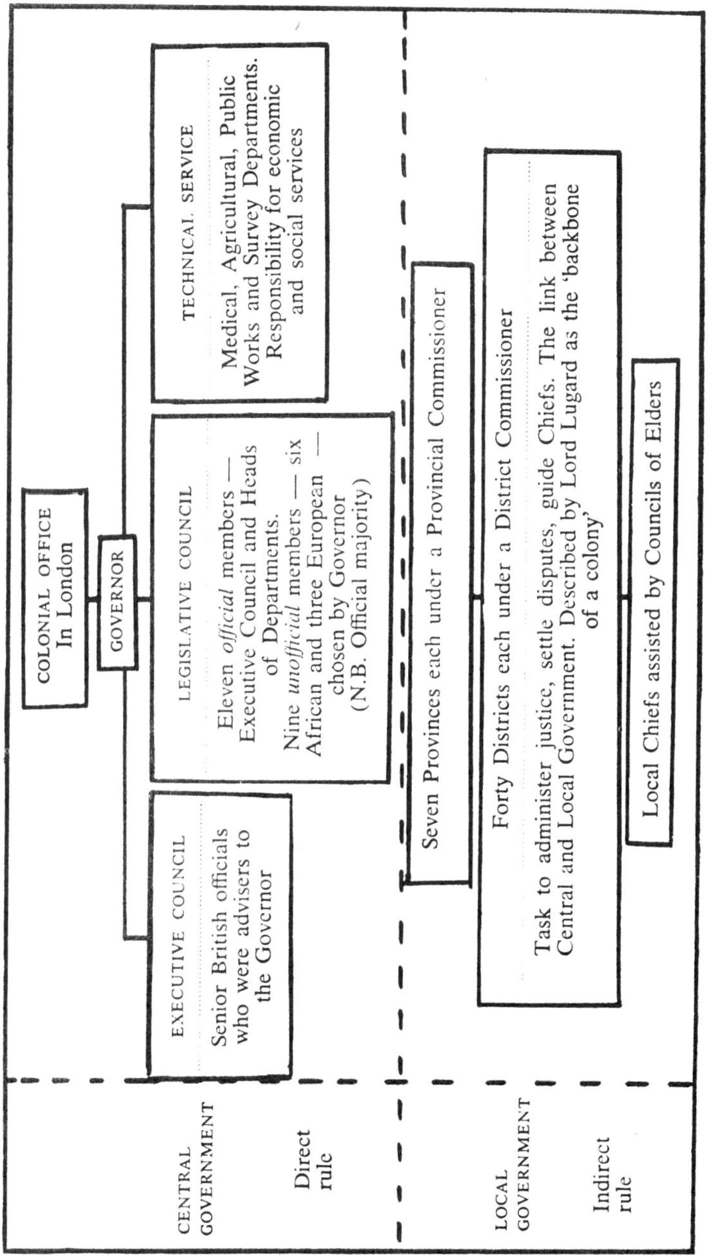

COLONIAL OFFICE In London

GOVERNOR

TECHNICAL SERVICE

Medical, Agricultural, Public Works and Survey Departments. Responsibility for economic and social services

LEGISLATIVE COUNCIL

Eleven *official* members — Executive Council and Heads of Departments.
Nine *unofficial* members — six African and three European — chosen by Governor (N.B. Official majority)

EXECUTIVE COUNCIL

Senior British officials who were advisers to the Governor

Seven Provinces each under a Provincial Commissioner

Forty Districts each under a District Commissioner

Task to administer justice, settle disputes, guide Chiefs. The link between Central and Local Government. Described by Lord Lugard as the 'backbone of a colony'

Local Chiefs assisted by Councils of Elders

CENTRAL GOVERNMENT

Direct rule

LOCAL GOVERNMENT

Indirect rule

sole reason for the difficulties of the cocoa farmers would be a dangerous and unwarranted simplification of an extremely complex problem. It is undoubtedly true that, under European controlled plantation methods, more efficient farming and marketing would have resulted. However, British colonial policy favoured the retention of land ownership by the native African people who, in their turn, often resented and opposed Government attempts to control marketing and to combat disease. As a result, agricultural progress was slower than in some other colonies, but in compensation for this, the African people still owned the land they farmed — even if individual titles were often confused!

Mining. By 1939 the Gold Coast was the third largest producer of diamonds and manganese in the world and also an important exporter of gold. Unfortunately these industries brought little profit to the colony because they were owned and controlled by European firms, and as the taxation on mining profits was paid in their respective countries the only revenue received in the colony was from the payments for mining concessions, usually a nominal amount. Repeated protests from African leaders brought no action from the Government for fear of discouraging foreign investment.

The world depression showed the danger of dependence on an export economy (where export earnings provide most of consumer goods and capital equipment) and African leaders began to press for the establishment of secondary industry in the colony. They argued that many imports, notably soap, foods and timber, could be manufactured or processed locally and so save valuable overseas earnings. Accusations that the government was more concerned with protecting British industry than with strengthening Gold Coast economy had no effect and it was not until the coming of war that encouragement was given for the development of local industries.

Economic progress. The determining factor for economic development was the amount of Government revenue as, until the passing of the first Colonial Development and Welfare Act in 1940, it was British policy for each colony to finance its own development.[1] During the prosperous twenties progress was rapid — 250 miles of railways, 3,500 miles of roads, and a large artificial harbour at Takoradi, as well as large expenditure on education and health. Throughout the interwar period Africans resisted the introduction of direct taxation (or income tax) so

[1] Between 1940 and 1960 Britain spent over £250 million through Colonial Development and Welfare Acts of which over £4 million was spent in the Gold Coast.

that, when Government revenue was halved in 1931 following the fall in cocoa prices, economic development and public works virtually stopped. In conclusion it can be said that the considerable political progress made during this period was not matched by similar progress in the economic field. The reasons for this may be attributed to insufficient Government assistance, the attitude of African farmers, and the impact of the world depression. Yet economic progress compared more than favourably with that in many other parts of Africa, both colonial and independent. Independent Liberia, with half the area and half the population, had only one twentieth of the revenue of the Gold Coast in 1939.

Progress in education. For Governor Guggisberg, who saw education as the 'keystone of progress', the opening of Prince of Wales College at Achimota (near Accra) in 1927, at a cost of over £600,000, was a personal triumph. This school, which catered for up to 800 pupils from kindergarten level to teachers' college, aimed to 'retain and improve the best things in Africa and couple them with the best things Western' and rapidly became one of the finest educational institutions in the whole of Africa. However, in general, education remained the responsibility of the various missions which, since the mid-nineteenth century, had played a major role in the improvement of native welfare. In particular the missionaries were chiefly responsible for stamping out many pagan practices, notably cannibalism, for the development of written languages by their work of Bible translation as well as for their establishment of schools and hospitals. Although only one child in seven was at school by 1939, the Gold Coast Government was spending almost ten per cent of its annual revenue on education, compared with eight per cent in Great Britain in the early sixties.

Social development. Although Korle Bu Hospital in Accra was the best in West Africa in 1939, there had been much less progress in health improvement than in education. Tuberculosis, leprosy and malaria were all increasing and, in all except a few areas, poor diet, bad sanitation and impure water remained the chief causes of disease. One baby in five died in infancy and almost half the children born in the Gold Coast died before reaching high school age. While these figures were typical of many parts of Africa, there were areas, notably the Belgian Congo, where much greater improvements had been made. Progress was hindered by shortages of trained doctors, nurses and dispensers, by lack of money, and by the ignorance and superstition of those living in the more remote areas.

ACHIEVEMENT OF INDEPENDENCE

During World War II, Gold Coast troops served with distinction in both the African and the Burma campaigns and many soldiers learned new clerical and technical skills which they were anxious to employ when they returned home. In the Dependency itself, the shortage of British officials gave opportunities for an increasing number of Africans to assume positions of responsibility, while the demand for raw materials for the war effort, especially minerals, greatly stimulated production. At the same time, because of wartime shortages, local industry finally received the encouragement that had been denied it before 1939. With the fall of France and the virtual closing of the Mediterranean, West Africa became strategically important as a supply base for the Allied desert campaigns so that the harbour at Takoradi and the airport at Accra were modernised and enlarged.

The war showed the tremendous loyalty of Britain's African people. Over 70,000 Gold Coast soldiers served overseas, out of a total population of only four million, and gifts and loans totalling more than £1 million were made to the people of England after the Battle of Britain. The war also gave the people of the Gold Coast a new confidence, new skills, a wider outlook, and a determination to achieve rapid political, social and economic progress in the immediate future. The stage was set for change.

Kwame Nkrumah. In 1947 Kwame Nkrumah returned to the Gold Coast after an absence of twelve years in the United States and England. A former student of Achimota, the thirty-eight-year-old Nkrumah was now a graduate of two American universities and he quickly assumed a leading position in the recently formed United Gold Coast Convention, the focus of opposition and discontent in the colony. Heavy cocoa losses (from swollen shoot disease) and the shortage of imported goods brought economic dissatisfaction to a head early in 1948. Serious rioting and looting broke out in Accra and rapidly spread to other towns. Nkrumah and five other leaders of the U.G.C.C. were arrested. Shortly after his release, Nkrumah resigned from the U.G.C.C. and formed his own political party, the Convention People's Party, pledged to secure independence and threatening, if necessary, 'strikes, boycotts, and non-co-operation based on the principle of absolute non-violence' — Nkrumah's policy of 'Positive Action'. Following further strikes and lawlessness, Nkrumah was again imprisoned in January 1950, but by this time he had established himself as the leader of the common people in the struggle for independence.

Meanwhile, the British Administration had been proceeding

with its plans for eventual independence. The war did not cause a change in British policy, it simply speeded it up. In 1942 the first two African members were added to the Executive Council. In 1945 elected African members were given the majority of seats on town councils. In 1946 the Gold Coast became the first colonial territory in Africa to have a majority of elected African members on its legislative council. Yet many argued that progress was still not quick enough. During the war urban population had been increased by the migration of many partly educated villagers to the towns. These new arrivals considered that they were too well educated to accept labouring or manual jobs but they were insufficiently educated to gain clerical positions. As in so many other countries, they became the leaders of discontent and were quick to follow any leader who would promise them a better future.

Self-government. An all-African committee was appointed by the Government in 1949 to consider the question of full self-government and, as a result of its recommendations, a new constitution was introduced in 1951. This provided for a Legislative Assembly (or Parliament) in which seventy-five of the eighty-four members were to be elected, and an Executive Council in which eight of the eleven posts were to be held by African Ministers elected from the Assembly. In the elections which followed, the Convention People's Party won a sweeping victory and, in a momentous decision, the Governor ordered Nkrumah's release from prison and invited him to take his seat in the Assembly as Leader of Government Business, a title that was changed to Prime Minister in 1952. (Although in prison, Nkrumah had been elected one of the members for Accra.) Following an overwhelming victory for the C.P.P. at the 1954 elections, Prime Minister Nkrumah formed the first fully African Cabinet which became fully responsible to a new Legislative Assembly entirely elected by the people of the Gold Coast. Self-government had been achieved. Independence was only a matter of time.

Republic of Ghana. In 1956 the British Government announced that the Gold Coast would receive its independence if this was favoured by a majority of the electors at the next election. One month later independence was assured when Dr Nkrumah and his party again won a sweeping victory at the polls and, on March 6, 1957, the Gold Coast became the independent Dominion of Ghana.[1] The independence of Ghana was a turning point in the history of the continent which 'electrified Africa south of the Sahara and became the nerve centre of African

[1] Ghana takes its name from an ancient North African kingdom.

nationalism'.[1] Three years later, Ghana became a republic with Kwame Nkrumah as its first president. Having now clearly demonstrated its complete independence, the new republic elected to remain a member of the Commonwealth of Nations.

INDEPENDENCE — PROGRESS AND PROBLEMS

One of the chief problems facing the newly independent country was the lack of national unity. The demand for independence had created a unity which lacked any real depth and, when the goal had been attained, old differences quickly re-emerged. One of the most serious of these was between the traditional authority of the chiefs, which had been protected under the British policy of 'indirect rule' (see page 235), and the power of the Central Government in Accra, which rested on the support of the new town working classes who had largely lost their tribal interests and loyalties. The picture was further complicated by regional and tribal jealousies, notably between the people of Ashanti and those of the southern coastal areas.

When Ghana became a dominion in 1957 its constitution included provision for an Assembly and a House of Chiefs in each region to satisfy the feelings of local people. But Nkrumah was anxious to develop a strong national government and, since Ghana became a republic in 1960, the powers of chiefs and regional assemblies have steadily declined in favour of those of the Central Government in Accra. Together with many other African and Asian leaders, he believed that his country must be organised and united if it is to solve the problems that face it both at home and abroad.

Democracy on trial. Ghana began independence equipped with all the machinery of British democracy. Whether the new State could operate the machinery remained to be seen (refer to page 231). From 1957 the more conservative opponents of the Convention People's Party joined together to form the United Party (representing mainly the chiefs and the city professional classes who regarded themselves as the rightful rulers of the country). Unfortunately Ghana had had no experience of a two-party political system on the British model. Under colonial rule, the African members of the Legislative Council had invariably voted together, so that with the coming of independence there was no understanding of a system which allowed the government of the country to pass from one party to another in accordance

[1]Hodgson, R. D. and Stoneman, E. A., *The Changing Map of Africa,* van Nostrand, New York, 1963, p. 89.

with the results of elections. For this reason the opposition resorted to the only methods it knew for opposing — threats of violence, non-co-operation and even regional agitation for self-government or secession.

Faced with the problems of disunity and increasing opposition, President Nkrumah adopted a policy of suppression. Political opponents were imprisoned for criticising the Government, foreign critics were deported, press censorship was introduced to prevent newspaper attacks on Government policy, and emergency measures allowed anyone considered 'a danger to public safety' to be detained without trial for up to five years. In 1961 it became a punishable offence to insult President Nkrumah either in speech or in print. When the Anglican Bishop of Accra criticised the Young Pioneer Movement (the youth wing of the C.P.P.) in 1962 because of its 'godless teachings' in such slogans as 'Nkrumah is our redeemer' and 'Nkrumah can do no wrong', he was promptly deported. (He returned after three months following worldwide criticism of the deportation.)

In 1964, following a 99.9 per cent vote of approval in a national referendum, Ghana officially became a one-party State. At the same time the President was given the power to dismiss Supreme Court judges if he considered this to be necessary 'in the national interest'.[1] The methods of conducting the poll were strongly criticised by foreign observers who alleged that, in many areas, the 'no' voting boxes were sealed or even removed from the polling booths. The absence of a single negative vote from many parts of Ashanti known to be strongly opposed to Dr Nkrumah would appear to support this contention.

Justification? 'Britain bequeathed to Ghana a black House of Commons, not in the belief that it was ideally suited to Africa, but because it was the only form of government she knew'.[2] As Ghana sought 'an African way of doing things', it was almost certain that its political system would be changed. How it would be changed was much less certain. Yet, as early as 1957, Nkrumah gave some indication of future trends, in the preface to his autobiography, when he stated that, 'Even a system based on social justice . . . may need backing up, during the period following independence, by emergency measures of a totalitarian kind . . . What other countries have taken three hundred or more years

[1] The protection of judges from political interference is regarded under British democracy as an essential safeguard of the rights and liberties of individual citizens. This protection was only secured after a long struggle.

[2] Sampson, A., *Common Sense About Africa,* Gollancz, London, 1961, page 92.

to achieve, a once-dependent territory must try to accomplish in a generation, if it is to survive. Unless it is jet-propelled, it will lag behind and thus risk everything for which it has fought'.

In common with the leaders of many other emergent nations, Nkrumah saw the restriction of liberty as the price that must be paid for rapid and positive action. To many observers his position as President and 'Father of the Nation' seemed more secure than that of most other African leaders. Yet in February 1966 he was deposed by the army during his absence in China. The new military regime was led by General Ankrah. In 1969, however, elections were called and Dr Busia, a former United Party opponent of Nkrumah, led his Progressive Party to victory. However the country's basic economic problems remained unresolved and a further military *coup* in 1972 brought the National Redemption Council to power. In the same year Nkrumah himself died after six years in exile in Guinea.

Economic problems. On page 231 we examined the economic problems that face developing nations. How is Ghana handling the difficult problem of financing the all important development of its industries, communications, and power resources? Direct taxation, which accounts for more than half of Government income in Great Britain, provides barely one-tenth in Ghana. This is hardly surprising in a country where the average annual income is little more than £150, but it forces the Government to seek other sources of revenue, principally from duties on imports and exports. Unfortunately, revenue from this quarter remains very dependent on the cocoa crop which still provides sixty per cent of the nation's export earnings. Since independence, the Government has attempted to stabilise prices by the establishment of a Marketing Board but world price fluctuations and the dangers from crop disease are a constant threat to this principal source of Government income.

Foreign aid. Because of these financial problems, foreign aid is essential for large-scale enterprises. The most important of these, and the central feature of the second National Development Plan introduced in 1957, were the Volta River Project and the Tema harbour scheme.

Nkrumah attached great importance to these prestige projects. The deep-water harbour was supposed to improve trade facilities and Tema was finally opened in 1962. The dam would provide power for a giant aluminium smelting works based on local bauxite deposits. A 250 mile lake was built up behind the dam and the project cost some £65 million of which half was raised abroad. Unfortunately the scheme did not produce the economic development on the scale which had been hoped for and the country remained heavily dependent on the fluctuating world price for its basic export commodity — cocoa.

Cocoa did well in the 1950s and this allowed Nkrumah to carry out his basic programme of school, hospital, and road building. On the other hand the decline in the cocoa market in the 1960s contributed significantly to Nkrumah's downfall. Sixty per cent of the population were engaged in agriculture and most cocoa was grown on the small plots of the peasant landowners who turned away from him as prices fell.

Despite the heavily agricultural nature of the country it had come to rely on food imports. After Nkrumah's fall the major emphasis in development plans has been to increase local food production and diversify exports into such things as tropical fruits and to encourage small local agricultural-based industries rather than major prestige projects.

Social services. Improvements in education, health, housing and general welfare services must accompany economic progress. Since 1961 primary education has been free and compulsory and mass literacy campaigns in the more remote villages have taught thousands of adults to read and write. The University of Ghana (1948) and the Kwame Nkrumah University (1952) play an increasingly important role in training future leaders although a large number of Ghana's students still attend overseas universities. Educational advances have helped to develop a greater awareness of health hazards, especially impure water and poor hygiene, while the network of Government and mission hospitals and clinics is being steadily expanded. The bringing of electricity and piped water to the villages helped to improve health standards. Nevertheless the towns, and especially Accra, attracted more and more young people despite the shanty towns and the lack of jobs. To relieve the acute housing shortage in many towns, a special Government Housing Corporation was responsible for developing sites and building houses for sale. The many fine schools, hospitals and public buildings in Accra and other cities provide striking evidence of the steady development of social services.

International relations. The clearly stated aims of Ghana's foreign policy are to follow a policy of non-alignment in world affairs and to work for the independence and eventual unity of all African States. Ghana was the second African state to recognise Communist China and the first to send troops under United Nations command to the Congo in 1960. It has also concluded trade agreements with the Soviet Union and other communist States as well as with Britain and the members of the Common Market. Similarly, Russian as well as Western financial aid, although on a smaller scale, has assisted with the nation's economic development. In the General Assembly of the United Nations, Ghanaian delegates seek solutions that will advance world peace and refuse to commit themselves to the unconditional support of any great Power.

As the first African State to secure its independence, Ghana was much in the spotlight of world affairs in the postwar era. Although small in size and population its achievements have been considerable and it has provided an inspiration to millions of African people who have since won their independence. However after the fall of Nkrumah the country has played a smaller part in world affairs and has been more concerned with its problems of internal development.

INDONESIA

Early history. Although the Portuguese were the first white men to visit the islands of the East Indies, arriving in search of spices in the early sixteenth century, they had been preceded by almost three hundred years by traders from India, China, and Arabia. These early eastern traders had spread the influence of Islam throughout most of the islands and the Portuguese, who had recently expelled the Moslem Moors from their European homeland, saw themselves not only as traders but also as crusaders against Islam. They failed in both their objectives and by the end of the century had been driven out, except for a single trading post on the small island of Timor, where they have remained until 1975. Dutch traders quickly replaced the ousted Portuguese, with much greater success. The Dutch were traders, not crusaders, and the commercial empire which they founded survived for more than three hundred years, apart from a short period of British rule during the Napoleonic Wars.

Dutch possession. The Dutch East India Company, formed in 1602, controlled the trade of the islands for almost two hundred years, and not until the start of the nineteenth century did the Dutch Government take direct control. During this period of 'company rule' other European rivals were driven out and Batavia (formerly Jakarta), in the northwestern corner of the island of Java, became a flourishing trading city. The influence of the company was restricted almost entirely to Java, with limited contacts in the Celebes and the Moluccas (see map, page 247), and it was not until the Dutch Government took control that Dutch influence spread to the other islands of the group, notably Sumatra. Consequently, many parts of the East Indies were only under direct Dutch control for much less than a hundred years.

In most areas the Dutch were neither welcome nor accepted and local resistance was seldom overcome without much fighting and loss of life.

Economic and social development. As in most primitive and medieval societies the peasant farmers of Indonesia paid taxes to their overlords with a share of their crops.[1] This system was extended by the Dutch who fixed strict production quotas for the crops they required. These included not only the spices for which they had originally come but also new crops which they introduced, especially coffee, tea and tobacco. During the nineteenth century this method of crop production, known as the 'Culture System', was considerably extended, with serious effects on local agriculture. Because the Dutch Government had a complete monopoly it was able to buy what it required at low prices and sell it on European markets at a handsome profit. At the same time local merchants and traders were steadily forced out of business by increasing numbers of Chinese who were encouraged by the Dutch.

By the start of the present century almost the entire wealth of the country was in the hands of foreigners — the ruling Dutch and their Chinese middlemen. Although the Culture System was gradually replaced by private investment after 1870 the position of the peasant was not improved. In order to pay the new taxes which replaced the compulsory crop quotas the peasants had to grow increasing amounts of export crops for the Dutch market. The new system also encouraged the development of large Dutch-owned plantations, and many peasants, whose families had farmed their land for centuries, were forced by economic necessity to give up their holdings and to become plantation labourers. Nor did

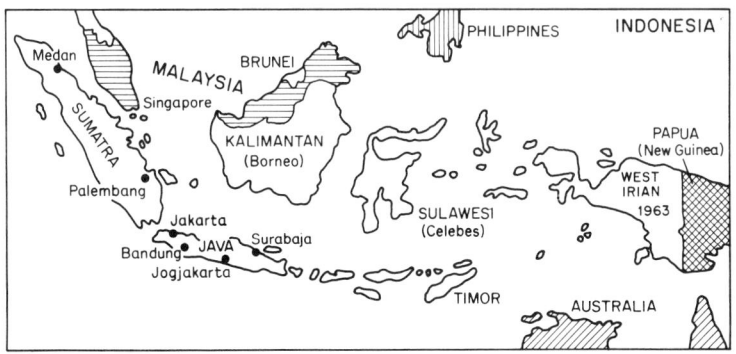

FIG. 36

[1]Indonesia means literally the East Indian islands.

the Dutch Government make any serious attempt to provide for the education or welfare of the Indonesian people. While the Netherlands prospered and grew rich from its East Indian trade, the native inhabitants remained without schools or hospitals or any of the improvements needed to advance their standard of living.

BACKGROUND TO INDEPENDENCE, 1900-39

When the Dutch assumed control of the country they found a well established system of government which, like the Norman feudal system in England, was based largely on the tributes and loyalties given by local rulers to their superiors. As the following chart shows, the Dutch superimposed their own highly centralised system of government on top of the existing pattern so that the decisions of the Governor-General in Batavia could be passed directly down a chain of officials until they reached the remotest villages. A system of this nature allows little hope of, or training for, eventual self-government.

Partnership policy. In the late nineteenth century a growing humanitarianism was apparent in Holland as in many other European countries. At the same time as Britain was seeing the need for a 'dual mandate' in tropical Africa (see page 230) the Dutch introduced a new 'ethical policy' in the East Indies. This policy was based on the belief that, as the Netherlands had grown rich at the expense of the Indonesian people, they had a moral duty to repay what was regarded by many as a 'debt of honour'. Unfortunately, this was easier said than done. Although this change in Dutch policy brought both social and political reforms in the Indies it came too late and was too limited in its scope to check the growing spirit of nationalism which appeared about the turn of the century. Dutch supporters of partnership envisaged the development of a new, westernised Indonesian society closely integrated with the Netherlands. They failed to appreciate that this might not be an acceptable solution to the people of Indonesia.

Political progress. Increasing Government concern for education, health, and general peasant welfare meant an increase in the number of decrees, directives, and regulations that were passed down the chain of officials to the village headman. Although this increased the participation of local people in the work of government, it did not increase their responsibility. At all levels Indonesian officials came to be regarded as representatives of the Dutch Government rather than of their own people. In 1918 the Dutch established a partly elected, partly appointed, national advisory council — the *Volksraad.* This was the first concession of any sort that the Dutch Government had made to the desire of the Indonesian people to share in the government of their country. In the early 1920s similar councils were set up in some of the towns and in regencies and provinces but they could do little more than offer advice to the local Dutch official, who usually acted as chairman. Even the enlargement of the Volksraad to provide for an elected Indonesian majority in 1925 was of little consequence because the Governor-General was not compelled to accept its decisions.

Plantation agriculture. We have already seen that, since the encouragement of private investment from 1870, there was a rapid expansion of the plantation system. One important effect of this was the rapid spread of Dutch influence to other islands in the group, especially Sumatra which, by 1900, had over half of the plantations. The new partnership policy had little effect on this economic pattern. Until the 1930s wealthy Dutch planters, producing rubber, tea, coffee and sugar, were the aristocracy of

East Indies Government, 1900

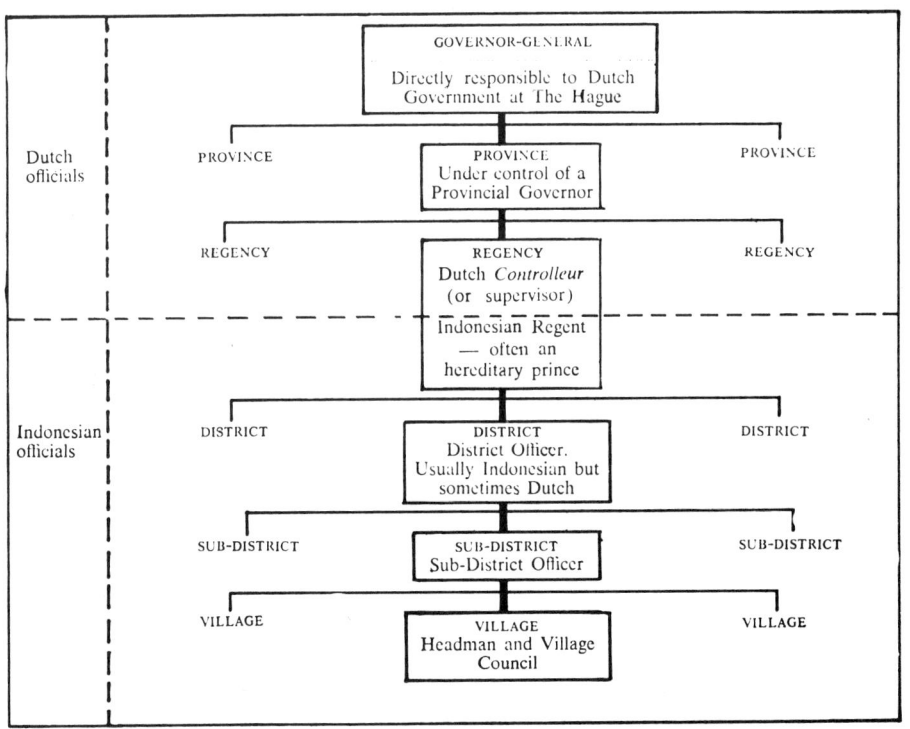

the Indies in much the same way that Southern planters had dominated the economy of the American cotton lands before the Civil War. But the Indonesian plantation workers, who returned to their villages when their labour contracts were completed, found they could no longer fit into the life of the village. The plantation system helped to destroy the traditional pattern of life by creating a new, unsettled, landless class which no longer fitted easily into Indonesian society.

From 1929, falling world prices for the major plantation crops struck at the prosperity of both the planters and the country as a whole. Although few Indonesians had a direct share in the profits of the plantations, the general development of the islands depended to a great extent on the profits of the export trade. The economic situation remained serious throughout the thirties but the Dutch Government failed to take any effective positive action.

Village life. The chief impact of the partnership policy was in the villages where the bulk of the people lived. New commercial crops were introduced to supplement the staple rice crop, irrigation and land clearance schemes were developed, and roads and communications were improved. The results were most unexpected. Because of the rapid increase in population (see below) these economic improvements did not produce the expected rise in living standards, while the breakdown of isolation and the introduction of commercial crops helped to destroy the pattern of village life that the Government was trying to preserve.

Furthermore, the increasing Government control and taxation that was necessary to accomplish these improvements was frequently resented by villagers. The presence of Government officials in the villages made the villagers realise that they were being controlled not by their headman and council but by some outside force. Thus they were forced to realise that they belonged to a society that was much larger than their own local area. Without realising it, the Government, by extending its activity at the village level, was creating a national awareness that had not previously existed.

Trade and industry. The expansion of plantation agriculture and the development of oil wells and tin mines led in turn to the growth in size of the main cities, especially Batavia, Bandung and Surabaja in Java, and Medan in Sumatra. Large foreign firms, mainly Dutch, British and American, provided the finance for this industrial and commercial expansion and the general trading of the cities was almost entirely in the hands of Chinese merchants. But with the breakdown of isolation and the increasing shortage of rural land, many Indonesians moved into the cities during the years between 1900 and 1939. They mostly found unskilled or semi-skilled employment, working long hours for low wages and living in slums on the outskirts of the cities.

Population pressure. Between 1860 and 1940 the population of Java increased from twelve million to almost fifty million. Much of this increase was due to the remarkable success of the Dutch health programme introduced in the early years of this century. Better housing and improved hygiene caused a sharp decline in the death rate. Once again the new policy of partnership had unforeseen effects. Although migration to other islands was encouraged, it did little to relieve the mounting pressure on the farmlands of Java, where by 1939 there were almost three-quarters of a million new mouths to feed every year. The Dutch Government was not able to find a solution to this problem of continuing poverty in the midst of prosperity. Nor was it able to provide sufficient doctors or hospitals for the growing needs of the people. By 1940 there were still only two doctors for every 100,000 people.

Education for the few. The change of Dutch policy after 1900 resulted in the first serious attempt to provide education at the village level, but with only limited success. By 1940 only one Indonesian child in six was attending school and then only for three years in most cases. Little attempt was made to cater for secondary and higher education which, when available, was in the Dutch language and in Dutch schools which charged high fees. Even those fortunate enough to benefit from further education found few opportunities for employment as the higher positions in the Civil Service were reserved for the Dutch. The lack of opportunities for higher education was one of the chief weaknesses of Dutch colonial policy. Few technicians or civil servants were trained for the future. The failure to use the abilities and to satisfy the ambitions of those who were trained may be considered an equal tragedy, typical of the majority of colonial policies.[1]

Growing nationalism. By the start of this century conditions in Indonesia favoured the appearance of organised opposition to Dutch rule. Commercial exploitation of Indonesian peasants and plantation workers, declining living standards, the breakdown of village isolation, the emergence of an underprivileged town working class, and the resentment of frustrated intellectuals contributed to the growing dissatisfaction. Educated Indonesians were also quick to appreciate the significance of events in Asia in the years between 1900 and 1914. Japanese success against Russia in 1905, the first of an Asian against a European nation (see page

[1] Compare with British policy in the Gold Coast. See page 236.

130), and the emergence of strong nationalist movements in China (the Kuomintang — see page 171) and India (the National Congress — see page 278) encouraged them to hope for similar developments in their own country.

The struggle of the Dutch to free themselves from Spanish control in the sixteenth century was a lesson not lost on Indonesian students who studied in Dutch universities three centuries later. Inspired by the success of their own masters and by more recent Asian examples, opposition groups quickly appeared and adopted nationalist aims with complete independence as their ultimate goal. Initially, these groups made no attempts at violence, but the success of the Russian Revolution led to the formation of an Indonesian Communist Party in 1919. When the reforms of 1925 failed to increase the power of the Volksraad (see page 249), communist-inspired strikes and demonstrations broke out. The Dutch Government promptly outlawed the Communist Party and other nationalist societies and executed, imprisoned or exiled thousands of those involved in the incidents. Although nationalist societies continued to grow during the 1930s they lacked any real unity and made little progress in the face of determined Dutch opposition.

ACHIEVEMENT OF INDEPENDENCE

Within weeks of the bombing of Pearl Harbour (see page 135) Japanese troops landed in Indonesia and the Dutch forces quickly surrendered. Indonesian offers of co-operation to defend the island had been rejected by the Dutch Government which had refused to train and arm local troops. Any hope of future co-operation with the Dutch was thus destroyed by Indonesian bitterness at their inability to defend their homeland. For the next three and a half years the islands of Indonesia were occupied by the Japanese. Although the new invaders were fellow Asians, the Indonesians soon found that they had simply exchanged one taskmaster for another — and a much more brutal and demanding one at that. Strong nationalist feeling was fostered not only by the Japanese anti-Dutch policy, which included the replacement of the Dutch language by Indonesian and Japanese, but also by their harsh suppression of all opposition, their seizure of crops and food supplies and their removal of thousands of Indonesians to forced labour camps in other parts of South-East Asia. Long before the Japanese withdrew in 1945 they were detested even more than the Dutch.

Of even greater significance was the training in self-government that the Indonesians received as a result of the Japanese occupation. The rapid expansion of the Japanese Empire (see page 135) created a serious shortage of officials to control newly won areas and of troops to defend them. In Indonesia many positions formerly held by Dutch civil servants were given to Indonesians and, in an attempt to win popularity, important national leaders, notably Sukarno and Hatta, were given important Government posts. Meanwhile, under Japanese officers, Indonesians received the military training and weapons denied them by the Dutch.

Japanese withdrawal. By the start of 1945 the war was going badly for Japan and plans were drawn up for the creation of an independent Indonesia in the event of a Japanese withdrawal. However, Indonesian leaders were not prepared to accept independence as a gift from the departing Japanese. The remaining Japanese were defeated by the troops they had trained and, on August 17, 1945, Dr Sukarno became the first President of the new Republic of Indonesia.

President Sukarno. The new President had been an important figure in the nationalist movement since the 1930s. Born in east Java in 1901, the son of a schoolteacher, Sukarno was one of the favoured few who was able to receive a first-class education in Dutch schools, and he graduated from the Bandung Technical Institute as a civil engineer in 1925. Almost immediately he turned his full attention to politics and in 1928 became chairman of a federation of political parties aiming at complete independence for Indonesia. In the following year Sukarno was arrested and charged with planning a rebellion, for which he was imprisoned until 1931. Further political activity after his release resulted in a second term of imprisonment from 1933 until the arrival of the Japanese in 1942. Although his collaboration (or co-operation) with the Japanese was later decried by the Dutch in their attempt to discredit him, he had already become a firmly established national hero and the natural leader of the new republic.

Fight for freedom. With the defeat of Japan, Dutch troops returned to regain control of the islands for the Netherlands. Neither the Dutch nor the Indonesian forces were strong enough to defeat the other and, after a year of intermittent fighting, Dutch troops were withdrawn on the understanding that a self-governing United States of Indonesia would remain linked to the Netherlands. Neither side accepted this solution as final and, in July 1947, the Dutch began a 'police action' involving a full-scale military attack and a naval blockade. United Nations intervention produced a temporary truce and an agreement that the future of those areas occupied by the Dutch would be decided by plebiscite.

The continuation of the Dutch blockade, in violation of the terms of the truce, led to a serious shortage of food and medical supplies in Indonesia. The ease with which the Chinese communists overthrew the government of Chiang Kai-shek during 1948 (see page 179) prompted their Indonesian comrades to take advantage of these serious internal problems to attempt a similar *coup* in September. Although the attempt was defeated, it weakened the country further and provided another opportunity for Dutch intervention to 'restore law and order'. In a surprise Dutch attack on the republican capital of Jogjakarta, President Sukarno and other leaders were captured. For the next six months the Indonesian people waged a guerilla war against the Dutch, by which time stalemate had again been reached, with the Dutch holding the major cities while the rest of the country was in the hands of the local people.

Freedom at last. By mid-1949 world opinion and even public opinion in the Netherlands was strongly opposed to the Dutch Government. Pressure from other Asian nations, led by India, and from the Government of the United States, persuaded the Dutch to give way and, in December, they agreed to evacuate the islands. The Republic of Indonesia, first proclaimed in 1945, was now established as an independent nation. The people of Indonesia had won their *Merdeka,* or freedom. They had fought for it in the same way as the people of America had fought for independence from Britain almost two centuries earlier. In each case the struggle for freedom hastened the development of a strong national spirit where it had previously not been marked.

The Dutch tragedy. Although the economic exploitation of previous centuries continued to some extent after 1900, there was also a sincere attempt made by the Dutch to improve the conditions of the Indonesian people. In fact, the 'ethical policy' (see page 248), which used Dutch funds to improve Indonesian living standards, was considerably in advance of the colonial policies of most other nations at the beginning of this century.[1] Unfortunately, as we have seen, the policy was not fully implemented, some of its results were unexpected, and it made no adequate provision for higher education or for training in self-government. The Dutch set out to help the people of Indonesia instead of helping them to help themselves. This was the Dutch tragedy in Indonesia.

INDEPENDENCE — PROGRESS AND PROBLEMS

Although the widespread acceptance of Islam and the general hostility to the Dutch were significant unifying forces, there were

[1]Compare with British colonial policy at this time. See pages 238-9.

equally important forces pulling in the opposite direction. One of the chief of these was the strong traditions and local loyalties that were typical of most of the islands of the group. This regional outlook was coupled, in many areas, with resentment and suspicion of Java which had always held a dominant position. The other serious political problem facing the new nation was the wide gap that existed between the small group of highly educated and partly Westernised leaders and the great mass of largely illiterate peasants. The Dutch policy of encouraging Chinese rather than local merchants had prevented the development of a middle class which has played such an important role in the advancement of democracy in Western nations. Even within the educated group there was no real unity, because communists, nationalists, Moslems, and soldiers favoured different approaches to the problems of government. The immediate need was for strong leadership. It has been provided by President Sukarno — the 'Father of the Republic'.

Failure of Parliament. In the troubled years between 1945 and 1950 when elections were impossible, President Sukarno appointed a Central National Committee to help him govern. This committee included representatives of all the main political groups in the country. When the Dutch withdrew, Sukarno agreed to the committee's request that a Cabinet responsible to it rather than to the President should be appointed. The first national elections to replace the committee with a properly elected parliament were held in 1955, suggesting that the development of a parliamentary system similar to that in Great Britain would only be a matter of time. Unfortunately, the election results vividly reflected the national disunity as no party secured a quarter of the seats. For the next two years weak coalition governments played political leapfrog until, in 1957, the President announced that 'liberal Western-style democracy', based on the control of the Government by Parliament, had failed to satisfy Indonesia's needs.

'Guided democracy'. Indonesians have a long tradition of reaching agreement through discussion and compromise before decisions of importance are made. Sukarno believed that this method, well established at the village level, should also be used at the national level in preference to what he called the 'fifty per cent plus one' type of democracy common in Western countries.[1] To secure a Government representing true national opinion he

[1] It should be remembered that, although many decisions in Western democracies are based on bare majorities, the success of democracy depends on (a) the full expression and consideration of minority views and (b) the acceptance of a majority decision as binding on all.

made two suggestions. First, he recommended the appointment of a Cabinet responsible to and chosen by the President which would include members of all the major political parties. Secondly, he proposed the appointment of a National Council, under his chairmanship, which would be representative of all groups in the country — village, commercial, religious and regional interests as well as purely political parties. A somewhat similar plan had been envisaged by Mussolini when he had attempted to establish a Corporate State in Italy in the 1920s and 1930s but the outbreak of war prevented its fulfilment.

President and army. The Indonesian Communist Party was the largest and best organised Communist Party in Asia outside China, claiming a membership of two and a half million. Sukarno's proposals for a truly representative national Government automatically involved the inclusion of communists. To many Indonesians, especially in Sumatra and Sulawesi (formerly the Celebes), this was unacceptable and serious revolts broke out in these areas in 1958. The suppression of these revolts by the army introduced an important new element into the already complex political situation. By its suppression of the revolts the army showed its support for the President and at the same time greatly increased its own prestige. But without the support of Sukarno, the army would not be nearly so powerful, as he was the national hero — the symbol of revolution and independence. For his part, the President had gained a valuable ally, but he could also not afford to ignore its strength as a possible opponent. This partnership between army and President had become the most important factor in Indonesian politics.

'Democracy with leadership'. Confident in the support of the army, Sukarno proceeded with his plans and, in 1959, abolished the constitution and introduced his proposals for 'guided democracy'. Future national policy would be decided by the President, in consultation with the Cabinet and the National Council, and would be based on the *Pantja Sila,* or Five Principles — belief in God, humanity, nationalism, representative government and social justice. (Compare with Sun Yat-sen's Three Principles in China on page 170.) After 1959 the Government of Indonesia was largely in the hands of Sukarno who was elected to the Presidency for life in 1963. With the abolition of emergency government in 1963 his need for army support became less apparent but the army remained an important, if less obvious influence in politics as events of 1965 were to prove.

Sukarno has been variously condemned by his opponents as a dictator and a communist. There is evidence to support both points of view. The limited authority of the Cabinet and the National Council can be interpreted as a disguise for his personal dictatorship, while his insistence in recognising and consulting the Communist Party can be used to justify the opposing view. On the other hand it can be claimed that, in the words of the motto on Indonesia's national symbol, Sukarno produced 'Unity in Diversity'. In its early years of independence Indonesia neither became a one-party State nor a military dictatorship. In spite of opposition in some quarters, Sukarno, somewhat in the manner of an Indonesian Mussolini, with his great ability as an orator and his magnetic appeal to the mass of the people, did guide the destiny of the nation through the critical period of the struggle for independence and its aftermath. The problem was that this style of leadership could not supply long-term solutions. The country faced massive economic problems and Sukarno's pro-Communist policies frightened away foreign investors while his attempts to divert attention from internal failure by confrontation with Malaysia (see page 259) only increased the economic difficulties.

Economic difficulties. In spite of the great wealth of its natural resources, especially the soil, Indonesia remained one of the poorest countries in Asia. The bulk of the population — over seventy per cent — are still peasant farmers living at subsistence level on farms of two acres or less, growing rice for their immediate needs, and bartering their surplus crops for goods which they cannot produce themselves. Because of the high fertility of the volcanic soil and the abundant rainfall and sunshine, there is little starvation as in much of Asia, but there is also little economic progress. It was easy to blame the Dutch for this but the *sandang pangan*, or good standard of living, promised by Sukarno in 1945 was not achieved. In fact in many areas, and especially in the cities, problems increased as the inflation of the postwar years tightened its grip on the national economy.

Foreign aid. Industrialisation could have solved many of the nation's problems but few factories were built since the coming of independence, and five-year plans, so effective in many other countries, achieved little success in Indonesia. As in many developing countries, foreign aid is essential for economic progress, but Indonesia was not an attractive field for foreign investment. The expulsion of the Dutch resulted in the departure of the majority of trained technicians and executives; the lack of higher education meant that there were insufficient qualified or experienced Indonesians to replace them; the seizure of Dutch businesses and plantations without compensation and the political instability of the country made foreign investors cautious and hesitant; and the fear that Sukarno was 'flirting with communism' made Western nations suspicious. Aid received through the Colombo Plan was used to meet immediate needs rather than to provide for the future, while much of the help from Russia and America was spent on armaments and on meeting the interest payments on the rapidly growing national debt.

Inflation. Progress can be measured in part by the increase in man's requirements as the luxuries of one age become the necessities of the next. Whereas a bamboo cottage, a single suit of clothes, a bamboo bed, a cow and a buffalo satisfied the needs of the prewar Indonesian peasant, his postwar counterpart hoped for much more. A brick house with a tile roof, a table, chairs, and other furniture, three suits of clothes, a bicycle and perhaps a radio, and education for his children, had become his basic requirements. In the cities the contrast was even more marked. The inability of the economy to supply sufficient consumer goods to meet this growing demand produced steadily rising prices and is an important cause of the serious inflation in Indonesia today.

A number of other factors helped to complicate the situation. Duties on imports and exports provided almost two-thirds of Government revenue and imports were therefore encouraged. But the heavy duties imposed on them helped to raise prices even higher and so further increase the cost of living. These imported goods had to be paid for from the country's export earnings, but fluctuating world prices for rubber, copra, oil, and tin have reduced these earnings in recent years. Yet the cost of imported manufactured goods was steadily rising. Overseas borrowing was needed to bridge the growing gap between spending and earning. Meanwhile, at home, although production was not expanding, the Government greatly increased the supply of money thus decreasing its value. When all of these factors are considered, it is little wonder that the cost of living in Jakarta trebled between 1957 and 1959, or that prices in some areas increased up to ten times in 1958–65.

Social services. In the new republic, education, so long denied, was eagerly sought after and the campaign against illiteracy was a remarkable success. Even while the war with the Dutch continued, high school students travelled from village to village teaching the people to read and write. UNESCO aid made possible the provision of cheap books and, with increasing literacy, there was a rapid increase in the circulation of daily newspapers, although these were controlled by a strict press censorship which prevented criticism of the Government. By 1965 literacy had been increased from the prewar level of seven per cent to an estimated sixty-five per cent, while four universities had been opened since independence. These universities did train the professional workers who were so urgently needed to overcome the desperate shortage of teachers, engineers and doctors. With the assistance of the World Health Organisation the attack on yaws, malaria, tuberculosis and other serious diseases began, but the general standard of health remained low and the shortage of hospitals was acute.

International relations. After the gaining of independence, Indonesian foreign policy fell naturally into two parts, separated by the increase in the personal power of Sukarno between 1957 and 1959. Until then the country followed a policy of strict neutrality in international affairs, seeing itself as the spokesman for the new nations of Africa and Asia, and taking the initiative in calling the conference at Bandung in 1955 (see page 210). After 1959 President Sukarno used foreign adventures to divert attention from increasing economic difficulties at home. In this he was not the first to seek remedies abroad for problems at home. Russia (page 97) and Japan (pages 127–8) are two other modern examples.

Confrontation. Mounting Indonesian threats against the continued Dutch control of West New Guinea culminated in its absorption as the province of West Irian in 1963 (see page 88). While there was general world sympathy for the Indonesian charge against the continuation of 'Dutch imperialism', few nations were willing to accept a similar charge against 'British imperialism' when the new State of Malaysia was formed in 1963. An attack on this relatively prosperous new State offered an obvious diversion from the growing inflation at home, especially as original plans for Indonesia had included the whole of Borneo and the Malayan peninsula! Commando raids, infiltration and trade boycott completely failed to destroy the new State, although the withdrawal of Singapore from the federation in 1965, while not basically the result of the policy of 'confrontation', was certainly an encouragement to its continuation.

In January 1965 Indonesia left the United Nations as a protest against the appointment of Malaysia to the Security Council (see page 81). Defection from the United Nations and the continuing policy of confrontation forced Indonesia away from the Afro-Asian nations and from Russia and the United States, and drew it closer to Communist China, the chief supporter of confrontation. In 1963 Subandrio stated that, 'Indonesia at present is deliberately neglecting her economy to concentrate on regaining her national unity.'

Counter-Coup. On October 1, 1965, a communist *coup* failed in an attempt to capture Sukarno's Government. Although many generals were kidnapped and assassinated, the army quickly restored order. In almost every Indonesian town communist buildings were burnt and communist slogans were ripped from hoardings and walls. The Communist Party, the largest in Asia after the Chinese, had suffered a devastating setback and a great many of its leaders were killed. A month after the *coup* Sukarno declared that those who wanted to eliminate communism in Indonesia were like a man who tried to bite an iron bar — 'eventually his teeth would be destroyed'. But Sukarno's attempt to blend nationalism, religion and communism in his policy of *Nasakom* had collapsed and his own ability to play factions off against each other with it.

At sixty-four years of age and in failing health, Sukarno was unable to resist the army officers who had put down the communist *coup*. The new Government was led by the vigorous General Suharto and Sukarno was progressively stripped of his powers and titles up till his death in 1970. More severe treatment befell his left-wing lieutenants such as Foreign Minister Subandrio who was convicted of treason, while many communist leaders were summarily executed. The large Chinese minority in the population suffered particularly badly in the anti-communist purge which the army encouraged.

Military Government. The new military Government proceeded to reverse the main strategies of Sukarno's policies. The purge of the left-wingers and the crushing of the mainly Chinese Communist Party was followed by a rapid reversal of foreign policy. As relations with Peking collapsed the new regime called off the confrontation and made every effort to win support in the West. In time Indonesia was able to resume her seat at the United Nations and Western economic aid and investment began to pour into the country.

With rich mineral deposits including oil and a highly productive agricultural system based on small farms, the country ought to be able to provide an increasingly good standard of living even allowing for the very fast growth in the population. The Japanese have been especially anxious to invest in the country and close trading links have developed with Australia.

The only current point of tension with Indonesia's immediate neighbours is in Timor, half of which was controlled by Portugal until the collapse of her colonial empire in 1975. The island consequently became a battleground between left- and right-wing factions and Indonesia was clearly tempted to seize the former colony herself.

Much more fundamental are the basic internal problems which Sukarno had failed to resolve. In particular the Chinese minority inevitably remains dissatisfied with its suppressed status and the growing middle class and intellectual élite are bound to press for more political rights.

EGYPT

Early history. The history of Egypt is almost as old as the story of mankind itself. For more than six thousand years the life-giving Nile has attracted to its banks people from the surrounding deserts, while the location of the Nile delta as a bridge between east and west and north and south has given Egypt an importance out of all proportion to its size or economic wealth. Western civilisation and the great religions of the modern world had their origins in the river valleys and deserts of the Middle East where, centuries before the birth of Christ, the Pharaohs had already established the greatness of ancient Egypt. However, by the seventh century B.C. Egypt was in decline and, in the two thousand years that followed, was conquered in turn by Assyrians, Persians, Greeks, Romans, Arabs, and Ottoman Turks. Almost three hundred years after the last of these invasions, Napoleon Bonaparte reached Egypt with a French army, but was forced to withdraw following the sinking of most of his fleet by Lord Nelson at the Battle of the Nile in 1798. The French occupation of Egypt was short but it was sufficient to bring Egypt into contact with the modern world.

Britain in Egypt. British interest in Egypt dates from the late nineteenth century. The opening of the Suez Canal in 1869 greatly increased the importance of the Red Sea route to the East and to the new lands of Australia and New Zealand. Since the withdrawal of the French, Egypt had been ruled by the Turks through governors, or *pashas*. In 1867 Ismail Pasha was granted the title of *khedive,* or viceroy, and rapidly made himself the virtually independent ruler of Egypt. By 1875 his personal extravagances and his ambitious plans for the westernising of Egypt had brought the nation's finances into such a desperate state that European investors were not prepared to invest any further money in the country. Even the sale of the Khedive's Suez Canal shares to Britain for nearly £4 million was insufficient to solve the country's financial problems.

Disraeli's purchase of almost half the canal shares gave Britain a much greater interest in Egyptian affairs but it did little to reduce the Khedive's financial embarrassment. By 1876 his debts totalled almost £100 million and an international commission was appointed to manage his affairs and to protect the interests of European investors in Egypt. Matters did not improve and, in 1881, the Khedive was overthrown by a military revolt. Following a French refusal to join forces, Britain occupied Egypt in 1882, restored the Khedive, and, under the leadership of Sir Evelyn Baring (later Lord Cromer), began the task of reorganis-

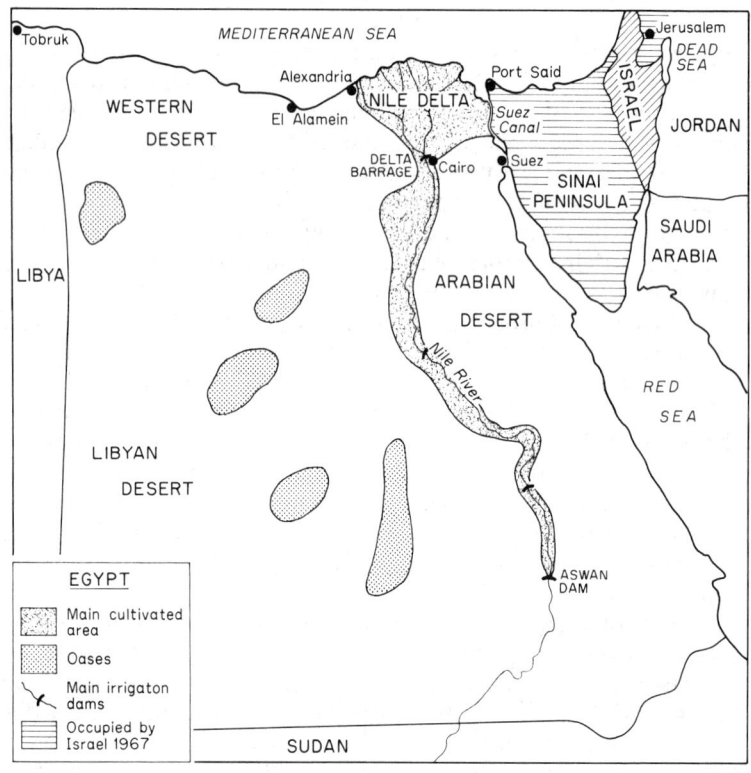

FIG. 37

ing the Government. Throughout this period Egypt remained nominally a Turkish possession, but when Turkey joined the Central Powers in 1914 it became a British protectorate.

Economic and social development. 'Egypt is the Nile and the Nile is Egypt.' Almost the entire population of Egypt lives within a narrow strip of land along the banks of the Nile. This strip is never more than ten miles wide and often only two. Realising the paramount importance of the Nile, Cromer concentrated first on controlling its waters to reduce flooding and to improve irrigation. In 1890 the delta barrage was opened and in 1902 the completion of the first Aswan dam brought similar benefits to upper Egypt. Modernisation of the larger towns was begun, some protection from moneylenders was provided for the peasants, and some improvements were made in public health. Much of the finance needed for these developments was provided from duties on cotton exports which, stimulated by the American Civil War, had grown steadily and almost doubled between 1890 and 1914. But social improvements were pitifully small and education remained almost entirely the privilege of the wealthy and of foreigners. Poverty was the greatest and largely unrecognised problem in the country.

BACKGROUND TO INDEPENDENCE, 1914-36
The ideals of racial self-determination (see page 52) which the statesmen endeavoured to implement at Versailles in 1919 were not lost on educated Egyptians. National feeling had been growing since the exile of Arabi Pasha in 1882, following an unsuccessful revolt, had made him a national hero. In 1919 a further revolt inspired by the *Wafd,* the Egyptian nationalist movement, demanded independence, and was only put down by the intervention of British troops. Its concern for the safety of the Suez Canal and the future of the Sudan prevented the British Government from agreeing to a complete withdrawal from Egypt but, in 1922, it granted independence with certain restrictions. To many Egyptians, and especially to the ardent nationalists, these terms were completely unacceptable. However, their wishes were not consulted as the ending of the protectorate was a British and not an Egyptian decision.

The British overlord. Although Egypt was now nominally independent under its own king, this independence was far from complete. The British Government remained responsible for the defence of Egypt and for the safety of the Suez Canal. It also retained the right to protect foreign interests and national minorities in Egypt and, in this regard, it informed other Powers that it would not allow any outside intervention in Egyptian affairs. Finally, Britain retained its controlling interest in the Sudan which had been jointly administered by the two Governments since 1899. Egyptian nationalists wanted British troops restricted to the Canal Zone in time of peace and the refusal of Britain to agree to this or to the evacuation of the Sudan remained a serious cause of dissatisfaction and resentment in Egypt.[1]

Political position, 1923. A constitutional monarchy was established in Egypt which left the greatest political power in the hands of the King rather than of Parliament. Although there was a Parliament of two Houses, the Cabinet was appointed by and responsible to the King, who also appointed almost half of the members of the Senate. The Chamber of Deputies was elected every five years by all adults but the elections were indirect, so

[1]British intervention in Egypt makes an interesting comparison with the activities of the United States in Latin America in the late nineteenth and early twentieth centuries (see pages 160-62).

Egyptian Government, 1923

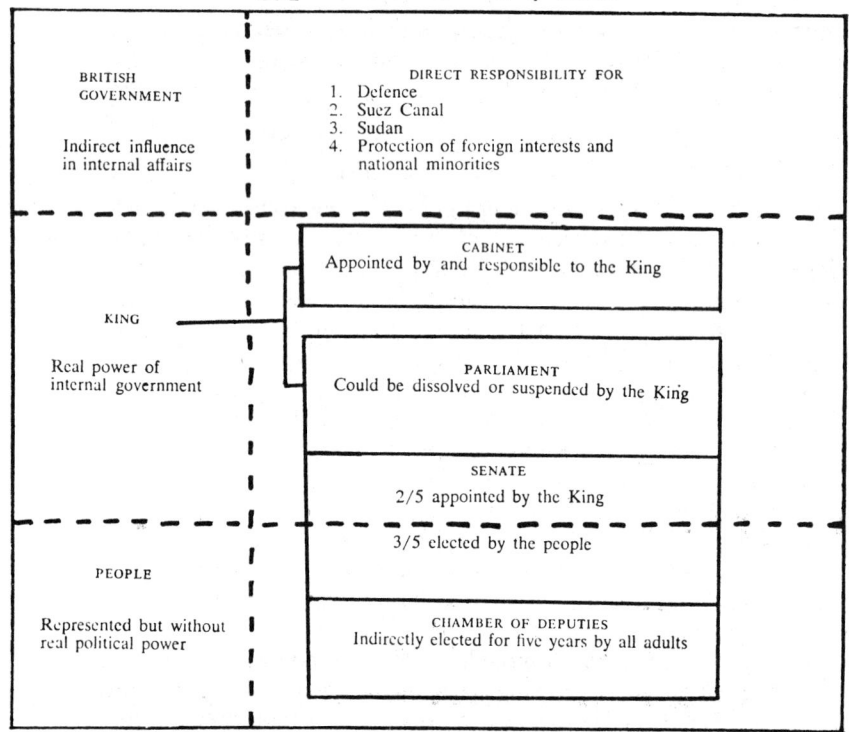

BRITISH GOVERNMENT Indirect influence in internal affairs	**DIRECT RESPONSIBILITY FOR** 1. Defence 2. Suez Canal 3. Sudan 4. Protection of foreign interests and national minorities

CABINET
Appointed by and responsible to the King

KING

Real power of internal government

PARLIAMENT
Could be dissolved or suspended by the King

SENATE
2/5 appointed by the King

3/5 elected by the people

PEOPLE

Represented but without real political power

CHAMBER OF DEPUTIES
Indirectly elected for five years by all adults

that the Chamber was not a true reflection of the wishes of the mass of the people.[1] A study of the chart makes clear the three factors in the government of Egypt. Although British influence was somewhat reduced after 1936, this triangular contest was the dominant feature of Egyptian politics until the overthrow of King Farouk in 1952.

In the 1920s Egypt had reached the stage of political development that had been attained three centuries earlier in Stuart England. King Fuad I, like James I and Charles I in England, sought to find a parliament that was to his liking. When this was not possible, he dissolved Parliament, suspended the constitution, and ruled by decree. For almost half of the period from 1923 to his death in 1936, Fuad ruled the country in this way. The chief opposition to the King came from the Wafd which dominated every Parliament elected. In an attempt to undermine its position, a new political party was formed with the support of the King, but to no avail. Although the Wafd obstructed all the royal pro-

[1] If, instead of all the citizens of a town voting to elect the borough council, all the people of each street elected one person to vote for them, this would be an indirect election. See page 103 for an example in Russia.

posals in Parliament after 1926 it made little progress towards a greater share in the government of the country.

The struggle for power between the King and the Wafd was complicated by the frequent intervention of the British Government. Sometimes this was in support of the Wafd because the British favoured an increase in the power of Parliament. But the Wafd was determined to secure the return of the Sudan and the expulsion of British troops from Egypt so that, on other occasions, Britain supported the King. In this way Britain maintained an uneasy political peace in Egypt, securing no real support from either side and earning the hatred of many educated Egyptians who accused her of seeking her own rather than Egyptian interests.

Foreign interests. Protection from the laws of non-Christian or less civilised States has always been a first concern of European traders. Such extra-territorial rights were demanded from Japan in the nineteenth century (see page 122) and had been required from the Ottoman Turks in the form of 'capitulations' in the sixteenth century. When peace was signed with Turkey at the end of World War I these capitulations were removed from all former Turkish possessions except Egypt. This unfair treatment was bitterly resented in Egypt, particularly as there was no valid reason for their continuation. As a result, the increasingly large foreign business community in Egypt was given almost complete immunity (or exemption) from Egyptian laws. This, in turn, gave Britain a standing excuse to intervene in order to 'protect foreign interests' — a further proof of the limited nature of Egyptian independence.

The Sudan. One of the chief issues between Britain and Egypt was the control of the Sudan — and, therefore, of much of the Nile waters — which had been granted to the Khedives of Egypt by the Sultan of Turkey in the mid-nineteenth century. Egyptian inability to suppress a revolution led by a religious prophet, the Mahdi, led to the reconquest of the Sudan by an Anglo-Egyptian force under Lord Kitchener between 1896 and 1898 (see page 18). Until 1924 the Sudan was ruled jointly by the two countries as a condominium, although in 1919 Egyptian nationalists began to demand full control. The refusal of Britain to agree to this in 1922 (see page 263) caused increasing ill-feeling in Egypt which culminated in the murder of the Governor-General of the Sudan, Sir Lee Stack, in 1924. Thereafter, until 1936, Britain retained almost sole control of the Sudan.

Few countries in the world had a greater range of wealth than Egypt in the period between the wars. The Egyptian peasant or *fellah* was among the poorest in the world. Those who were fortunate enough to own any land at all generally possessed less than one acre. On the Nile delta, the richest farming land in Egypt, ninety per cent of the *fellahin* owned nothing. A mere hundred thousand wealthy *pashas,* less than one person in two hundred, owned almost a third of all the farm lands in the country. With little interest in their lands, apart from the rents they returned, these wealthy aristocrats dominated the economic and political life of the nation. This economic pyramid, built on the poverty of the masses, had at its apex the largest single land owner in the whole kingdom — the King himself. The luxury of the Egyptian Court provided a bizarre contrast to the poverty of the farmers who lived in one-roomed, thatch-roofed, mud cottages on a diet of bread, vegetables and tea.

Economic development. Throughout its long history the economy of Egypt has been tied to the River Nile. In a land where eighty per cent of the people remained peasant fa mers, agriculture continued to dominate the national economy, with cotton and sugar the principal exports. As national affairs were controlled by the landowning classes there was little development of industry between the wars. However, after 1930 an important change took place. In that year the last of the old commercial treaties, which had fixed the duties on all imports and exports, expired. (Compare with Japan, page 131.) Protected by new tariffs, local industries began to develop, especially for the manufacture of textiles. But, by 1939, large city industries, which could have given employment to thousands of Egyptians, had not appeared. Meanwhile, the dues from the Suez Canal traffic were paid to English and French shareholders with no benefits to Egypt.

Widespread illiteracy was a natural accompaniment of widespread poverty. Although the constitution of 1923 had made education compulsory for both boys and girls, only half of the children of Egypt were at school in 1939 and adult illiteracy remained very great. The political problems which we have already described (see page 263) did not encourage social reforms. Nor were such reforms evident in Stuart England where poverty and illiteracy were equally common. Unless a country's social progress is considered in relation to its political development it is easy to make both an unfair and an unsound judgment.

The Moslem Brotherhood. Rapid westernisation and the development of industry was considered by many to be the best solution to the economic and social problems of Egypt. Others had exactly the opposite view. The Moslem Brotherhood, formed in 1928, believed that all of Egypt's problems would be solved if the nation turned its back on the Western world and returned to the faith of its fathers — Islam. One of the significant features of Islam is that it sees no division between Church and State. Thus the Moslem Brotherhood believed that, if the laws of the Koran became the laws of the State; if the emancipation and education of women was stopped and they returned to their 'former modesty'; if cinemas, bars, and other products of Western civilisation were destroyed; if devout Moslems remembered their religious duty to set aside part of their income to help the poor — then all would be well in Egypt. Understandably, this movement was tremendously popular with the conservative peasants and it grew rapidly in strength.

All but one of the elements of the Egyptian revolution were now present in the national life. The British Government, the King, the landowners, the peasants, the Wafd, and the Brotherhood. Only the leaders were missing. Neither the nationalist Wafd nor the Moslem Brotherhood was strong enough to overthrow the existing system. It was the critical years of the late thirties that provided a situation in which new and powerful leaders could emerge — the young officers of the new Egyptian army.

ACHIEVEMENT OF INDEPENDENCE, 1936-52

Mussolini's attack on Ethiopia in 1935 (see pages 58-9) and increasing international tension in Europe made it imperative that Britain should settle her differences with Egypt to ensure the safety of the Suez Canal. In 1936 an Anglo-Egyptian treaty was signed in London which was intended to last for the next twenty years. It provided for the withdrawal of British troops from Egypt, except from the Canal Zone, and Britain promised to defend Egypt in the event of war. Of equal importance was the British promise to assist with the removal of the hated capitulations (see page 265). Their removal in the following year gave Egyptians a greater feeling of independence than they had previously enjoyed in modern times. In the same year, Egypt was admitted as a member of the League of Nations. Although the future of the Sudan was not settled, the co-operation that had existed before the murder of Sir Lee Stack was restored (see page 265). A few months before the treaty was signed King Fuad died. The new King, seventeen-year-old Farouk I, quickly gained in popularity, and there seemed some hope of the development of a parliamentary monarchy on the British model.

Enter the army. Control of the army had previously been in the hands of the aristocracy whose sons had provided the officers, but this position was altered by the withdrawal of British troops from Egypt in 1936. To provide sufficient officers for the larger army now required, it became necessary to recruit officers from other classes. The effect of this was to convert the army from a stronghold of aristocracy into a national force led by young officers dedicated to the expulsion of foreign power from Egypt, the reform of the Government and the army, and the establishment of complete independence. These Free Officers were to be the leaders of the Egyptian revolution in the years immediately following World War II.

Effect of World War II. Egypt remained neutral throughout the greater part of the war although, under the terms of the 1936 treaty, the country was used as a base and a supply centre by Britain. However, there was much sympathy for the Axis Powers in Egypt, where the German invasion of Crete and the rapid advance of Rommel's panzer divisions across the North African desert were welcomed by many who believed that these events foreshadowed the defeat and withdrawal of British troops from Egypt. The obstructive tactics of the Egyptian Government brought matters to a head in February 1942 when British tanks surrounded the royal palace and demanded that Farouk appoint a more co-operative Prime Minister. Eight months later the victory of Montgomery's Eighth Army at El Alamein swung the Middle East campaign in favour of the Allies and the danger of a British defeat in Egypt had passed. But, in Egypt, February 1942 had been a fateful month. Enraged by the insult to their national pride, the Free Officers vowed to avenge this humiliation. In their eyes, the Egyptian revolution had begun.

Gamal Abdel Nasser. One of the first of the new officers to graduate from the Egyptian Military Academy in 1938 was Second Lieutenant Nasser. Already, at high school in Alexandria, he had begun to demand the expulsion of the British, and the submission of February 1942 made him even more determined. Nasser saw 'imperialism, monarchy, and feudalism' as the three great evils in Egypt and, by 1945, had become the leader of the highly secretive and well organised Free Officers' movement. Bitter experience in the Palestine War convinced him that the overthrow of the monarchy was essential and he began to plan for a military coup d'etat. In 1952 the Free Officers secured the support of General Mohammed Naguib, a well known and much respected officer, whose high rank and popularity made him acceptable as a revolutionary leader. But the real power remained in the hands of Colonel Gamal Abdel Nasser.

The Palestine War. Although Egypt had joined the Allies in the dying stages of the war, the Egyptian army had not been called on to fight. The Arab invasion of Israel in 1948 (see page

FIG. 38 — Haile Selassie, the Emperor of Ethiopia with President Nasser of the United Arab Republic in 1959.

211) was the first real test for its leadership, courage, equipment, and efficiency. It proved to be a disaster for Egypt, the Arab League (see page 210), and for King Farouk. Courage and sound leadership were insufficient to make up for the defective equipment purchased cheaply by the Egyptian Government. Although outnumbered eighty to one by the Arab forces, the Jewish army was victorious. When the armistice was signed in 1949, Israel retained more territory than it had been allotted in the original partition in 1948. Nasser and the Free Officers returned from the front determined that the King must go.

The disaster of the Palestine War also greatly increased the popularity of the Moslem Brotherhood but, at the same time, proved its undoing. Riots and assassinations in Cairo led to its suppression and the imprisonment of thousands of its members. The destruction of the Brotherhood removed the only properly organised and truly national body in the country because the

Wafd, in spite of its earlier importance, was by now seriously divided and hopelessly entangled in the triangular political struggle we examined earlier (see page 264). Only the Free Officers could provide the leadership necessary for the Egyptian revolution.

Republic of Egypt. Meanwhile, relations with Britain had once again deteriorated. In the Sudan, independence rather than union with Egypt seemed probable, while in the Canal Zone, the Palestine War had further aroused British fears for the safety of the sealanes. Clashes between British troops and Egyptian police became frequent and, in January 1952, riots broke out in Cairo, almost four hundred foreign businesses were destroyed, and a number of British residents were murdered. The Wafdist Government, which had held office since 1950, was completely discredited. Six months later the Free Officers were able to seize power, without bloodshed. Farouk officially abdicated in favour of his infant son. In June 1953 the country became a republic. Farouk, now grossly fat and concerned only with his own pleasure and soft living, had rapidly lost popularity after the humiliation of 1942 and the defeat in the Palestine War. When the blow fell in 1952, not a hand was raised to save him, and he passed quietly out of Egyptian history to finish his days in dissolute living in the casinos of the Riviera coast of southern Europe.

INDEPENDENCE — PROBLEMS AND PROGRESS

Revolution was easier than reform. Nasser quickly discovered that Egypt needed 'social and economic strengthening by authoritarian methods and political purge . . . before a democratic constitution'. His disagreement with President Naguib, who favoured a rapid return to parliamentary government, resulted in the latter's removal in November 1954. Nasser was now the undisputed military dictator of Egypt. All political parties were dissolved, dishonest politicians were imprisoned, the loyalty of army officers was scrutinised, and military law was introduced. Egypt has had a long history of dictatorship but the new regime was distinguished from its predecessors by the dedication of its leaders to the cause of national unity and social and economic progress.

Democracy 'in trust'. A new constitution in 1956 provided for a nationally elected Parliament, with limited powers, elected from candidates approved by the National Union, the only political party in the country (it was renamed the Arab Socialist Union in 1962). Freedom of speech, of public meeting, and of the press were allowed, 'within the limits defined by the law', but in 1960 the press was nationalised, so ending what little liberty it had enjoyed. The constitution placed few restrictions on the powers of the President so that Nasser, who was also the leader of the National Union, was in an extremely strong position. The division of the country into twenty-four provinces under the control of governors appointed by the President further increased this power and ensured a centralised control of national policy. At the village level, affairs were to be conducted by elected councils, with definite responsibilities, including the maintenance of law and order. Experience at the local level would eventually lead to a greater share in the government of the country as the illiteracy and poverty of the mass of the people was reduced. In practice, however, elections have been postponed more often than they have been held, both at local and national levels.

Justification? Egypt is both a one-party State and a military dictatorship. But Nasser appeared to be a dictator by force of circumstances rather than by personal choice, as it was the original intention of the Free Officers simply to ensure sound and honest government for Egypt. The impossibility of this task forced Nasser and his supporters to assume control of the country themselves. Although Nasser was most certainly inspired by the highest ideals of service to his country, international involvements led him to be increasingly authoritarian and after his death in 1971 his successors continued the same style of authoritarian but popular government.

Nasser once said that, 'Every one of us is able in his own way to perform a miracle.' The most urgent miracle needed in Egypt is social and economic reform. Whether progress in these fields will be helped or hindered by a vigorous foreign policy which seeks to dominate the Arab world remains to be seen. There can be no doubt that Nasser's successes in his foreign ventures, especially in the Suez Crisis (see page 212), have helped create a sense of national pride that was formerly lacking in Egypt. Yet unless there are rapid and extensive social and economic reforms in Egypt, justification of Nasser's Government and that of his successor Sadat will become increasingly difficult. Sadly, the conflict with Israel has constantly directed resources from the desperate needs of the Egyptian people.

Economic problems. The greatest single problem in Egypt is increasing population pressure on a limited area of arable land. Of a total area of almost 400,000 square miles, less than four per cent can be cultivated and the population density on this area is already over 1,500 per square mile.[1] With an extra half a

[1]Apart from Indonesia, few purely agricultural countries have population densities on their *cultivated* land that even approach this figure.

million mouths to feed each year, it is difficult enough to maintain the present standard of living, let alone to raise it, when almost one-third of the population is already unemployed for the greater part of the year. Even with an extension of irrigation there is a limit to the amount of land which would be suitable for agriculture in this infertile land. As in Japan, industrial expansion could do a great deal to solve the nation's economic problems and the Egyptian Government is also encouraging birth control to ease the population pressure.

One of the first actions of the new Government was to destroy the land owning monopoly of the Egyptian aristocracy (see page 266). The title of *pasha* was abolished and properties larger than two hundred acres were seized and subdivided for distribution to landless peasants as Government co-operative farms. In 1961 the maximum area for private ownership was reduced to 100 acres. The extension of irrigation is another possible solution which has been sought by the Government. Between 1957 and 1961 the Government nationalised over eighty per cent of industries and businesses. Many of these, notably banks, insurance companies, and textile factories, were previously owned by foreign firms. Although ambitious national development plans were launched at the same time, progress by the mid-sixties had not been spectacular.

The High Dam. The key to a revitalised Egypt in Nasser's view was the Aswan High Dam, which would increase the amount of irrigated land by almost one-third (compare this with the Volta Dam project, see page 244). This would not only allow an important increase in food production, but the water power stored behind the dam — in the world's largest man-made lake — would provide urgently needed hydro-electricity for industrial expansion. This vast undertaking could not possibly be financed by a poor nation such as Egypt. In seeking finance for the project, which he regarded as 'essential for Egypt's survival', President Nasser became embroiled in world politics and the Cold War. The Egyptian purchase of arms from Czechoslovakia in 1956 ended negotiations for loans from the United States, Britain, and the World Bank. The nationalisation of the Suez Canal failed to provide sufficient revenue for the building of the dam but the offer of Russian financial and technical assistance in 1960 allowed a start to be made. The dam was finally opened by President Podgorny of U.S.S.R. in 1971.

Trade and aid. Raw cotton and cotton goods account for over three-quarters of the value of Egypt's annual exports. This dangerous overdependence on a single crop made the Egyptian economy most sensitive. Because of its long staple, Egyptian cotton is generally in

Fig. 39 — Soviet President Podgorny and Egyptian President Sadat attend the opening of the Aswan Dam.

demand on world markets, but worsening relations with the West following the arms deal and the Suez crisis, and the increased indebtedness to the Soviet Union following the Aswan dam loan, seriously upset the Egyptian balance of trade. After 1960 the bulk of the cotton exports were sold to Russia and China but over half of Egypt's imports came from the United States and West Germany. To add to its difficulties, the Egyptian Government was faced with a regular trade deficit and has already received over £350 million in foreign aid from nine different countries, principally Russia and America.

Social services. Although the revolution only slowly improved the standard of living of the average peasant, it nevertheless did begin the attack on some of the most pressing social problems, particularly health and education. An important achievement was the establishment in many areas of Rural Combined Centres each providing for up to twenty thousand people in neighbouring villages. These centres co-ordinate the work of village councils in providing better schools, improved water supplies, medical aid, advice for farmers, and other social services. Considerable progress has been made in the fight against some of the more common diseases, especially smallpox, malaria, and cholera (see page 86) but much remains to be done and hookworm and trachoma (a serious eye disease) still occur widely. A tremendous effort has been made to raise the standard of education and fifteen per cent of the annual Government expenditure is taken for this work. Although school attendance is compulsory to the age of twelve, shortages of teachers and schools still prevent many children from attending. However, illiteracy has been enormously reduced from seventy-five per cent in 1945 and adults flock to the special evening classes provided for them.

Social Progress. Nasser destroyed, imperialism, monarchy, and feudalism, but the 'new society' which he envisaged in 1952 has not yet emerged. An attempt to create an experimental new province based on the irrigation of the desert and the development of industry, as an example of the achievements of the new Egypt, ended in failure. On the other hand the introduction of a national system of insurance to provide for sickness and old age has given some social security to factory and office workers in Egypt's growing cities. Nasser was neither a communist nor a capitalist. He saw the 'new society' in Egypt as based on co-operation. He explained his ideals in 1956 when he said, 'At present our society . . . is still based on exploitation . . . In the exploitative State, if you want to raise your income . . . you don't resort to work, but you resort to trickery. But in a co-operative society, if you want to raise your income, you resort to work and not to trickery. You raise the quality of your work and get more pay. This is the society I want for my country.' Obviously progress towards such an ideal can only be slow as it will involve the re-education of an entire nation, and a radical departure from an economic system that has been unchanged for centuries.

Suez and Sudan. Under the terms of the 1936 treaty (see page 267) occupation of the Canal Zone had been settled for twenty years and no final decision had been made about the future of the Sudan. The failure of the British and Egyptian Governments to agree on the future of these two areas after the war worsened relations between them and intensified the already strong anti-British feeling in Egypt. Matters came to a head in 1950 following the Palestine War, when Egypt demanded the complete evacuation of British troops from the Canal Zone and the reunification of the Sudan with Egypt. This the British Government refused to do, believing that co-operation was essential for the defence of the canal and of the Middle East generally.

President Nasser was determined to settle these two matters as soon as possible. There was much disappointment in Egypt in 1953 when the Sudan used the opportunity provided by Britain to decide its own future by choosing independence rather than union with Egypt. This decision caused bad feeling between Egypt and the Sudan until 1958 when, realising the need for Sudanese approval of the High Dam project, Nasser adopted a more friendly attitude towards his southern neighbour. However, the evacuation of the Canal Zone in 1954 (see page 212) more than compensated for this disappointment and allowed Nasser to claim that Egypt was finally and completely an independent nation.

The fateful events of 1956 have already been described (see page 212). Although the nationalisation of the canal appeared as an immediate triumph for President Nasser it also had far-reaching consequences which were not at first apparent.

Leader of the Middle East? Among the nations of the Middle East, Egypt gained greatly in prestige from its diplomatic victory in 1956. In the following year Syrian fear of communist expansion resulted in the formation of the United Arab Republic with Nasser as President. But Egyptian methods soon proved unpopular in the more prosperous Syria and in 1963 the union was dissolved, although Egypt has retained the name of the United Arab Republic. The Six Days War was a heavy blow to Nasser's prestige in the Arab world as a whole although his position in Egypt was never really threatened. After the war he had to rely increasingly on Russian military aid and advice and this to some extent limited his freedom of action in international affairs.

At his death in 1971 he was in many ways a disappointed man. The Canal was still closed and the dam had not yet fulfilled the great hopes that had been pinned on it. On the other hand he had fundamentally transformed Egyptian society and was a leader not only for his own people but for people throughout the Arab world whom he had enthused with the spirit of nationalist unity.

Egypt after Nasser. After his death it was assumed that a period of political instability would follow the disappearance of such a powerful figure. In fact his successor Sadat soon established his own status, pushing his rivals from power and forging effective new policies for the country. In the negotiations which followed Sadat won a series of further concessions. Egypt regained control of both sides of the Canal which was finally re-opened in 1975. In a further agreement that year the Israelis withdrew further east in Sinai, handing over control of the vital strategic passes to the United Nations observers and the Sinai oil-fields to Egypt. Now backed by the wealth of the oil states such as Saudi Arabia, Egypt was able to secure much greater freedom of action from their Russian allies. The Americans came to regard Sadat as the most moderate leader amongst the embattled states surrounding Israel.

Sadat appeared to be prepared to settle for a gradual solution to the conflict with Israel which might allow him to pursue Nasser's plans for internal reconstruction. To this end he was also prepared to moderate Nasser's form of socialism and to encourage private enterprise and foreign investment. However these policies at home and abroad did leave Sadat open to criticism from the more radical Arab leaders and especially from the Palestinian refugees. Moreover Sadat, like so many leaders of developing countries, had to face the difficulty of reconciling the need to have strong government to bring about the necessary development of the country with the demands for political rights from an increasingly well-educated and politically aware population.

The 1973 war and its aftermath (see page 214) brought an enormous increase in Sadat's stature. Though the war had not been a clear-cut victory, it was certainly the most effective performance by any Arab army against the Israelis and brought immediate gains even at the armistice in October 1973.

INDIA

Early history. Before the Aryan invasions of India began, almost two thousand years before the birth of Christ, a flourishing civilisation had already been established in the valley of the Indus River. Although little evidence remains today, the excavated ruins on the lower Indus bear silent witness to well-planned cities and the high standard of living that these people must have enjoyed. The Aryans were followed in their turn by the Greek armies of Alexander the Great, the Persians, the Turks, the Arabs, and the Mongols. While Drake and the English seadogs were vying with the Spaniards for the treasures of the New World, the Mongols were establishing the great Mogul Empire in India which lasted for more than 150 years. When English traders of the British East India Company followed Vasco da Gama's route to India early in the seventeenth century they found Portuguese and Dutch influence in decline and a strongly ruled Mogul Empire controlling the greater part of the sub-continent.

British India. For almost a hundred years the British traded peacefully from their 'factories', or trading posts, around the Indian coast, notably at Madras, Bombay and in Bengal. By the end of the seventeenth century the situation had changed. Weakened by religious disputes and the ambitions of local princes and hampered by poor communications, the Mogul Empire was in a state of collapse. Factories became forts to protect British trade from the effects of frequent civil wars and also from the threat of French competition now appearing.

During the eighteenth century the British tightened their control on India. Under the leadership first of Robert Clive and later of Warren Hastings, the English drove the French out of India and the power of the East India Company was greatly extended. When the Indian Mutiny occurred in 1857 the whole of the sub-continent was either under direct British rule or was governed by princes 'advised' by British officials. Following the suppression of the mutiny the British Government took control of Indian affairs and, twenty years later, Prime Minister Disraeli proclaimed Queen Victoria Empress of India.

Social and economic development. Company rule had brought many benefits to India. It had also created problems. The establishment of law and order and the improvement of communications were important achievements in themselves in a country eighteen times the size of Britain and divided by racial and religious differences. Trade flourished in nineteenth century India but it was based on the sale of English manufactured goods in exchange for Indian raw materials, and brought large profits to the Company rather than to the Indian people. Little was done in the field of education before 1854 but this is understandable when it is recalled that Government concern for education in England was scarcely apparent before 1870. After 1854 a school system was established and grants were given to mission schools, but to many Indians this new western education seemed to be undermining their culture and their religious traditions. Also, there were few positions available for educated Indians. Again, the suppression of *suttee* (widow burning) was opposed by many as an attack on Hindu teaching, but the suppression was justified on Western humanitarian grounds.

British rule in India was obviously a mixed blessing. In the view of one Englishman, 'We are in India not for any love of the Indians, but for what we can make out of it.' In the opinion of another, 'British greatness should be founded on Indian happiness . . . The first and primary object of my heart is the benefit of the Hindus.' The events of the succeeding century were to show that the truth lay somewhere between these extremes. If we accept the European penetration of India as inevitable, it can be strongly argued that India gained more than it lost from British rule.

BACKGROUND TO INDEPENDENCE, 1858-1919

In the latter half of the nineteenth century there was considerable difference of opinion on the extent of self-government that should be allowed in India. On the one hand, Lord Ripon, who became Viceroy in 1880, favoured the extension of local self-government as part of the political education of the Indian people, while on the other, many British civil servants and statesmen believed that they belonged, 'to a race whom God has destined to govern'. In spite of some minor concessions to Indian national feeling, there was little evidence of growing powers of self-government before 1900. The continuation of official majorities and the importance of Government officials is shown in the chart that follows. Through the work of its officials the power of the Government extended from the capital in Delhi to the remotest villages.

While this system was undoubtedly efficient, it gave little opportunity for the expression of Indian opinion. Provincial Councils could discuss but not vote on matters referred to them by the Viceroy, and all legislation introduced into the Legislative Council was proposed by him. The reigns of government were still tightly held by the British Administration.

Indian National Congress. The failure of the British to provide representative institutions in India led to the formation, in 1885, of the Indian National Congress. There were many matters on which educated Indians were anxious to express their opinions. Although Indians had been eligible for the Civil Service since 1879, the holding of the examinations in England debarred all but a small minority from entering. Those educated Indians who had studied abroad were also familiar with the operation of the British parliamentary system and believed that the Congress could provide a lead for the development of representative institutions in India. Its members expressed their concern about the lack of social reform, the effect of imported cotton goods on local cottage industries, the absence of a Government programme to combat famines, and many other matters that affected the lives of the Indian people.

The Moslem League. Supporters of the Congress hoped that it would speak for the whole of India but, from the outset, few Moslems took part. Fear of domination by the Hindu majority in any system of representative government prompted the Moslems to form a separate organisation in 1906. The religious divisions that were to play such an important part in shaping the history of modern India were already becoming significant.

For centuries these two great religions had existed side by side in India, the one rooted in Indian history, the other with its origin in the Arabian desert and the teachings of Mohammed. The developing sense of nationalism in India was largely a Hindu revival. The Moslems saw themselves as part of a religious rather than a national State. This basic difference in outlook reached its climax with the partition of India in 1947.

The Morley-Minto Reforms, 1909. The Japanese victory against Russia in 1905 (see page 130) had an immediate effect in India, where the invincibility of the European had been generally accepted. The demand for further reforms was accompanied by a boycott of British goods and the outbreak of violence in many areas. Realising that further concessions were necessary, the Viceroy, Lord Minto, and the Secretary for India, Lord Morley, introduced an Indian majority on the Provincial Councils in

Indian Government, 1900

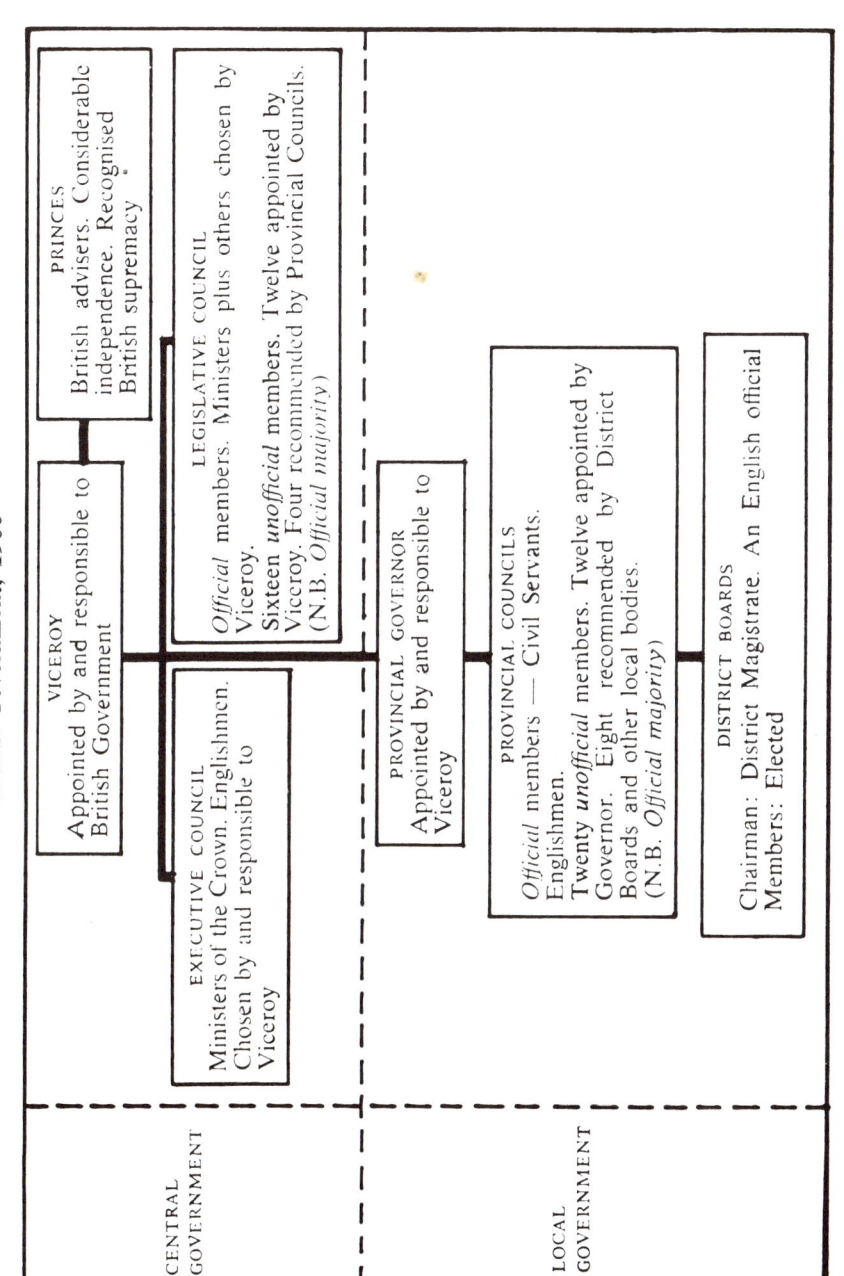

CENTRAL GOVERNMENT

VICEROY
Appointed by and responsible to British Government

PRINCES
British advisers. Considerable independence. Recognised British supremacy

LEGISLATIVE COUNCIL
Official members. Ministers plus others chosen by Viceroy. Sixteen *unofficial* members. Twelve appointed by Viceroy. Four recommended by Provincial Councils. (N.B. *Official majority*)

EXECUTIVE COUNCIL
Ministers of the Crown. Englishmen. Chosen by and responsible to Viceroy

LOCAL GOVERNMENT

PROVINCIAL GOVERNOR
Appointed by and responsible to Viceroy

PROVINCIAL COUNCILS
Official members — Civil Servants. Englishmen.
Twenty *unofficial* members. Twelve appointed by Governor. Eight recommended by District Boards and other local bodies. (N.B. *Official majority*)

DISTRICT BOARDS
Chairman: District Magistrate. An English official
Members: Elected

1909. However, this change had little effect on the government of the country which still remained in the hands of the Viceroy and his Executive Council. The English attitude towards India at this time can perhaps be best understood by examining reaction to a proposal to include an Indian Minister as a member of the Viceroy's Council. The English press, former Viceroys, most Conservative and some Liberal members of Parliament, many members of the Indian Civil Service, and even the Prince of Wales, expressed strong disapproval. In spite of the objections the appointment was made, but the opposition was indicative of the general attitude of superiority that still existed among many Englishmen.

Government of India Act, 1919. The example of the Irish revolt in Dublin in 1916 was not lost on Indian nationalists. In the same year, the Moslem League and the National Congress combined briefly, in the Lucknow Pact, to demand home rule for India. They achieved some success because the Government of India Act of 1919 was an important step in this direction. It established a national Parliament with an elected majority and a series of elected Provincial Councils. Although the major responsibility for governing the country remained with the Viceroy and the Provincial Governors, the new Act provided for important training in responsible government at the local level by giving the Provincial Councils full powers to deal with agriculture, industry, education, health, and local government. At the national level, representative government was introduced.

British colonial policy has been based on the development of responsible self-government *by stages* (see page 229) and the 1919 Act pointed to the acceptance of a similar policy in India. Extremists in India refused to accept this principle and demanded immediate home rule. Their demands led to further violence which had to be suppressed. Unfortunately, over-severe measures in some cases, notably in the Amritsar massacre in 1919 when 1500 unarmed people were killed or wounded, intensified the growing anti-British feeling in many areas. India's political problems were apparently far from being solved.

Railways. The breaking of village isolation, with the associated social, political, and economic consequences, has been one of the most significant results of the British occupation of India. One of the principal agents in the destruction of this isolation has been the railways. By 1914 over 25,000 miles of railways had been laid. Village raw materials could more easily be transported to distant ports for export, food could be moved quickly to areas where famine threatened, imported manufactured goods could reach formerly isolated markets, all to the benefit of the Indian peasants. Also with the breakdown of isolation came the destruction of village self-sufficiency with serious effects for cottage industries, notably spinning, weaving, pottery, and metal crafts, which could not compete with the cheap factory-made articles from Manchester, Birmingham and Sheffield. Railways helped in the maintenance of law and order by allowing the rapid movement of troops to troublesome areas. They also helped in the development of an Indian national spirit by speeding the spread of ideas and by making it easier for people to travel to and from the large cities.

Peasant problems. The land has been the basis of existence in India for centuries. In the second half of the nineteenth century pressure on the land increased as the population rose steadily in the new era of peace that accompanied the establishment of British rule. By 1914 extensive Government public works had brought some fifteen million acres under irrigation, but by this time the population had passed the 300 million mark and was increasing at the rate of almost two million a year. The problem of land shortage was intensified by the common Indian practice of sub-dividing a father's holding among his sons so that many units were too small to be farmed efficiently. Financial problems often followed, and in bad times the peasant was often forced to borrow from the village moneylender. Once in his power it was difficult to escape for interest rates were usually such that the debt continued to grow, in spite of repayments! The introduction of village co-operative credit societies by the Viceroy, Lord Curzon, in 1904 proved a great boon to the peasants who, henceforth, were able to borrow at low interest rates.

Industrial problems. Industry was slow to develop in India, largely because British investors were more interested in the profits from trade and from British industry than in the establishment of new factories in India, or 'anywhere else in the Empire for that matter. Nineteenth century economists believed that colonies should supply raw materials for home industries and act as markets for finished products. They also believed that governments should not interfere in trade or industry. The effect of their beliefs can be seen in the establishment of free trade in the British Empire after 1868 and the reluctance of British Governments to impose regulations and restrictions in British factories. The first cotton factory was established in India in 1851. By 1914 there were 250 textile factories employing almost half a million workers. The jute industry had also been established, in the delta of the Ganges River, and in 1907, the Tata Iron and Steel Company began production at Jamshedpur. Almost all of these enterprises were financed with Indian capital. The persistent British refusal to allow the imposition of a protective tariff, though in keeping with trade and economic theories just described, was not understood in India where it was seen as a deliberate attempt to continue British exploitation and to prevent Indian industrial progress.

Attempts to improve village health were frequently unsuccessful because ignorance, superstition, and religious beliefs often prevented the acceptance of new ideas. The work of Sir Ronald Ross allowed an attack on malaria to begin at the turn of the century but general progress in the field of public health was limited in this period. When war broke out in 1914 there were 100,000 Government schools in India providing education for almost four and a half million children. In some areas Christian mission schools had also been established. These figures do not appear as impressive when it is realised that only one person in eight could read and write, but even this low figure compares more than favourably with that in many other colonial areas at this time. Furthermore, the establishment of five universities in India provided educational opportunities for a growing number of able Indian students. It was these men, and others who had studied in English universities, who were to become the leaders of Indian agitation for independence in the years between the wars.

ACHIEVEMENT OF INDEPENDENCE, 1919-47

Mahatma Gandhi. Few national leaders can claim a greater place in the history of their country than can Mohandas Karamchand Gandhi. The Mahatma, or Great Soul, as he is generally known, had become a legendary figure long before an assassin's bullet cut him down in 1947 shortly after India gained its independence. Born of lowly Hindu parents in 1869, Gandhi later studied law in England before settling in South Africa where he championed the rights of the Indian minority. It was in South Africa that he perfected the technique of opposing authority without violence that was soon to make him famous not only in India but throughout the entire world. A devoutly religious man, Gandhi believed, 'in the supremacy of the moral law, the law of truth and love'. *Satyagraha* — non-violence or civil disobedience — is 'the force which is born of truth and love' and it was this weapon that was used by Gandhi to such good effect in his struggle against the British for Indian self-government.

When Gandhi returned to India in 1915, he quickly became the leader of the National Congress. His answer to the Amritsar massacre was a two-year campaign of non-violent, non-co-operation which resulted in his imprisonment until 1924. Throughout the 1920s and 1930s he continued his policy of *Satyagraha* and, as a result, spent frequent periods in prison. Gandhi spent much of his time travelling, often on foot, among the villages of India where his campaign on behalf of the outcastes, or Untouchables, won him the support of millions and made him a national leader. He believed that the future of India depended on the return to the simple village life of the past. The spinning wheel, at which he worked for some hours almost every day, became the symbol of his opposition to modern, and especially British, industry. More than any other leader he reached into the hearts and minds of the millions in the villages of India and created a national awareness and a new self-respect that inspired rich and poor, educated and ignorant to suffer in the cause of their country. Perhaps this was his greatest contribution to the nation to which he dedicated his life.

The Simon Report, 1930. Growing awareness of Indian dissatisfaction prompted the British Government to appoint a Royal Commission in 1927 to report on the political situation and to make recommendations. Unfortunately, not a single Indian was included in the commission's membership. This continued refusal to recognise the right of Indian leaders to speak on behalf of the people of India was one of the most disturbing features of British policy. It is little wonder that Gandhi and other national leaders flatly rejected the commission's recommendation that the system of diarchy already operating in the provinces (see page 280) should be extended to the Central Government. Such progress was much too slow for the National Congress. Even before the Simon report was presented, the Congress had adopted the recommendation of Mr Jawaharlal Nehru that it should accept nothing less than complete independence outside the British Empire!

If the British were not sure about the future of India, neither were the Indians themselves. The princes feared for their position in a united India and demanded a loose federation in which most of the power would be retained by the individual States. The Moslems were also concerned for their position. Comprising, as they did, almost a quarter of the population, they demanded 'weightage' or over-representation to ensure that their interests were protected. This system has no parallel in Great Britain where each member of Parliament represents a more or less equal number of people, however up until 1945, a similar system operated in New Zealand whereby those living in rural areas had more representatives in Parliament than their actual population entitled them to. There too, Maoris, who would normally form a minority in an ordinary electorate are provided with four communal electorates. Moslems were in a similar position in India and were concerned by the revival of National Congress demands for the abolition of the communal electorates which they feared would leave their special interests totally unprotected in a predominantly Hindu State.

Civil disobedience again. Gandhi's reply to the Simon report was a renewal of his policy of *Satyagraha*. In 1930, in defiance of the British salt monopoly, he set out to walk sixty miles to the sea to collect salt. He was joined by thousands of followers as he walked and his deliberate civil disobedience forced the Government to imprison him and 60,000 others. Such mass demonstrations of passive resistance were an inspiration to the people of India, who saw in Gandhi's example an effective method of embarrassing the Government and forcing reforms and concessions. However, even Gandhi was unable to control his followers completely and sustained civil disobedience often led to the outbreak of violence. The British Government could not ignore the growing public opinion and popular agitation in India. Events had proved that the imprisonment of its leaders was no solution. Other measures had to be considered. A series of round table conferences in London between 1930 and 1932 simply drew new attention to the complexity of India's problems. Gandhi returned from London and an audience with the King to a new civil disobedience campaign and further imprisonment.

Government of India Act, 1935. In the prevailing climate of distrust it is hardly surprising that the new Act, embodying the proposals of the Simon report, was not well received. An attempt to establish a federal government failed because the princes refused to take part. In the provinces new fully responsible councils were established to have virtually complete control over local affairs. Although it was not then realised, the division of India dates from this Act. In the provinces where there were Hindu majorities, National Congress leaders refused to allow the Moslem League to be represented in the Provincial Governments. They argued that the Congress was not a religious body; that it stood for the independence of *all* Indians; that it would protect the rights of minorities; and that membership was open to Moslems as well as Hindus. But this argument was not acceptable to Moslems who saw the Hindu dominated National Congress as a threat to their very survival.

Jinnah and Pakistan. By 1939 all hope of an independent, united India had gone although British officials continued to work for this ideal for a further eight years. Moslem fear of Hindu domination was expressed by the leader of the Moslem League, Mohammed Ali Jinnah, who declared that, 'Moslems can expect neither justice nor fair play under Congress government . . . Moslems are a nation . . . they must have their homelands, their territory and their State.' In fairness to the Congress it must be said that the idea of Pakistan[1] as a separate Moslem national State grew not out of ill-treatment of Moslems but out of their fear of being ill-treated. The British political system is based on majority rule with respect for minority views. It was a fear of the 'tyranny of the majority' that drove the Moslems out of India.

Effect of World War II. Continued refusal of Congress and League to co-operate with each other, or with the Government, dominated the early years of the war. Offers of complete independence after the war were rejected. 'Quit India', said Gandhi who saw the fall of Singapore and the Japanese invasion of Burma in 1942 as a threat to the safety of India and also as the end of British power in Asia. The abandonment of passive resistance and the outbreak of a rebellion in 1942 resulted in the imprisonment of Gandhi, Nehru, and other Congress leaders for the remainder of the war. Peace brought little improvement in the situation. British missions to India failed to accomplish anything and tension mounted steadily. The election of a Labour Government in Britain in 1945 proved to be of considerable significance for India. If the war had done nothing else, it had convinced the new British Government that, while independence would not necessarily solve India's problems, it was, nevertheless, the only acceptable solution. Britain was finally prepared to do as Gandhi wished and, 'leave India to God'.

Republic of India. From 1909 onwards India had been moving slowly but inevitably towards self-government — far too slowly for many Indians and rather too inevitably for some British statesmen. As recently as November 1942, Winston Churchill had declared that he had not become Prime Minister, 'in order to preside at the liquidation of the British Empire'. British reluctance to hand over control of the country until stable government was assured was typical of its colonial policy during this century.[2]

[1]Punjab, Assam, Kashmir, and Baluchistan were the provinces claimed by the Moslem League.
[2]Similar problems delayed a settlement of the future of Rhodesia.

But, in India, every effort to achieve a settlement had failed. Early in 1947, Prime Minister Attlee announced that Britain would leave India in June 1948, whether the League and the Congress had resolved their difficulties or not. Under the guidance of the wartime hero, Earl Mountbatten, whom Attlee appointed the last Viceroy of India, a settlement was quickly reached and in August, the Indian Empire ceased to exist, becoming instead, the Dominions of India and Pakistan. Three years later India became a republic. To the surprise of many, it chose to retain its membership of the Commonwealth of Nations.

INDEPENDENCE — PROBLEMS AND PROGRESS

Minorities and violence. The expected violence was not long delayed. After the partition over 40 million Moslems remained in India while almost half that number of Hindus were left as a minority group in Pakistan. The three months following independence were among the blackest in the history of the sub-continent. A wave of arson, looting, and murder swept through the frontier districts while a further eight million refugees moved from one country to the other. (About seven million had crossed the frontiers before partition was announced.) Carrying nothing but a few personal belongings, with nowhere to live, and nowhere to work, these pitiful refugees were the tragic result of the partition. In the midst of this bloodshed and misery Gandhi celebrated his seventy-eighth birthday, with 'nothing but anguish in my heart'. In January 1948 he began his last fast, to encourage the people of both India and Pakistan to 'turn the searchlight inward' in order to 'purify their hearts' so that they would be best able to work for the good of their countries. His life had been devoted to the struggle for independence. He lived long enough to see the horrors that accompanied its achievement but not to share in the triumphs that followed.

A united India. The spread of education, the rise of Hindu unity, the expansion of railways and the growth of nationalism had largely destroyed the significance of the boundaries of the independent States where the princes of India still ruled. These influences affected rulers as well as people so that by 1949 all but the Maharajah of Kashmir had voluntarily surrendered their power to the new Government of India, in exchange for pensions and the retention of their titles and personal privileges. The importance of this development for the future of India can best be realised when it is appreciated that the princes had ruled over an area almost equal in size to that which had formerly been known as British India. Without their co-operation the unity of

FIG. 40 — Jawaharlal Nehru and Mahatma Gandhi.

FIG. 41 — An Indian bullock cart moves slowly past an atomic energy
installation near Bombay.

the new nation would have been seriously affected and its future imperilled.

Democracy in action. In 1952, the world watched while more than 100 million Indians went to the polls in the largest free elections ever held. How could these illiterate peasants hope to operate successfully the most complicated system of government in existence? Perhaps they could neither read nor write, but at least they could hear! As seventeen thousand candidiates for seats in the local and national governments toured the countryside to tell the people what they would do if elected, the people of India came to listen and to decide. Each party was given its own symbol which every candidate had prominently displayed while he spoke. Even the least educated voter could associate the speaker he preferred with the party symbol. On polling day he simply placed his voting paper in the ballot box that belonged to the 'cow' or the 'flower' party. The elections of 1957 and 1962 proved to be even more successful than the first. India had proved to the world that educated voters were not an essential prerequisite for the conduct of successful democratic elections.

Both worlds. The constitution of India reflects both the ideals of Gandhi and the heritage of British rule. The provision that prevents discrimination, on the grounds of 'religion, race, *caste,* or sex', derives directly from Gandhi's campaign on behalf of the Untouchables. Preservation of freedom of speech and of meeting is a direct continuation of the British tradition. These two provisions illustrate the fact that India is a national rather than a religious State (such as Pakistan), determined to preserve the rights and to recognise the views of minority groups. Herein lies one of the greatest strengths of the Indian Republic. Furthermore, the National Congress had had thirty years of training in democratic methods and, through its nationwide agitation for independence, had produced a large number of educated and experienced leaders well known to and trusted by the local people.

Like the United States and Australia, India has a federal constitution but, unlike these two nations, only limited powers are given to the State Governments.[1] The strong central government that results from this system has enabled the Indian Government to take the lead in national planning and development. At the same time, there are definite local loyalties based on differences of race, language, religion, and traditions. India is thus one nation but many people. On the one hand strong central control offers some

[1]In the United States and Australia there has been a long struggle between the Federal and State Governments because the central Governments have only possessed those powers specifically allocated to them in the constitution. In India the position is exactly the opposite.

guarantee of effective government while, on the other, local loyalties and a federal constitution provide safeguards against the danger of a *coup d'etat*. The position of many other emergent nations is much less secure.

Starving millions. The most immediate and pressing problem that faced independent India was the increasing gap between population and food. Rice production per acre was only a quarter of that in Japan, yet for two-thirds of the people rice was the staple food. Meanwhile, the population was growing by almost five million every year. Under British rule, irrigation had been steadily extended so that, when independence was gained, one-fifth of the cultivated land was being irrigated. But irrigation itself was not enough to solve the problem of starvation in India. Conservative, illiterate peasants were suspicious of Government officials and foreign specialists, often from the specialised agencies of the United Nations, who came to demonstrate new ideas and to offer aid. Furthermore, the Hindu religion taught an acceptance of life as it was and a contempt for material wealth. Against this background of suspicion, indifference, and ignorance, the Indian Government faced the task of feeding the starving millions.

The first Five-Year Plan, introduced in 1952, placed the emphasis on agriculture, especially on the extension of irrigation and the associated development of hydro-electric power schemes. In industry aid was given to the establishment of a vast fertiliser works, and to many other industries which were of direct importance in increasing food production. The first plan was immediately followed by a second and, by 1961, food production had been increased by forty per cent while population had only grown by half that amount. Subsequently food production has not increased reliably or at a pace with the population. There have been serious famines in bad years such as 1973–4 despite the 'green revolution' which introduced local irrigation plans and high yield grain.

Industry and trade. While industrial production, notably of textiles and steel, had developed during British rule, there had been no serious or planned attempt to establish industry in India. Because of the rapid development necessary to make up this leeway, the State has had to play an important role in industrial expansion. And as a result many basic industries are now under State control. These include the production of steel, chemicals, and heavy machinery. Private investment is also being encouraged for the establishment of the many other industries essential for a modern nation — textiles, cement works, motor car assembly, sugar refineries, and so on. At the same time, the Indian Government is ensuring that industry is developed in all parts of the country so that the advantages of increased employment and wealth will not be restricted to any one region. As industrial expansion continues, the value of India's exports will also increase, and thus help to reduce the country's large trade deficit, at present being met by foreign loans and grants.

Community projects. Eighty-five per cent of the population of India live in villages of fewer than five thousand people, and there seems little likelihood of any significant alteration in this figure for many years to come. For this reason, any scheme that does not reach down to village level and win the support of the mass of the peasants can hope for only limited success. This explains the tremendous importance of the community projects which were first started in 1952 and which have since reached over half of the villages in India. Each of these schemes includes about a hundred villages and provides for the improvement of housing, sanitation, education, roads, wells, agriculture, and other amenities, and for the development of co-operative farms to replace tiny individual plots.

No other scheme better illustrates the spirit of the new India. Educated young men and women, often the sons and daughters of peasants, have returned to the villages in their thousands to show their own people new ways of solving old problems. With their enthusiasm and ability they have captured the imagination of millions who see the chance of new life, if not for themselves then at least for their children. At the same time, the Government is encouraging the expansion of small scale village industries, based on the traditional skills of the Indian peasants, to bring increased employment and a higher standard of living to the mass of the people. Critics may argue that progress is slow in comparison to the more spectacular achievements of China, but Indian statesmen, who believe in democratic methods, believe that a movement which grows from the 'grass roots' of society will eventually have a greater permanence and a wider acceptance from the people they represent.

A social revolution. The determination of Indian statesmen to build a national State has brought them into sharp conflict with many Hindu customs. At the same time a reformation within the Hindu religion itself has shown that many of these customs had no true religious origins or justification. Also, the achievement of independence, the rapid growth of new industrial towns, and the problem of finding new homes for more than nine million refugees from Pakistan, have helped to create a public opinion favourable to social change. The result has been a social revolution equal in magnitude and significance to the emergence of capital and labour in nineteenth century industrial England or to the re-modelling of Russian and Chinese society after 1917 and 1948. Its effect on the growth of a national spirit in India has been incalculable.

The establishment of equality for women and the destruction of the caste system were embodied in the constitution (see page 288), but this did not guarantee their achievement, which depended on the introduction and enforcement of new national laws.[1] Probably the most outstanding of these is the Marriage Law. By removing the barrier to marriage between people of different castes, and by making marriage a civil contract between two persons instead of a family compact, the law removed with one stroke the disadvantage of Untouchability and the inequality of the sexes. Laws such as this which are a true reflection of the spirit of Gandhi are the finest tribute that the Indian nation can offer to the memory of its beloved Mahatma.

In common with many developing countries Indians have found it hard to bridge the gap between major prestige projects such as dams and steel works and the life of the mass of the population at village level. At the basis of the problem was the need to educate this enor-mous and rapidly increasing population. Without this it will be im-possible to introduce effective birth control, to emancipate the mass of women who still despite legal reforms occupy a suppressed position in Indian society, to break the hold of a traditional society or to intro-duce improvements in agriculture and industry at village level.

Social services. The Government of the Republic has adopted British proposals, prepared during the war, for the long-term improvement of public health in India. Community projects and schemes initiated by the World Health Organisation and the Children's Emergency Fund are making an important contribution to this work, but results will be unspectacular for many years in this land of desperate poverty. There are still only twenty doctors per 100,000 people, and most of these are in the large cities.[2] In education, progress has been more rapid. Since inde-pendence, literacy has risen from one in eight to one in four while the number of universities have increased from twenty-four to sixty, with over one million students in 1964. Educational advances have been somewhat hampered by the different local languages in India. English served as the official language until 1965 but in that year Hindi (or Urdu) became the official language. However, Hindi is spoken by less than half of the

[1] The United States Constitution recognises the civil rights of Negroes but many of these rights are still denied in some States.

[2] Most industrial states have at least 1 doctor per 1,000 people.

population and it is apparent that English will continue to be used as an associate language for many years.

Kashmir and the Indus. Two immediate problems bedevilled relations between the newly independent India and Pakistan. Although the Indus River is almost entirely within Pakistan, many of its important eastern tributaries originate in the Punjab and provide irrigation water for Indian farmers. Pakistan's fears that India might divert further water eastwards were finally allayed in 1960 when the two nations agreed to accept a United Nations settlement which allocated eighty per cent of the water from the Indus system to Pakistan and twenty per cent to India.

Unfortunately, the dispute over possession of Kashmir has not been so peacefully settled. In 1947, the unpopular Hindu ruler of Kashmir chose to remain independent rather than join either of the two new States (see page 286) but his people, the majority of whom were Moslems, clamoured for union with Pakistan. The entry of Pakistani volunteers into Kashmir precipitated an Indian invasion and war between the two countries appeared to be imminent. A cease-fire line was drawn with the assistance of the United Nations and, in 1951, it was agreed that the future of Kashmir should be decided by plebiscite. But such questions as who would conduct the plebiscite and whether it would include independence as one of the alternatives, were never decided. In practice, therefore, it would have been extremely difficult to conduct a plebiscite that would have satisfied the wishes of all parties. So a theoretically simple solution was never adopted and until 1965 United Nations observers patrolled the cease-fire line and maintained an uneasy peace.

Meanwhile, India, which had occupied the more fertile and densely-populated part of the State, declared Kashmir to be part of India, while Pakistan continued to press its claims in the General Assembly of the United Nations. Fighting again broke out in August 1965 and quickly developed into a full-scale war which was only stopped by the intervention of the Security Council. After eighteen years of partition the problem seemed to be little nearer a solution, but Russian mediation in January 1966 gave some hope for the future (see page 88). However this was not to be. The next cause of conflict was to be internal conflict in Pakistan itself. The western wing of the country had always dominated the army, the government, and the economy to their own advantage. In 1970 after unrest in the east the Pakistan army began a programme of violent repression and there was a massive movement of refugees from East Pakistan into India. India itself backed the Bengali guerillas and mobilised against Pakistan. The Pakistan army in the East collapsed and an independent state of Bangla Desh was established. Indian policy had been successful, but the economic cost of the war and the refugees had been devastating and the new state of Bangla Desh was to be plagued with economic crises and political instability.

Foreign aid. Like most other emergent nations, India has depended largely on foreign aid. Because of its great size and population, and its widespread poverty, its needs have been correspondingly great. American aid, including enormous loans, grants, technical assistance and food surpluses has far exceeded that of any other country, although many have given help. India was the first non-communist country to receive aid from the Soviet Union and Russian loans have financed much heavy industrial development as well as providing military equipment. Under the Commonwealth Colombo Plan, India has also received assistance from Britain, Canada, Australia, and New Zealand and many Indian students and technicians have been trained in the universities, hospitals, teachers colleges and technical institutes of these countries. A strong India can make an important contribution to the future peace of the world. It could well provide the sheet anchor of the Third Force of the Afro-Asian world (see page 219). But its strength is largely dependent on economic growth and this, in turn, must rely in part on the continuation of considerable foreign aid.

International relations. Under the leadership of Pandit Nehru, India adopted a policy of determined non-alignment in 1947. Nehru's 'Five Principles', or *Panch Shila,* declared that India would respect the territory and independence of other countries, would treat all nations as equals, would not interfere in the internal affairs of other countries, would follow a policy of peace and would make peaceful coexistence the basis of all its dealings with foreign nations. Until the mid-1960s India clung to this policy of neutralism and spoke boldly and independently in the United Nations and other world councils on all matters affecting world peace, the rights of oppressed peoples (especially the native people of South Africa), colonialism, and aid to underdeveloped countries. India also championed international disarmament and the outlawing of nuclear tests. In spite of its present economic weakness, India speaks for almost one-seventh of the world's people. Its voice cannot be ignored.

Pandit Nehru. In 1964 the world mourned the death of Pandit Nehru, one of the greatest statesmen of this century. For seventeen years 'Father Jawaharlal' had been the symbol of Indian unity, loved and respected by millions. At an early age he had come under the spell of Gandhi and, in 1947, when India needed a strong and able leader, the mantle of Gandhi had fallen on his shoulders. As Prime Minister of India his fame spread far beyond the shores of his own country. To millions of underprivileged people he appeared as the champion of freedom, equality, and peace. To his own countrymen he offered hope for the future. Perhaps the greatest tribute that could be paid to his statesmanship and leadership of his people in the difficult years following independence was the ease with which he was succeeded as Prime Minister by Lal Bahadur Shastri. The sudden death of Mr Shastri only a few hours after he had signed a peace pact with Pakistan provided further proof of the political stability of India as, within a week, a successor had been found in Mrs Indira Gandhi, the only child of Pandit Nehru, who became the second woman in the world to become a Prime Minister.

The unresolved problems. For Mrs Gandhi the political situation was even more complex than that which faced her father. Unlike most developing countries India has stood by the democratic parliamentary system of government inherited from the British, along with a non-political army and an independent judiciary. In all post-independence elections at national level and most State elections the Congress Party has won convincing majorities. It was faced by socialist and communist groups on the one hand and Hindu traditionalist parties on the other, but neither opposition groups were a possible alternative government nor did they produce political leaders with a national following. As a result much political activity has taken place within the Congress Party between left- and right-wingers and there has been a constant danger of separatism in this vast sub-continent spanning many linguistic and racial differences.

In 1975, faced by an attempt to oust her in a dispute about election irregularities, Mrs Gandhi assumed emergency powers and imprisoned many of her opponents. This was a setback for the principles on which India has been established and it remains to be seen whether she will be able to take the country back to a full parliamentary system. On the other hand there are those who argue that such a system is in practice corrupt and quite incapable of the social and economic transformation of the country.

India is inevitably in competition with the other Asian giant, China. In 1962 they came into physical conflict in a border dispute and minor brushes continued in 1975. India has enjoyed much greater outside help both from the West and from the Soviet Union. In foreign affairs she continues to adopt a strictly neutralist line and, despite her explosion of a nuclear bomb in 1974, clearly has no aggressive intention against any of her neighbours. In India, as in most developing countries, the most urgent battle that has to be fought is against poverty, famine, ignorance and disease within her own borders.

NOTEBOOK SUMMARY

New Nations in Africa and Asia

Reread the introduction to this chapter, pages 225 to 233, and note the following *general points* as a basis for a more detailed national study.

COLLAPSE OF COLONIALISM
1. Extent of collapse
2. Arguments against colonialism
3. Arguments in support of colonialism
4. Reasons for collapse

GROWTH OF NATIONALISM
Note effects of
1. Economic conditions (especially contrasts in living standards)
2. Education
3. World War II

BACKGROUND TO INDEPENDENCE
Note the major differences between the colonial policies of
1. Britain
2. France
3. Other countries

PROBLEMS OF INDEPENDENCE
Note under the following headings the chief features of each of the main problems facing newly independent nations.
1. Political
2. Economic
3. Social
4. International

NATIONAL CASE STUDY
The national case studies all conform to the following general pattern. When making notes it is important to record
1. The *policy* of the colonial Power
2. *What was done* by the colonial Power
3. *What was not done* by the colonial Power
4. The *effect* of (2) and (3) on the colonial people

Introduction
This gives a short early history, explains how the territory became a European colony, and outlines early social and economic developments. Any notes should be *very brief*.

Background to independence

1. Political developments — both local and central. What was their purpose? What was their effect?
2. Economic developments — agriculture, industry, trade. Who benefited? With what effects?
3. Social development — education, health, living standards, etc. How much was achieved? Who benefited? With what effects?
4. Growth of nationalism — From the notes you have made on this section, what *evidence* can you summarise to show the growth of nationalism? What factors favoured its development? If in doubt as to what to look for, check back to *general notes* under the first three headings to see which factors apply to the study you have chosen.

Achievement of independence

Look for the following main points, not necessarily in this order.
1. The effect of World War II
2. The influence and contribution of a great national leader
3. The method by which independence was achieved. Try to find reasons for this method being used
4. The stages by which independence was achieved

Independence — problems and progress

Examine both the *problems* and the *progress* under the following headings. In some cases problems result from former colonial policy, in others progress has been aided by the former colonial Power. These instances should be noted. Use the *general notes* (Problems of Independence) as a guide. You should seek to discover the problems faced, the methods adopted to deal with them, the success achieved, and, where possible, the reasons for the policy.
1. Political
2. Economic
3. Social
4. International

WORDS TO KNOW

The following words used in this chapter need to be understood. Most of them have been explained in the text but all of them should form part of a history student's vocabulary. Make a list in the back of your notebook, with meanings, of those words which are new to you. Learn these and use them in your essays:

Assimilation, civil disobedience, colonialism, communal electorate, confrontation, 'culture system', 'dual mandate', emergent nation, exploitation, federal government, fellah, indirect rule, infiltration, interdependence, Khedive, mixed economy, nationalism, neo-colonialism, neutralism, non-alignment, outcaste, pasha, plantation agriculture, plebiscite Wafd.

BOOKS TO READ OR CONSULT

General

Catchpole, B. *A Map History of the Modern World*, London, Heinemann Educational Books, 1974.

Crowley, D. W. *The Background to World Affairs*, London, Macmillan, 1967.

Ghana

Anderson, J. *A History of West Africa in the Nineteenth and Twentieth Centuries*, London, Heinemann Educational Books, 1973.

Fage, J. D. *A History of West Africa*, London, Cambridge, 1969.

Webster, J. B. and Boahen, A. A. *The Revolutionary Years: Africa since 1800*, London, Longman, 1970.

Indonesia

Grant, B. *Indonesia*, London, Penguin, 1964.

Egypt

Mansfield, P. *Nasser's Egypt*, London, Penguin, 1965.

Rodinson, M. *Israel and the Arabs*, London, Penguin, 1969.

India

Crocker, W. *Nehru*, London, Allen and Unwin, 1966.

Thapar, R. and Spear, R. *A History of India*, London, Penguin, 1966.

Watson, F. *Gandhi*, London, Oxford, 1969.

QUESTIONS FOR ESSAYS OR DISCUSSION

The following questions can be used with *any* of the different national studies from this chapter.

1. (a) What were the chief political, social, economic and international problems facing .... when it gained independence?

   (b) Select the problems under any *one* of the above headings and describe how and with what success the government has attempted to solve them.

2. (a) What advantages did .... gain from colonial rule?

   (b) What problems were created in .... as a result of colonial rule?

   (c) What have been the relations of .... with its former colonial rulers since independence?

3. (a) What foundations for independence were provided in .... by the colonial government?

   (b) Briefly describe the main stages by which independence was achieved in ....

4. Choose any one great national leader in ....

   (a) Briefly outline his career.

   (b) Discuss his importance in the achievement of independence.

   (c) What policy has he (or his party) followed since independence, for what reasons and with what success?

5. (a) What do you understand by nationalism?

   (b) What factors hindered and favoured the growth of nationalism in ....?

   (c) How and for what reasons was independence gained in 19.....?

GENERAL LIST OF RELATED READING

Calvorcoressi, P. *The Background to Current Affairs*, London, Macmillan, 1970.

Catchpole, B. *A Map History of the Modern World*, London, Heinemann Educational Books, 1974.

Cornwell, R. *World History in the Twentieth Century*, London, Longman, 1969.

Crowley, D. W. *The Background to Current Affairs*, London, Macmillan, 1970.

Duffy, M. *The Twentieth Century*, London, Blackwell, 1964.

Henderson, J. W. *Since 1945*, London, Methuen, 1966.

Knapton, E. and Derry, T. *Europe and the World since 1914*, London, Murray, 1967.

Richardson, P. *Britain, Europe and the Modern World*, London, Heinemann Educational Books, 1974.

Wales, P. *World Affairs since 1919*, London, Methuen, 1967.

INDEX

ABYSSINIA, 18, 58-9, 76
Adowa, 59
Afro-Asian bloc, 80, 191, 210
Agadir crisis, 25
Albania, 25, 56, 65, 78, 117, 190
Alexander III, Tsar, 94
Algeciras Conference, 25, 151
Algeria, 81
Alsace-Lorraine, 15, 21, 33
Anglo-Japanese Alliance (1902), 24, 130
Angola, 230
Anschluss, 62
Anti-Comintern Pact, 60
ANZUS Pact, 138
Appeasement, 61
Arab League, 210-13
Archangel, 110
Aswan Dam, 212, 272, 274
Atlantic Charter, 78-9, 196
Atomic bomb, 137, 191, 205, 215-16
Attlee, Clement, 286
Austria, 56, 62, 197, 200, 201; in Triple Alliance, 21; in World War I, 26-8

BAGHDAD Pact, 212
Baldwin, Stanley, 61
Balkan crises, Bosnia (1908), 25; Sarajevo (1914), 25
Balkan Pact, 202
Balkan Wars (1912-13), 25
Bandung Conference, 191, 210, 259
Bangla Desh, 293
Basic Treaty, 199
Battle of Britain, 65, 156
Benelux Union, 203, 205
Berlin-Baghdad Railway, 19
Berlin, partition, 198; blockade, 198; Wall, 199
Bernadotte, Count, 87
Bismarck, Otto von, 21
Boer War, causes, 18
Bolsheviks, 99-101
Bonn, 198
Borodin, 171, 173
Boxer Rebellion, 130, 170
Brezhnev, Leonid, 113-14
Briand-Kellogg Pact — *see* Pact of Paris
'Brinkmanship', 198
Brüning, Heinrich, 42
Brussels, Treaty of, 203

Bulganin, Marshal, 112
Bulgaria, 56, 78, 197
Burma Road, 135, 178
Bushido, 129

CANTON, 170, 171
Caroline Islands, 132
Casablanca crisis, 25
'Cash and Carry', 155-6
Castro Fidel, 217
Central Treaty Organisation (CENTO), 212, 218
Chamberlain, Neville, 61, 64
Chiang Kai-shek, 79, 134, 171-9, 188-9, 208
Chiang Kai-shek, Madame, 174
China, 166-92; and Japan, 128-33, 175-9; Communist, 179-89; in 1900, 169-70; in world affairs, 190-2; Kuomintang Revolution, 170-3; Kuomintang v. Communists, 173-5, 178-9; Taiwan, 189-90
China Incident, 134
Chou En-lai, 185, 189, 210
Chuh Teh, 173
Chungking, 134, 178
Churchill, Winston, 61, 64, 79, 93, 157-9, 196, 199, 215, 285
Clemenceau, Georges, 32
Cold War, 113-14, 198, 203, 212, 217
Collective farms, China, 183-5; Russia, 107-8
Colombo Plan, 258, 293
Colonial Development and Welfare Acts, 238-9
Common Market — *see* European Economic Community
Commonwealth of Nations, 230
Communes, 183-6
Communism, world, 117, 190
Communist International (Comintern), 104, 173
Communist Manifesto, 96
Communist Party, Chinese, 173-5, 179-89; German, 41-5; Indonesian, 252, 256-60; Japanese, 139; Russian, 103-21
Confucius, 167, 180
Congo, 87, 230, 245
Convention People's Party (CPP), 240-4
Coolidge, President, 154
Coral Sea, Battle of, 136